LIBRARY *of* GREAT AUTHORS

The

LIBRARY *of* GREAT AUTHORS

series explores the

intimate connection between writing and experience, shedding light on the work of literature's most esteemed authors by examining their lives. The complete LIBRARY *of* GREAT AUTHORS brings an excitingly diverse crowd to your bookshelf:

Albert Camus
Lewis Carroll
Fyodor Dostoevsky
Barbara Kingsolver
Gabriel García Márquez
Toni Morrison
Vladimir Nabokov
J.K. Rowling
J.R.R. Tolkien
Virginia Woolf

Each book in the LIBRARY *of* GREAT AUTHORS features full-length analysis of the writer's most famous works, including such novels as *Crime and Punishment*, *Lolita*, *The Lord of the Rings*, and *Mrs. Dalloway*. Whether you are a reader craving deeper knowledge of your favorite author, a student studying the classics, or a new convert to a celebrated novel, turn to the LIBRARY *of* GREAT AUTHORS for thorough, fascinating, and insightful coverage of literature's best writers.

Library *of* Great Authors

Toni Morrison

Her Life and Works

W. John Campbell, Ph.D.

EDITORIAL DIRECTOR Justin Kestler
EXECUTIVE EDITOR Ben Florman
SERIES EDITOR Emma Chastain

INTERIOR DESIGN Dan Williams

Produced by The Wonderland Press and published by SparkNotes

Spark Publishing
A Division of SparkNotes LLC
120 5th Avenue
New York, NY 10011

10 9 8 7 6 5 4 3 2 1

Please submit comments or questions, or report errors to www.sparknotes.com/errors

Printed and bound in the United States of America

ISBN 1-58663-838-6

Library of Congress Cataloging-in-Publication Data available on request

Contents

Introduction ix

I.
The Life of Toni Morrison
1

People, Events, and Trends 7
Morrison's Literary Context. 10

II.
The Bluest Eye
13

An Overview 15
Key Facts 15
Style, Technique, and Language. 15
Characters 18

Reading *The Bluest Eye* 21
Introduction 21
AUTUMN
Section 1. 23
Sections 2–3: HEREISTHEHOUSE. 29
WINTER
Section 1. 33
Section 2: SEETHECAT. 36
SPRING
Section 1. 39
Section 2: SEEMOTHER. 41
Section 3: SEEFATHER. 44
Section 4: SEETHEDOG. 46
SUMMER 48
Conclusions 50

III. Sula 51

An Overview 53
Key Facts 53
Style, Technique, and Language 53
Characters 55
Reading *Sula* 58
PART ONE
Prologue and Chapter 1: 1919 58
Chapter 2: 1920 62
Chapter 3: 1921 64
Chapter 4: 1922 67
Chapter 5: 1923 70
Chapter 6: 1927 72
PART TWO
Chapter 7: 1937 73
Chapter 8: 1939 76
Chapter 9: 1940 79
Chapter 10: 1941 81
Chapter 11: 1965 84
Conclusions 86

IV. Song of Solomon 87

An Overview 89
Key Facts 89
Style, Technique, and Language 89
Characters 91
Reading *Song of Solomon* 95
PART ONE
Chapter 1 95
Chapter 2 100
Chapter 3 105
Chapter 4 109
Chapter 5 111
Chapter 6 114

Chapter 7 117
Chapter 8 119
Chapter 9 123
PART TWO
Chapter 10 125
Chapter 11 129
Chapter 12 133
Chapter 13 135
Chapter 14 136
Chapter 15 137
Conclusions 142

V.
Beloved
143

An Overview 145
Key Facts 145
Style, Technique, and Language 145
Characters 147

Reading *Beloved* 151
PART ONE
Chapter 1 151
Chapter 2 158
Chapter 3 160
Chapter 4 163
Chapter 5 164
Chapter 6 167
Chapter 7 169
Chapter 8 171
Chapter 9 173
Chapter 10 176
Chapter 11 177
Chapter 12 178
Chapters 13–14 178
Chapters 14–15 180
Chapter 16 182
Chapter 17 185
Chapter 18 186
PART TWO
Chapter 19 187
Chapter 20 190

Chapter 21 191
Chapter 22 192
Chapter 23 193
Chapter 24 194
Chapter 25 196
PART THREE
Chapter 26 197
Chapter 27 201
Chapter 28 204
Conclusions 205

Suggestions for Further Reading 207

Index 211

Topics In Depth

Bill "Bojangles" Robinson 24
Black Power 28
The Maginot Line 34
The Great Migration 38
Living in Lorain 42
World War I 60
Mules and Men 74
The Biblical Shadrach 82
Freedmen's Bureau 104
A Brutal Hate Crime 108
Malcolm X 116
Four Little Girls 120
On Wax Wings 122
The Biblical "Song of Solomon" 128
Wise and Supernatural 138
Inspired by Margaret Garner 152
The Black Book 156
The Middle Passage 166
Traveling on the Underground Railroad 172
The Four Horsemen of the Apocalypse 184
The Colored Regiments of the Civil War 202

LIBRARY *of* GREAT AUTHORS

Toni Morrison

I

THE LIFE OF TONI MORRISON

Toni Morrison was born **Chloe Anthony Wofford** on February 18, 1931, in Lorain, Ohio, a small steel-mill city west of Cleveland. She was the second of four children. Her parents were **George Wofford**, an emigrant from Georgia who worked as a shipyard welder, and **Rahmah Willis Wofford**, whose parents had come to Ohio from Kentucky, where they had been sharecroppers.

At home, Morrison was brought up amid a rich oral tradition of folklore, fables, and songs. Ghost stories were especially popular in the house, and the future author's maternal grandmother believed in the supernatural and the interpretation of dreams. Music, too, was a constant presence in the Wofford home. Morrison's maternal grandfather, **Solomon Willis**, played the violin, and her mother, a member of the church choir, often sang jazz, blues, and gospel around the house.

Most households in Lorain were relatively poor, especially during the Great Depression when Morrison was a child. The city had a sizeable, tight-knit black community, but since the town was less segregated than many towns in the North, the Woffords had white neighbors, most of whom were Greek and Italian immigrants. While parts of Lorain were segregated, such as its public parks, claims of discrimination and racial violence could be brought to the courts, where blacks relied on a certain measure of justice.

Lorain's public schools were integrated. In school, Morrison immersed herself in literature. She excelled in high school and, in 1949, became the first woman in her family to go to college. She began attending Howard University, the esteemed, predominantly black institution in Washington, D.C. Once she had arrived at Howard, however, Morrison felt ambivalent about it. She studied the classics and American literature, but she read few black writers, and those black writers she did read were men such as **Richard Wright** (1908–1960), and later **Ralph Ellison** (1914–1994) and **James Baldwin** (1924–1987). Not until years later did she read the work of novelist and folklorist **Zora Neale Hurston** (1901–1960). When Morrison proposed writing a paper on Shakespeare's black characters, her professor told her that it was not an appropriate topic for academic study. Moreover, Morrison found the student body materialistic and more interested in socializing than in pursuing academic excellence.

As solace, Morrison joined the school's drama club, the Howard University Players. During her college summers, she traveled throughout the South with the troupe, performing to all-black audiences while witnessing the peculiarly

Southern brand of Jim Crow segregation. At this time, Morrison also began calling herself "Toni," a shortened version of her middle name, Anthony. She used this name instead of her first name, since many people mispronounced "Chloe."

After graduating from Howard with a bachelor's degree in English literature in 1953, Morrison entered graduate school at Cornell University in upstate New York. There, she earned a master's degree in English and completed her thesis on the role of suicide in the novels of **William Faulkner** (1897–1962) and **Virginia Woolf** (1892–1941), two writers whose rich styles and experimental narrative techniques would greatly influence her own novels.

In 1955, Morrison accepted her first teaching job at Texas Southern University, a predominantly black institution that was decidedly more Afrocentric than Howard. Texas Southern University focused on African and African-American cultures as bodies of knowledge in their own right. Morrison would later explain that the university instilled in her a sense of "black culture as a subject, an idea, as a discipline." She left Texas Southern after two years and returned to Howard to join its English faculty. In Washington, she met **Harold Morrison**, a Jamaican architect, and married him in 1958. Three years later, she gave birth to their first son, **Harold Ford**.

The Civil Rights movement had gained strength in the late 1950s. Black America was galvanized by events such as the Montgomery Bus Boycott of 1955, which was prompted by **Rosa Parks** (b. 1913), whom Morrison credits with sparking the entire movement. By the early 1960s, civil rights had become the foremost issue facing the country, and the Howard campus was alive with protests and demonstrations.

Morrison did not actively take part in civil disobedience. Not only was she busy raising her children, she was uncomfortable with the movement's philosophy of integration. She sensed that integration would come only through the kind of black solidarity she had found at Texas Southern. Her beliefs resembled those animating the Black Power movement, which grew out of frustrations with the larger Civil Rights movement. The Black Power movement was most concerned with creating a black consciousness and unity. One of Morrison's students at Howard was **Stokely Carmichael** (1941–1998), a founder of the Black Power movement.

In the early 1960s, Morrison's marriage began to sour. Partly as an escape, she joined a small circle of poets and fiction writers who met monthly to share their work and criticism. Morrison usually brought some of her old writings from high school, but before one meeting, she quickly jotted down a short story about a young black girl who longed for blue eyes. This story, eventually revised and published as *The Bluest Eye*, would launch her writing career a few years later.

By the mid-1960s, Morrison had arrived at a crossroads. While expecting her second child, **Slade Kevin**, she resigned from Howard and toured Europe with her husband. The two separated during their travels and divorced soon thereafter. After a brief period back in Ohio in 1965, Morrison was hired as a fiction editor at the L.W. Singer Publishing Company, a subsidiary of Random House in Syracuse, New York.

> "Morrison gives us a fresh, close look at the lives of terror and decorum of those Negroes who want to get on in a white man's world...she puts her compassionate finger on the roles of crude fantasy in sustaining hope."
>
> L. E. SISSMAN

By 1967, Morrison had been promoted to senior editor and relocated to Random House's New York City headquarters. She worked there for eighteen years, specializing in the literary works of black authors including **Gayl Jones** (b. 1949), **Henry Dumas** (1934–1968), and **Toni Cade Bambara** (1939–1995). Morrison published the landmark autobiographies of civil rights leader **Angela Davis** (b. 1944) and boxing champion **Muhammad Ali** (b. 1942). She collaborated on *The Black Book* (1974), a groundbreaking scrapbook of sorts that included photographs, documents, and articles collected from 300 years of African-American history and culture. Her goal as an editor was to help create a canon of African-American literature.

In the late 1960s, as Morrison's prominence as an editor grew, her literary career also began to flourish. Before leaving Syracuse, she had reexamined her old short story after showing it to a receptive editor, **Alan Rancler**. Rancler encouraged her to expand the story into a full-length novel. After soliciting the revised final manuscript, now called *The Bluest Eye*, Rancler published the book in 1970.

The Bluest Eye, a tragic story of childhood and black identity, made a strong impression on the mainstream literary establishment. Despite being mostly neglected by black reviewers, Morrison was praised by many white critics as an important new voice in African-American literature. As she began writing for magazines and book reviews, she established herself as an authoritative, independent voice on racial matters as well as on women's issues.

In 1973, Morrison's second novel, *Sula*, was published. The story of nonconformity in a black community, the novel received wider critical attention than *The Bluest Eye* had, especially from black critics. However, it failed to find a broad readership and was not a commercial success, despite its nomination for the National Book Award for Fiction in 1975.

Morrison's third novel, *Song of Solomon* (1977), was her breakthrough work. It made her a household name in America. The Book-of-the-Month Club chose it as a main selection, the first novel by a black author to be given that honor since Richard Wright's *Native Son* was chosen in 1940. *Song of Solomon* went on to win the prestigious National Book Critics Circle Award. A year later, it became a bestseller in paperback, and Morrison was honored with the Distinguished Writer Award from the esteemed American Academy of Arts and Letters.

Morrison gained further renown with her next novel, *Tar Baby* (1981), the first in which she featured white characters in prominent roles. Shortly after the novel's publication, Morrison became the second black woman to appear on the cover of *Newsweek* magazine. (Coincidentally, the first was another writer, Zora Neale Hurston.)

In 1984, Morrison gave up her editing job at Random House, which she had held throughout the beginning of her literary career, and accepted a professorship at the State University of New York (SUNY) at Albany. There, she dedicated the next three years to researching and writing her fifth novel, *Beloved*, based in part on the life of ex-slave Margaret Garner, whose story she had discovered while researching *The Black Book* a decade earlier. *Beloved* was an instant bestseller, but it failed to win either the National Book Award or the National Book Critics Circle Award, a perceived slight that prompted a protest by a group of black writers and scholars. The injustice was redressed a few months later when *Beloved* received the highest honor in American literature: the Pulitzer Prize in Fiction.

In 1989, Morrison left SUNY Albany to accept the Robert F. Goheen professorship at Princeton University, becoming the first black writer, male or female, to hold an endowed chair at an Ivy League university. In 1992, she published two new books, one fiction and one nonfiction, which simultaneously climbed the bestseller lists. *Jazz* is a novel set in Harlem in the mid-1920s, and *Playing in the Dark: Whiteness and the Literary Imagination* is a study of racial attitudes expressed in the works of white American writers such as Edgar Allan Poe and Mark Twain. Later that year, Morrison compiled and edited *Race-ing Justice, En-Gendering Power,* an examination of the racial and sexual issues stirred up by the controversy surrounding **Anita Hill** (b. 1956) and the confirmation hearings for **Clarence Thomas** (b. 1948), America's second black Supreme Court justice.

In 1993, Morrison won the Nobel Prize in Literature, becoming the eighth woman and the first black woman to receive the honor. The Nobel committee praised her entire body of work, giving special mention to *Song of Solomon*, *Beloved*, and *Jazz*, and noted that Morrison gave life "to an essential aspect of American reality."

In 1995, Morrison published a new novel, *Paradise*, which explores the dynamics of all-black American towns of the early twentieth century. In the second half of the 1990s, Morrison's early novels enjoyed a renaissance sparked by the enthusiasm of television talk-show host **Oprah Winfrey** (b. 1954). Winfrey starred in the 2000 film adaptation of *Beloved*, and, through her high-profile book club, introduced *The Bluest Eye* and *Song of Solomon* to a new generation of readers. This widespread attention cemented Morrison's place in American and world literary history.

People, Events, and Trends

That Influenced Morrison's Work

Slavery and the Middle Passage: The "peculiar institution" of slavery (a term coined by pro-slavery southerner John C. Calhoun) brought millions of Africans to American soil between the seventeenth and mid-nineteenth centuries. As part of the "triangular trade" between Europe, Africa, and the Americas, slave ships brought as many as 100,000 slaves per month to the New World during the peak of the slave trade in the eighteenth century. The dreaded Middle Passage—the transatlantic trip in which future slaves were packed tightly into disease-infested ships—claimed the lives of more than 200 million men, women, and children. Slavery existed in every state and territory in America, including the northern states. The economic and moral issues surrounding slavery were one of the causes of the **Civil War** (1861–1865), which pitted the northern Union against the southern Confederacy. The **Emancipation Proclamation** of January 1, 1863 freed slaves in all but the border states (i.e., slave states that were loyal to the Union), and the **Thirteenth Amendment** to the U.S. Constitution ended slavery altogether in 1865.

Abolitionism and the Fugitive Slave Laws: Abolitionist (antislavery) movements, spearheaded in northern states by whites such as newspaper editor **Horace Greeley** (1811–1872), sprang up all over America before the Civil War. A loose network of sympathetic whites and free blacks formed the **Underground Railroad**, which brought runaway slaves to freedom in the North and Canada. The Fugitive Slave laws, instituted by the federal government in 1793 (and renewed in 1850), called for runaway slaves to be tracked down and returned to their owners.

Margaret Garner: The story of runaway slave Margaret Garner was the inspiration for Morrison's novel *Beloved*. In 1856, Garner escaped with her four children from Kentucky into Ohio, but was tracked down a few weeks later. To prevent herself and her family from being forced back into slavery, she killed one of her children and attempted to kill the others and herself.

Reconstruction: The period after the Civil War was a critical time for African-Americans. The **Freedmen's Bureau** (1865–1872) built public schools and hospitals, provided food rations, and in some cases donated land to former slaves and their families. Blacks gained the right to vote under the **Fifteenth Amendment** (1870) and were elected to local, state, and federal offices across the South, even holding a majority in the South Carolina state legislature. Despite these advances, angry white Southerners made Reconstruction a divisive and gruesome period. White supremacist organizations like the **Ku Klux Klan**, sometimes sanctioned by state and local governments, burned black schools and lynched thousands of black people. The institution of segregationist **Black Codes** and **Jim Crow** laws led to a separate and unequal system of public and private services that were later upheld by the Supreme Court's landmark ***Plessy v. Ferguson*** decision of 1896. Meanwhile, landowners used the farming system called **sharecropping** to force black farmers into a vicious cycle of debt and poverty.

The Great Migration: Throughout the early decades of the twentieth century, African-Americans slowly moved from the rural South to the industrial North in search of jobs and relief from Jim Crow segregation. Between 1900 and 1930, more than one million blacks relocated to major cities from Chicago to New York. Known as The Great Migration, this mass relocation peaked between the 1940s and 1970s as four million blacks came north into the urban centers of the Great Lakes region.

World War II: The Second World War was a major impetus for The Great Migration. In December 1941, the United States entered World War II, siding with England, France, and later, Italy against Japan and Nazi Germany. As hundreds of thousands of American men, black and white, fought in Europe and the Pacific, the homeland suffered a labor shortage. Blacks in the United States found new job opportunities in the North, filling vacancies left by whites and, at times, crossing the picket lines of whites who demanded higher wages.

Civil Rights Movement: By the mid-1950s, black civic and religious organizations like the Congress of Racial Equality (CORE) and the Southern Christian Leadership Conference (SCLC)—led by **Dr. Martin Luther King, Jr.** (1929–1968)—began a series of demonstrations and protests against segregation and demanded greater enforcement of civil-rights laws. The movement gained the support of white liberals, and after numerous violent clashes between demonstrators and police or public officials in places such as Birmingham, Alabama, the federal government intervened with National Guard troops. By 1965, new legislation was introduced that protected the voting rights of blacks and led to the nationwide desegregation of public schools and public services.

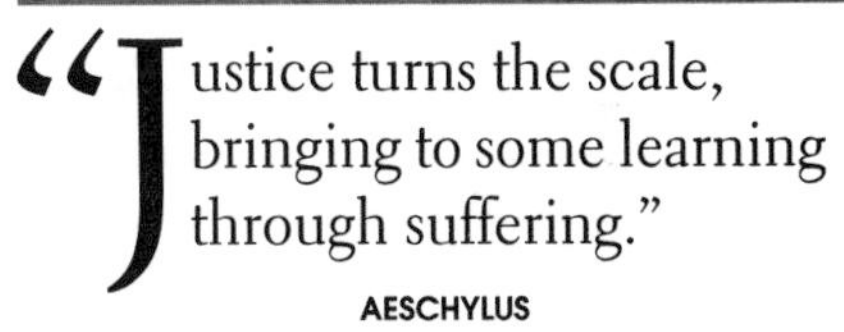

Black Nationalism and Black Power: Black leaders who were frustrated by the Civil Rights movement and its integrationist stance created new organizations to stir black consciousness and political power. Black Muslims such as **Malcolm X** (1925–1965), who was first a leader of the Nation of Islam and later led his own organization, advocated black separatism and nationalism in the face of what he perceived as a white-dominated society that did not want peaceful coexistence. In the mid-1960s, **Stokely Carmichael** (1941–1998) and others initiated the **Black Power** movement in response to what they saw as compromises within the Civil Rights movement. Black Power promoted black self-determination. It called for black control of organizations, a united political party, and the reexamination and renaissance of African and African-American culture. This movement eventually led to the rise of African-American studies as an academic discipline in high schools and colleges.

Morrison's Literary Context

Her Influences and Impact

Toni Morrison's novels can be placed in the category of African-American literature, but confining them to one category diminishes their richness and the vast, diverse readership they attract.

Morrison's novels lyrically depict the black experience, whether in racist white culture, nonconformist black culture, or post-slavery folk culture. Her novels merge elements of magical realism and regional dialect, and feature well-developed relationships among friends, mothers, and daughters.

Considered a preeminent African-American writer, a groundbreaking female writer, and one of our finest contemporary writers, Morrison has earned praise from almost every literary camp, as evidenced by her Nobel Prize in Literature, her Pulitzer Prize, and her National Book Critics Circle Award.

> "I am not *like* James Joyce; I am not *like* Thomas Hardy; I am not *like* Faulkner. I am not *like* in any sense.... My effort is to be *like* something that has probably only been fully expressed in [black] music.... Writing novels is a way to encompass this—this something."
>
> TONI MORRISON

Morrison's literary influences include American novelists **Willa Cather** (1876–1947) and **Ernest Hemingway** (1899–1961), nineteenth-century European novelists **Gustave Flaubert** (1821–1880) and **Jane Austen** (1775–1817), and Russian writers **Leo Tolstoy** (1828–1910) and **Fyodor Dostoyevsky** (1821–1881). As part of her formal education, she studied the classics and American literature, but she read the work of few black writers. Not until years later did she encounter the work of novelist and folklorist **Zora Neale Hurston** (1901–1960), another groundbreaker of African-American literature depicting life in the South. Morrison's master's thesis explored the role of suicide in the novels of **William Faulkner** (1897–1962) and **Virginia Woolf** (1892–1941), two writers who greatly influenced her own work.

II

THE BLUEST EYE

The Bluest Eye

An Overview

Key Facts

Genre: African-American novel; coming-of-age novel

Date of First Publication: 1969

Setting: 1940–1941 in Lorain, Ohio; Kentucky, Georgia, the Caribbean

Narrator: Multiple narrators: third-person omniscient, Claudia MacTeer (third-person), and Pauline Breedlove (first-person)

Plot Overview: A black girl yearns for blue eyes, hoping that if she gets them, someone might love her and consider her worthwhile.

Style, Technique, and Language

Style—Four Seasons, Four Parts, Three Narrators: *The Bluest Eye* is divided into four parts corresponding to the four seasons of one full year, the autumn of 1940 to the summer of 1941. A short, two-part introduction precedes the main body of the novel. The first half of the introduction is an excerpt from the *Dick and Jane* reading primers, and later chapters of the book are prefaced with corrupted versions of this primer's content. The four seasons do not have any significance in and of themselves, except, perhaps, for the impregnation of Pecola Breedlove in "Spring," a season traditionally associated with birth and renewal.

> "The seasons are not only surface movement in the novel; they are ironic and brutal comments of Pecola's descent into madness."
>
> BARBARA CHRISTIAN

Significantly, the yearlong story ends in the fall of 1941, an ominous date that marks the eve of the United States' entrance into World War II. Ending on this date suggests a grim future for the nation and for Pecola Breedlove.

Morrison uses three distinct narrators: a third-person, omniscient narrator; Claudia MacTeer, who uses present-tense and past-tense narration at different times; and Pauline Breedlove, who gives a first-person testimonial about her life. This fractured story, told by different narrators, reflects Pecola Breedlove's fractured nature and her eventual disintegration into madness.

Technique—Imagery and Metaphors

Blue Eyes: Pecola's desire for blue eyes symbolizes her racial self-hatred and her belief that becoming beautiful by white standards will win her acceptance. Pecola's identity is defined solely in terms of how other people see her.

Shirley Temple: Shirley Temple symbolizes the white ideal of beautiful girlhood. Pecola aspires to look like Shirley Temple, the blonde, blue-eyed film star. Claudia rebels against this image by imagining herself taking Temple's place and dancing with the black Bojangles. Other symbols of white beauty include the movie stars Jean Harlow and Ginger Rogers.

Soil and Marigolds: The barren soil is a metaphor for Pecola's barren environment. Just as the marigolds that Claudia and Frieda plant do not flourish in the desolate earth, Pecola does not flourish in her desolate family. Her family and community neglect her, and she withers.

The Breedloves' Home, Furniture, and Stove: The storefront that serves as the Breedloves' house does not have the usual comforts of home, and the rundown things that clutter it stand for the family members' unhappy relationships. The old, ratty furniture has no memories or history. A tear in the sofa symbolizes the growing rift among family members. The fire in the stove suggests the endless, violent battles between Pauline and Cholly.

Dandelions: Dandelions stand for Pecola's unstable sense of self-worth. When Pecola hopes to discover beauty within herself, she feels optimistic about life and sees the dandelions as beautiful flowers. But in moments when she feels shame and emptiness, she sees the dandelions as ugly weeds.

Dick and Jane: The *Dick and Jane* primer is a recurring symbol of white middle-class utopian existence. The happy world of the white children in the primers has nothing to do with Pecola or her life. The distorted versions of the primer that preface many chapters are ironic commentaries on how little the mangled existence of the Breedloves resembles Dick and Jane's carefree life.

Language—The Oral Tradition: The story of *The Bluest Eye* is told as if it is a piece of gossip or a secret revealed. The prose mimics the passing of rumors from neighbor to neighbor or family member to family member. This novel is Morrison's written version of the oral tradition of storytelling. Claudia MacTeer is the first character to use the phrase "quiet as its kept," a phrase that characterizes the story of Pecola Breedlove as something sisters would whisper about. "Quiet as its kept" is usually a spoken phrase, similar to "Ssh, it's a secret," and Morrison's use of it in her novel exemplifies her skill at transposing spoken language onto the page. Her dialogue is colloquial, intimate, and evocative of the American English her characters would have spoken in the time and place they lived. ("Did you hear about that girl?" / "What? Pregnant" / "Yas. But guess who?")

> "There are many novelists willing to report the ugliness of the world as ugly. The writer who can reveal the beauty and the hope beneath the surface is a writer to seek out and to encourage."
>
> HASKEL FRANKEL, ON *THE BLUEST EYE*

In this novel, individual narrators speak in unique voices. When speaking as an adult, Claudia MacTeer conceptualizes and philosophizes. ("But what is really like that? As painful as I remember?") When speaking as a child, the nine-year-old Claudia focuses on the sensory perceptions of the world around her. ("Our house is old, cold, and green"; "My mother's voice is not talking to me.") Pauline Breedlove's first-person narrative in the "Spring" section captures her unique voice. ("I was sitting back in my seat, and I taken a big bit of that candy, and it pulled a tooth right out of my mouth. I could of cried.") The passages in which she speaks seem almost like a testimony.

Morrison introduces one of the novel's key themes by using the language of the *Dick and Jane* primer and showing how painfully it clashes with the life of the Breedlove family. As each chapter of *The Bluest Eye* opens, mangled passages of the *Dick and Jane* primer preface the story. For instance, the chapter about the Breedloves' storefront house is prefaced by a contorted version of the primer ("HEREISTHEHOUSEITISGREENANDWHITE..."). This part of the primer describes Dick and Jane's idyllic house: "Here is the house. It is green and white." By mangling this sentence, Morrison shows that comparing Dick and Jane's existence to Pecola's is a gruesome, sad, surreal exercise.

Characters in *The Bluest Eye*

Blue Jack: An old man who was a slave when he was growing up. Blue Jack works with Cholly at the feed store. He is Cholly's childhood best friend and role model.

Bob: The mangy mutt that belongs to Soaphead Church's landlord. Soaphead tells Pecola that if she wants blue eyes, she should feed poison to the dog as an "offering" to God.

China: One of three prostitutes who live in the apartment above the Breedloves' home.

Cholly Breedlove: Pauline's husband and Pecola's father. Cholly is described as "[a]n old dog, a snake, a ratty nigger." Often drunk, he rapes and impregnates Pecola. He burns down the Breedlove home.

Pauline Breedlove: Pecola's mother and Cholly's wife. She is known to most people, including her own family, as "Mrs. Breedlove." She works for the Fishers, a white family, who call her "Polly."

Pecola Breedlove: The novel's protagonist. A black girl of about twelve, she believes that blue eyes will make her worthy of love. She is raped and impregnated by her father, but her child dies at birth.

Sammy Breedlove: The fourteen-year-old son of Cholly and Pauline. He runs away.

Darlene: The girl to whom Cholly loses his virginity. Two white men interrupt Darlene and Cholly, and Cholly directs his hatred and anger at her instead of at the men. He leaves Georgia partly because he fears that Darlene is pregnant.

The Fishers: The white family who employ Pauline Breedlove as a maid and cook. They call her "Polly."

The Fisher Daughter: A young white girl with blonde hair and green eyes. Mrs. Breedlove attends to her instead of Pecola after Pecola accidentally knocks over a pie.

Samson Fuller: Cholly's father. Samson spitefully shoos Cholly away after Cholly finds him in Macon, Georgia. Cholly realizes after meeting his father that he has nothing to lose in life.

Geraldine: The mother of Louis, Jr. Geraldine is an archetypal black middle-class woman who straightens her hair, keeps her house immaculate, and does not enjoy sex if it means indulging an inattentive, thoughtless partner.

Mr. Henry: A boarder at the MacTeers'. Claudia and Frieda catch him in the house with two prostitutes, but they do not tell their mother about it. He is later thrown out of the house after fondling Frieda.

Great Aunt Jimmy: An old relative of Cholly Breedlove. She saves the infant Cholly after his mother abandons him on a junk heap.

Louis, Jr. (Junior): A sadistic young boy who lures Pecola to his house and then throws his mother's cat at her.

Claudia MacTeer: A childhood friend of Pecola Breedlove. She is about nine. She is one of the novel's narrators.

Frieda MacTeer: Claudia's older sister and playmate. She is about ten years old. After Mr. Henry fondles her, she worries that she has been "ruined."

Mrs. MacTeer: A stern mother who occasionally whips her daughters, Claudia and Frieda. When she is in a bad mood, she tends to ramble aloud to her children about her troubles and the problems in the world. The children try to avoid her when she is in these moods.

Miss Marie (Maginot Line): One of the prostitutes who lives above the Breedloves' storefront home. She is "a mountain of flesh" whom the MacTeer girls call "Maginot Line." Pecola knows her as "Miss Marie" and befriends her.

Maureen Peal: A haughty, well-bred black schoolmate of Claudia, Frieda, and Pecola. The daughter of a well-off family, Maureen wears nice clothes and is impeccably groomed. She thinks of herself as pretty and considers the other girls ugly.

Poland: The third prostitute who lives above the Breedloves' storefront home. She drinks a lot and often sings the blues.

Soaphead Church: An old, light-skinned, celibate resident of Lorain whose real name is Elihue Micah Whitcomb. Soaphead was born in the Caribbean and settled in Lorain as a fortune-teller and interpreter of dreams. He "grants" Pecola's wish for blue eyes.

Velma: Soaphead Church's one love. She breaks up with him because she finds his melancholy moods too intense to bear. After Velma leaves, Soaphead remains celibate.

Rosemary Villanucci: The white girl who lives next door to Claudia and Frieda and who sometimes plays with them.

Mr. Yacobowski: The gray-haired owner and proprietor of the grocery store where Pecola buys Mary Jane candies. Pecola imagines that he cannot see her.

Reading *The Bluest Eye*

Introduction

The novel opens with an excerpt from the children's reading primer *Dick and Jane*. The excerpt ("Mother, Father, Dick, and Jane live in the green-and-white house. They are very happy.") is read aloud three times. The second time the excerpt is read, all punctuation is removed. The third time the excerpt is read, the spacing between words is removed and the sentences begin to spiral into a blur of unintelligible words and letters.

An adult narrator, **Claudia MacTeer**, then begins to tell a story from her childhood. The story takes place in the autumn of 1941 in Lorain, Ohio. Claudia's friend, **Pecola Breedlove**, is pregnant by her own father, **Cholly Breedlove**. The girls' innocence has been shattered by this pregnancy.

Claudia and her sister **Frieda** want Pecola's baby to be born healthy and strong, so they plant marigolds. They think that if the marigolds blossom, there may be hope for the baby's life. But no one's flowers grow that year in Lorain, their flowers included. The baby dies, and all that remains is Pecola and the "unyielding earth." Claudia says there is nothing more to say about the story except: "why?" Since "why?" is too difficult a question to answer, she will tell the story of "how" everything happened.

UNDERSTANDING AND INTERPRETING

Introduction

Fractured Narration: The novel opens with distorted language from the *Dick and Jane* primer, followed by a first-person narration. Both of these introductory narrations prepare the reader for the novel, which uses a number of different narrative techniques. The story of Pecola will be told from various viewpoints, including that of Claudia MacTeer, who narrates as an adult looking back on her childhood. At other times, the story is told through a series of first-person testimonials from different characters, or through the voice of the more traditional omniscient (all-knowing) third-person narrator. Morrison immediately reveals the pivotal event of the novel—Pecola's pregnancy and the death of the baby—thus removing some of the suspense from the story and allowing us to focus on how the events happened.

> "So precise, so faithful to speech and so charged with pain and wonder that the novel becomes poetry…I have said 'poetry,' but *The Bluest Eye* is also history, sociology, folklore, nightmare and music."
>
> JOHN LEONARD

"Quiet as Its Kept": The existence of multiple narrations demonstrates how oral traditions influence Morrison's work. Claudia begins the novel by saying "quiet as its kept," a phrase that shows how Pecola Breedlove's story grew from rumors and gossip, from secrets exposed. Claudia's narration provides an intimacy that only an insider could have. The phrase "quiet as its kept" is one that Morrison has said she remembers from her own childhood, from the whispers of adults and children telling stories.

Untended Plants: In Lorain in 1941, marigold seeds did not sprout, just as Pecola's baby did not grow into a healthy human being. The soil represents Pecola's "unyielding" and barren upbringing in a family that does not love her and in fact, as in the case of her father, does violence to her. Other factors affect Pecola too, factors such as the prevailing notions of beauty in white America, which stunt Pecola's growth and make her unhappy.

The Cruelty of *Dick and Jane*: The use of passages from the reading primer is one of the key narrative techniques Morrison employs in the novel. Many sections are preceded by a mangled excerpt from the *Dick and Jane* story, which depicts an idyllic life of white, middle-class perfection. "Mother" and "Father" happily preside over the family, who live in a colorful, "pretty" house. Everyone is "nice." Mother laughs, and Father is strong. Everyone plays with kittens and dogs. The children have good friends. It is a story of blissful family life. When contrasted with the family life of Pecola Breedlove, the world of the primer seems unimaginable, and cruel in its perfection. The disintegration of the primer's language in the first section becomes a commentary on Pecola herself. Pecola worships the Dick and Jane icons of the white world, with their pretty blue eyes, and when her own life becomes the precise opposite of their perfect world, Pecola descends into madness, unable to accept the gap between her experience and her fantasy.

Ohio in 1940–1941: The novel is set during a crucial moment in modern American history, just before the nation entered World War II. Although the war itself is never mentioned in the novel, the ideals of the Nazis lurk in the background as a political subtext. The Nazis' physical ideal of white, blonde, blue-eyed Aryan pureness sounds just like American notions of beauty as they are described in Morrison's novel. Morrison makes the point that having one rigid idea of physical beauty can actually be dangerous when it is linked to notions of ideal racial makeup and enforced by violent people.

AUTUMN
Section 1

Claudia narrates the novel's first section, beginning with a present-tense narration of her life as a young girl in 1940, then switching to her adult, past-tense recollections. The young Claudia describes her family's house as old and cold, its windows stuffed with rags to keep in the heat. Autumn is usually a time of illness for Claudia and her sister, **Frieda**. Their mother, **Mrs. MacTeer**, takes care of them by rubbing salve on their chests. Claudia remembers her mother as "somebody with hands who does not want me to die."

That autumn, the MacTeer family takes in a boarder, Mr. Henry Washington, known as **Mr. Henry**. Claudia overhears her mother gossiping with a neighbor about Mr. Henry's arrival and does not understand all that is said because she is too young. Claudia remembers only Mr. Henry's wonderful smell and how he, unlike other boarders and grown men, talks to her and to Frieda. Mr. Henry teases the girls, calling them "Greta Garbo" and "Ginger Rogers" after the white American movie stars of that time.

BILL “BOJANGLES” ROBINSON

Shirley Temple’s dancing partner, **Bill “Bojangles” Robinson** (1878–1949), was a tap dancer extraordinaire whose skill allowed him to transcend racial boundaries. Born Luther Robinson, he first found an audience dancing for whites on the streets of Richmond, Virginia. For years, he made a career dancing in nightclubs and in vaudeville acts across the country, becoming one of the most famous performers of the early twentieth century. His films with Shirley Temple increased his international renown. Robinson invented his famous “stair dance” (tap dancing up stairs) when he improvised a way to receive an award from the King of England, who met him at the top of a flight of steps. The meaning of Robinson’s nickname, “Bojangles,” was interpreted in two very different ways: to whites, the name meant “happy-go-lucky,” but to blacks it recalled the more derogatory word “squabbler” (in film, Robinson often played the role of a butler). After his death in 1949, Robinson was given one of the largest funerals in the history of New York City, where black and white mourners alike eulogized him.

Pecola Breedlove also comes to stay with the MacTeers for a few days. Her father, Cholly Breedlove, burned down their house one night, and county welfare officials have placed Pecola with the MacTeers until the Breedlove family can be reunited in a new house. Claudia says being forced outside is the "real terror of life." Outside means the "end of something, an irrevocable, physical fact, defining and complementing our metaphysical condition." To put your family outdoors by an act of your own volition, as Cholly Breedlove did, is terrible.

Black people who own property, like the MacTeers, spend all of their energy and money on their homes, overdecorating, filling the cupboards, and planting flowers. Their houses are like "hothouse sunflowers among the rows of weeds that were the rented houses," like the Breedloves' former home. While a guest in the MacTeers' home, Pecola drinks quarts and quarts of milk and gazes fondly at the image of the blonde, blue-eyed child movie star **Shirley Temple** (b. 1928) on her cup.

Claudia furiously hates Shirley Temple and believes that she, not Temple, should be the one dancing in the movies with Shirley's black dance partner, **Bill "Bojangles" Robinson** (1878–1949). Claudia says, "I hated Shirley. Not because she was cute, but because she danced with Bojangles, who was *my* friend, *my* uncle, *my* daddy, and ought to have been soft-shoeing it and chuckling with me." Claudia had once received a blonde, blue-eyed baby doll as a gift. She hated the doll so much that she broke it into pieces and then dismantled the mechanism inside to make it stop crying "Mama." She says, "I could not love it."

One Saturday, Claudia, Frieda, and Pecola are sitting on the steps of the MacTeers' porch with nothing to do. Suddenly, Pecola jumps up, her eyes wide with fear. Menstrual blood runs down her leg, and she has no idea what it is. The girls try to take care of the problem themselves, but the neighbor girl **Rosemary** spies on them and tattles to Mrs. MacTeer. Mrs. MacTeer figures out what has happened and helps Pecola. Later that night, Pecola marvels at the fact that she can have a baby. She still wonders how babies are made. Frieda tells her "somebody has to love you," and Pecola wonders how she can get somebody to love her.

UNDERSTANDING AND INTERPRETING
Autumn, Section 1

Girlhood and Womanhood: The narrative voice of Claudia slips back and forth between the past and present tenses. In the present tense, she shows how she reacted to events as a child, and in the past tense, she adds the wisdom of her adult years to the narration. For example, girlish Claudia associates vague notions of death with being outdoors, while adult Claudia clearly articulates

> "Never able to achieve existence in her own eyes—her own 'I'—[Pecola] exists only in the image reflected by others—by other eyes/Is. Existentially, she is an object, never a subject."
>
> ROBERTA RUBENSTEIN

the terror of being homeless. The mixture of girlish and womanly reflections emphasizes the fact that in 1940–41, Claudia was a girl approaching womanhood.

The Nurturing MacTeer Home: The MacTeer household, while somewhat stern, is presented as a model of good family life. The house is cold but well-kept, and Claudia remembers her mother as someone with healing hands—an indication of positive physical contact in the family. The MacTeers take pride in being homeowners. They do not endure the frightening prospect of being "outdoors," and their status as homeowners represents a sharp contrast to the Breedloves' situation. A father burning down his own house is the worst thing that young Claudia can imagine. Home, meaning both the physical building and the family living in that building, signifies the entire universe to children.

Pecola Breedlove's White Love: Pecola's defining feature is her attraction to all things white. She gulps down quart after quart of white milk and is fascinated by the picture of the white actress Shirley Temple on her cup. She identifies closely with the image on the cup, as if it is a living part of her. She seems to lack awareness of her own body, which reflects a greater lack of self-knowledge. When she has her first period, she has no idea what it is happening to her and becomes terrified. She fails to see herself as she is, preferring to have no identity (by not knowing herself) or to co-opt the identity of someone else (like Shirley Temple) than to accept herself.

Shirley Temple on a Cup: The Shirley Temple cup is the novel's first symbol of the dominant, arbitrary standards of American beauty: cloyingly cute, blonde, and above all, white. In the same way that Mr. Henry tries to flatter Claudia and Frieda by calling them **Greta Garbo** (1905–1990) and **Ginger Rogers** (1911–1995), the young girls admire Shirley Temple as the epitome of a cute white girl. That the Shirley Temple cup is usually filled with milk underlines this aspect of the importance of whiteness.

Racial Standards of Beauty: Two of the novel's central themes are the role of beauty and the different standards by which it is measured. Morrison has said in interviews that she believes our ideals of physical beauty are one of western civilization's most destructive elements. Significantly, Morrison was writing *The Bluest Eye* in the mid- to late 1960s, a time when the Black Power movement and similar groups demanded a new black consciousness. Black Power urged its followers to redefine and reclaim standards of beauty and success, which had always been defined by whites. Pecola Breedlove tries to define herself according to white notions of beauty, and the impossibility of fulfilling those blonde, blue-eyed standards burdens her with shame.

SHIRLEY TEMPLE

Her dimpled, smiling face, blonde locks, and high-pitched lisp made **Shirley Temple** (b. 1928) an instant sensation in pre–World War II America. As a child star, she sang and danced her way to fame in fifty-seven feature films such as *Little Miss Marker* (1934), *Baby Take a Bow* (1934), and *The Little Colonel* (1935). Temple received a special Academy Award in 1934 "in grateful recognition of her outstanding contribution" to American film. Later in life, as Shirley Temple Black (her married name), she pursued a career in politics as a delegate to the United Nations and as the U.S. Ambassador to, successively, Ghana and the Czech and Slovak Republics.

Claudia MacTeer's Idea of Beauty: Unlike Pecola, Claudia rejects the standards of white beauty as epitomized by Shirley Temple. Instead, she imagines herself in Shirley's place, dancing next to her black "uncle" Bojangles. She hates the blonde, blue-eyed baby doll and dismantles it. Claudia rejects symbols of white beauty. A wise little girl, she understands that there is no reason why Shirley Temple belongs next to Bojangles and she, Claudia, does not. Her unwillingness to love her white doll shows her refusal to hold herself to an arbitrary standard of beauty.

Dismembering the Baby Doll: Claudia's treatment of the doll is a way to examine the doll's identity by literally looking inside it. *The Bluest Eye* examines the identify of Claudia and Pecola and others by metaphorically peering into them, and Claudia examines the identity of the white doll by literally tearing it apart and trying to find its voice. In some way, when she rips open the doll she is looking for her own voice, not just the doll's.

BLACK POWER

Stokely Carmichael (1941–1998) first used the phrase "black power" in 1965 during a voter-registration march in Mississippi. Black Power became the name of a group that split off from the larger Civil Rights movement, shunning Dr. Martin Luther King, Jr.'s calls for integration and promoting black control of rights organizations and community-based initiatives aimed at forming black political parties and institutions separate from the national, white-controlled establishment. Other, more militant activists endorsed the creation of an independent black state within the United States' borders. Ultimately, Black Power stressed black pride, an exploration of blacks' African heritage, and black self-determination. Many whites and integrationists (including Dr. King) saw Black Power as a form of "reverse racism" aimed at disparaging whites. But Carmichael and others argued that the beginnings of black liberation lay in a new, independent black consciousness that would provide the grounds for true equality.

AUTUMN
Sections 2–3: HEREISTHEHOUSE...

The second and third sections of Autumn are narrated by an omniscient third-person narrator. The second section opens with another mangled excerpt from the *Dick and Jane* primer ("HEREISTHEHOUSE . . . "), which introduces the Breedloves' new home. They move into an old storefront with two rooms, no bath, and a coal stove for heat and cooking. Their furniture is a ragtag assortment of used and worn pieces, plus a new sofa whose fabric frays on the very day it is delivered. The house has no history. The "only living thing" is the stove, and even it seems to live by its own designs, since it always dies in the morning no matter what the family does to keep it burning.

The third section begins with another *Dick and Jane* excerpt ("HEREISTHE-FAMILY . . . "). The Breedloves are described as a "relentlessly and aggressively ugly" family. They have irregular hairlines, crooked noses, heavy eyebrows, and pointed ears. It is as though "some mysterious all-knowing master had given each one a cloak of ugliness to wear, and they had each accepted it without question." In the outside world, everything the Breedloves see confirms their conviction that they are ugly.

It is a typical Saturday morning in the Breedlove home. Cholly has passed out after coming home drunk. **Pauline Breedlove**, whom everyone (including her own family) calls "Mrs. Breedlove," gets up to feed the cold stove. She wakes up Cholly and complains that they need coal. They threaten each other, and their quarrel turns violent. Quarrels are the only identifying feature of Cholly's and Pauline's lives, and the arguing is what makes life tolerable. Mrs. Breedlove uses it to feel morally superior and martyred in contrast to her base husband. Fighting is one of her only sources of pride and pleasure. Cholly enjoys arguing because Pauline, of all the people and things he hates, is one of the only ones he can hurt.

Pecola's older brother, **Sammy**, pretends to be asleep. Sometimes he adds fuel to his parents' quarrels, encouraging Mrs. Breedlove to kill Cholly. On other occasions, he runs away. He has run off twenty-seven times already. During her parents' fights, Pecola usually lies in bed, tense and breathing quietly. She closes her eyes and prays that she will vanish. She imagines that all of her body disappears except for her eyes, which she thinks are her ugliest feature.

At school, Pecola is the only one who sits alone at a double desk. Everyone else has a partner. Teachers never call on her. She may as well not be there. Whenever the children want to pick on someone, they invoke Pecola's name.

Pecola imagines that if she had pretty blue eyes, she would see pretty things and everyone would love her. No one would want to hurt her or say bad things to her. Each night, she prays for blue eyes.

Morrison inserts an italicized passage: "*Pretty eyes. Pretty blue eyes. Big pretty blue eyes. / Run, Jip, run. Jip runs. Alice runs. Alice has blue eyes*." The narrator says that because Pecola thinks only a miracle would help her, she cannot understand the beauty she already has. One afternoon, Pecola goes to a local store owned by the white, gray-haired **Mr. Yacobowski**. She wants to buy some candy. On the way there, she walks by a thicket of dandelions. She thinks they are pretty and wonders why people call them weeds.

When Pecola arrives at the store, she decides to buy Mary Jane candies. She loves the picture of the blue-eyed Mary Jane on the package. ("To eat the candy is somehow to eat the eyes, eat Mary Jane. Love Mary Jane. Be Mary Jane.") Yacobowski looks down at her from the counter, but he doesn't seem to see her. The vacuum in his eyes reminds Pecola of the disgust she sees in the eyes of all white people when they look at blacks. As she pays for the candy, Pecola is overcome with shame.

While walking home, she notices the dandelions again and thinks they are ugly. She trips on the sidewalk and feels ashamed again, but this time her shame turns into anger. She decides that anger is better, since it is real. But when she thinks back to Mr. Yacobowski's eyes, she feels shame again.

Now and then, Pecola visits the three prostitutes who live in the apartment above the Breedloves' storefront home. The women are named **China, Poland**, and **Miss Marie**. They are proud survivors, ugly women who hate men. Pecola watches the prostitutes primping and dressing, hoping to glean from them something about the nature of love. The three women accept her and would not object if she decided to work with them. All Pecola knows of love is the painful noises her father makes in bed with her silent mother.

UNDERSTANDING AND INTERPRETING
Autumn, Sections 2–3

The Breedloves' Dilapidated House: The sorry state of the Breedloves' new home is the physical manifestation of their unhappy family life. The storefront home has no memories, life, or meaning. The dilapidated furniture reflects the neglect and lack of affection that the family members exhibit toward one another. It is an ugly place, like the ugly people who inhabit it. It is a storefront, not an actual house, and is usually referred to as the "Breedloves' storefront," which underscores the idea that the Breedloves can barely be called a family. The sofa, which represents their one hope for possessing something beautiful, arrives with a tear in the upholstery—a tear that grows bigger and bigger. The tear symbolizes the rift between Pauline and Cholly, and between the parents and their children. It grows bigger and bigger as the years go on.

The Dying Stove: The stove, an important image, explains the nature of the relationship between Cholly and Pauline. Just as the couple fights every day and then collapses into silence, the stove is brought to life each morning, only to die out at night. Despite the spark of life that the Breedlove parents give off when they talk, eventually they lapse into silence. No matter what the family does to the stove, the fire still dies out.

The Ugly Breedloves: The ugliness of the Breedlove family is their defining feature. When they compare themselves to the billboards and people they see, they feel sure that they are ugly. What cloaks them in ugliness is the society around them, which they allow to define them. Everything they see is a byproduct of white society's standards of beauty. The Breedloves think of themselves as they compare to these byproducts, letting others determine their identities rather than claiming ownership of themselves.

Cholly and Pauline: Pauline defines her identity mostly through her interactions with Cholly. She enjoys playing the martyr and can play that part most easily by giving herself up to Cholly's spite and bad treatment. Similarly, Cholly lets his hatred for Pauline become the feeling that defines him. He is angry at many people and things, but for the most part he is powerless to injure these things. Pauline he can injure, and he lets himself luxuriate in this feeling. Over the years, Cholly's and Pauline's quarrels have "identified, grouped, and classed" their lives.

Abandoning the Body: Just as Cholly escapes into drink and hatred and Pauline escapes into martyrdom, Sammy escapes the pandemonium at

INVISIBLE MAN

Ralph Ellison's novel *Invisible Man* was a groundbreaking work of postwar American fiction. It won the National Book Award in 1953. Set in New York City in the 1940s, it is the story of a nameless, faceless black man driven underground by the pressures of a society that ignores him. ("I am invisible . . . because people refused to see me.") The narrator struggles with his identity while being buffeted between white Communists and black nationalists, who seek to convert him to their separate causes amid the race riots of black Harlem.

> "More than the melancholy story of a little girl driven mad by the world's hostility, *The Bluest Eye* tells the story of the community and society that persecutes her. Pecola may be the central character, but she is far from the only victim of the blue eyes."
>
> KEITH E. BYERMAN

home by running away. Pecola escapes in her own way, indulging in a disquieting fantasy. She dreams of disappearing. She imagines that her entire body, except for her eyes, vanishes into thin air. This fantasy brings Pecola's hatred of her own body into relief. She feels uncomfortable in her own skin, and longs to leave her physical self behind.

Fading Away: To other people, Pecola is invisible. Her peers and her teachers act as if she does not exist. Because Pecola defines herself based on other people's perceptions of her, she begins to think of herself as invisible—i.e., if no one sees her, she cannot exist. She does not have the ability to see herself and will herself into existence.

Longing for Blue Eyes: Pecola imagines that if she has blue eyes, she will be able to see the world as a beautiful place for the first time. Her parents will be loving, affectionate, strong, and beautiful, and everyone will be happy. She will live life as it is depicted in the *Dick and Jane* primers. She will crawl into the fantasy of a perfect white society. The italicized passage—"*Alice runs. Alice has blue eyes*"—is Pecola's version of *Dick and Jane.* The omniscient narrator points out, however, that Pecola will never know her own beauty if she continues to fantasize about blue eyes and to see herself only through others' eyes.

Mr. Yacobowski as Society: When Pecola confronts Mr. Yacobowski at the grocery store, we see how whites beat down blacks at every turn, in every blank stare, in every small interaction. Pecola understands that Mr. Yacobowski's blank disgust upon seeing her is what all of white society feels toward all of black society. Pecola feels invisible to Yacobowski. His eyes are what define her, and when he sees nothing, Pecola feels like she is nothing.

Mary Jane Candies: In the same way that Pecola finds meaning in the Shirley Temple cup, she considers the Mary Jane candies a means of transforming herself into something white and blue-eyed. Each candy wrapper bears the image of another Temple-like character. Pecola sees each of the nine candies she buys as "nine lovely orgasms with Mary Jane." Pecola superimposes herself into the scene on the paper wrapper and tries to experience life by "eating" the blue eyes and "being" Mary Jane.

Pretty/Ugly Dandelions: Pecola's opinion of the dandelions changes according to her feelings of self-worth. On the way to the store, she is filled with hopeful anticipation about eating the Mary Janes and having blue eyes, so she finds beauty in things that are normally considered ugly. But after her numbing experience with Mr. Yacobowski, she finds the dandelions ugly.

Poland, China, and Miss Marie: The conversation with the three prostitutes is a reminder that Pecola is still a young girl who is inexperienced in matters of love and sex. Like Pecola, the whores are outcasts. The conversation also shows that even though Pecola is a still a little girl, she could easily become a prostitute. She is more desperately unhappy than these women, and they sense that she could become one of their own.

Warring Whores: The names of the prostitutes (China, Poland, and Marie) remind us that in the background of this novel reverberates World War II, an unseen but ominous force. All three of the countries for whom the women are named were invaded and conquered by the Axis Powers: China by Japan in 1937, and Poland and France ("Marie" is a French name) in 1939 and 1940, respectively. Naming the prostitutes after invaded countries shows how the prostitutes are victims, unable to fend off attackers. Just as World War II subjected nations to Hitler's Nazi regime, the devastating ideals of beauty prey on outcasts like the prostitutes and Pecola.

WINTER
Section 1

Claudia remembers winter as the most difficult season, full of cold mornings and endless boredom. The only disruption is the appearance of a new light-skinned black girl, Maureen Peal. Maureen flaunts her wealth. She wears nice dresses and kelly-green knee socks. Her long hair is braided into "two lynch ropes." Her skin has a yellowish hue, and the sisters nickname her "Meringue Pie." Maureen is popular with everyone and eventually befriends Claudia and Frieda, who are amused and fascinated by her.

One day, when the weather turns warmer, the sisters walk home with Maureen. Claudia remembers how she and her sister noticed even tiny changes in the weather. As the three girls leave the schoolyard, a group of boys circles Pecola, mocking her with a chant: "Black e mo Black e mo Ya daddy sleeps nekked." Frieda tells them to stop teasing Pecola, but they ignore her. When Maureen steps forward, the boys back off.

THE MAGINOT LINE

Miss Marie, the prostitute known as the Maginot Line, is in part a symbol for France. After World War I, France vowed never again to let Germany breach its borders, so they conceived and built the Maginot Line, named for André Maginot (1877–1932), the French minister of war from 1929 to 1931. The Maginot Line was a series of forts and bunkers stretching along the border between the two countries, from Luxembourg to Switzerland. The Line was supposed to be impenetrable by enemy armies, but although it was cleverly designed and engineered, Nazis successfully bypassed it in the spring of 1940, entering France from the north through the Ardennes. They captured Paris soon thereafter. The Maginot Line today remains a symbol of an expensive and elaborate plan that provides little more than a false sense of security.

Later, Maureen buys Pecola some ice cream. She asks Pecola if she has ever seen a naked man. The boys were teasing Pecola, Claudia knows, because Pecola's family is so poor she probably shares a bedroom with her father. Claudia tries to stop Maureen from teasing Pecola anymore. Finally, Claudia takes a swing at Maureen, but she misses and hits Pecola by mistake. Maureen runs across the street and taunts the three of them, saying "I am cute! And you ugly! Black and ugly black e mos."

After the incident, Claudia reflects that Maureen Peal is "not the Enemy." The enemy is whatever makes Maureen beautiful and the girls ugly. When Claudia and Frieda arrive home, they peek through a window and see Mr. Henry with the neighborhood prostitutes, China and Marie. They call Marie **the Maginot Line**. The girls know their mother would not approve of Mr. Henry receiving prostitutes, but they decide not to tell her.

UNDERSTANDING AND INTERPRETING
Winter, Section 1

Bloom and Grow: The idea that Claudia and Frieda sense the slightest change in the weather reminds us of the marigolds at the beginning of the novel. Whereas the marigolds would not bloom in the autumn, Claudia and Frieda easily blossom even in the winter, sniffing out changes like hardy plants. They live healthier emotional lives than Pecola, because they are planted in the healthy soil of a functional family. The flower imagery is also a reminder of the girls' imminent puberty, a time of rapid growth and change that knows no seasons.

Multicolored Maureen Peal: In contrast to Pecola, Maureen Peal is rich, pretty, well-dressed, self-confident, and aggressive. She enjoys reminding everyone else of her superiority. Her yellow skin and kelly-green stockings make her another color altogether from Pecola and the MacTeers.

"Black e mos": The use of "black" as a synonym for "ugly" shows the extent to which white notions of beauty are used against blacks, even by other blacks. As an adult, Claudia sees the racial self-hatred of the boys and of the light-skinned Maureen as a sign that they are all suffering from "smoothly cultivated ignorance." It is a warped form of self-determination when they take the language of children, the schoolyard chant, and turn it against themselves as an insult.

Pecola's Surrender: Pecola folds instantly under the scorn of Maureen and the boys. She does not see, as Claudia does, that Maureen is not the real problem. She does not see that Maureen is only a tiny speck swept up in the torrential storm that is actually the problem. The storm is the white standard of beauty that says Maureen is cute because of her paler skin, and the other girls are ugly because of their darker skin. Pecola watches sadly as Maureen taunts her and skips away. Pecola never sees herself through her own eyes, so if Maureen thinks she is ugly, Pecola thinks herself ugly.

WINTER
Section 2: SEETHECAT...

This section opens with a mangled *Dick and Jane* excerpt ("SEETHECAT . . . "), followed by the narrator's description of a distinctive archetype of a black woman. This archetypal woman comes to Ohio from the South. She comes from Mobile, Alabama; Marietta, Georgia; or Meridian, Mississippi. The influences of her hometown never leave her. She is tall and thin, straightens her hair, has good manners and high morals, goes to college, never drinks or smokes, and never ever enjoys sex. She marries, lives a proper life, and learns how to get rid of passion, nature, and the wide range of human emotions. She always has some other living thing, such as a cat, to whom she shows affection.

> "This novel is a book about mythic, political, and cultural mutilation as much as it is a book about race and sex hatred."
>
> BARBARA CHRISTIAN

One such woman is **Geraldine**, who lives with her husband **Louis**, her son **Louis Jr**. (known as **Junior)**, and her cat. They reside in an immaculately clean house next to the local school's playground. When Junior was young, Geraldine made sure that his physical needs were met, but as he grew older, Geraldine began to transfer her affections from her son to her cat. Junior felt neglected and learned to direct his hatred toward the cat instead of toward his mother.

Geraldine told Junior to play with white children, never with "niggers." In her view, "colored people were neat and quiet; niggers were dirty and loud." Junior longed to play with other black boys, but he grew up playing only with a white boy. He also liked to terrorize girls.

One March afternoon as Pecola is walking through the playground, Junior lures her into his family's house on the pretense of showing her some kittens. Pecola notices right away how beautiful and tidy the house is. Junior then violently throws his mother's cat in Pecola's face. The cat claws her face and jumps to the floor. Pecola tries to escape the house, but Junior blocks her way. Crying, she notices that the cat has black fur and blue eyes. She bends down to pet it. Junior grabs the cat and swings it around by one of its legs. Pecola tries to stop him, but succeeds only in ripping her dress. When Junior loses his grip, the cat crashes against a window and collapses into a motionless heap.

At that instant, Geraldine walks in and looks on the scene with horror. She sees Pecola, with her torn clothes and her uncombed hair, and thinks of a whole class of poor black girls she has seen in her lifetime. She yells at Pecola, "Get out you nasty little black bitch!" Pecola backs out of the room and walks home in the cold wind.

UNDERSTANDING AND INTERPRETING
Winter, Section 2

Tidy, Spiteful Geraldine: In attempting to be socially acceptable, Geraldine overshoots her mark and winds up hating members of her own race. Her hatred might not be immediately apparent, since it lurks under cover of domesticity, cleanliness, and good behavior, but it is dangerous. She hates all black people who do not strive, as she does, to "be white." This attitude infects Junior, who comes to hate black women. Geraldine is beautiful, according to some standards, with her straight hair and light skin, but her family life is devoid of meaning. Sex with her husband is mechanical, not passionate, and her relationship with her cat is more important than her relationship with her only son. Her exit from the South was an escape from the "dirtiness" of her rural past. She tries to cover up any trace of her Southern roots, as if they are shameful. The narrator suggests that Geraldine is not an exception, but almost a cliché, an archetypal woman.

Two Groups: Geraldine voices her hatred by classifying other blacks as either "colored people," like herself, or "niggers." She will not let her son play with "niggers" because, according to Geraldine, they are dirty and loud, whereas she and her family members are cultivated and refined. Geraldine classifies Pecola as a specific type of "nigger." When she sees Pecola, Geraldine remembers all the pathetic, poor black girls she has seen in her past—girls who sleep six to a bed and break things in the five-and-dime stores. She distances herself from Pecola by calling her a "nasty little black bitch," as if reassuring herself that she has nothing in common with this black girl.

THE GREAT MIGRATION

Between 1940 and 1970, five million black Americans left the rural South and moved to the urban North in the largest mass migration in American history. They sought to leave behind the brutal legacies of Reconstruction, such as the vicious, violent, racist attacks by segregationists and the inequities of sharecropping. They moved into racially segregated neighborhoods of cities in the Midwest and the Northeast. Other social forces that fueled the migration included World War II and the need for labor in the northern manufacturing and steel industries of the post-war economic boom. Toni Morrison's maternal grandparents moved to Ohio from Kentucky in the years preceding the Great Migration, and in *The Bluest Eye*, Pauline and Cholly Breedlove moved North.

Geraldine as Society: Geraldine reacts to Pecola much as Mr. Yacobowski does. When she looks at Pecola, she sees a mere stereotype, not a unique human being. Pecola sees the look in Geraldine's eyes and finds the same expression she saw in Mr. Yacobowski's face—distaste and disgust bordering on hatred. Pecola sees herself through Geraldine's own self-hating eyes and leaves the house full of self-hatred.

Black Cat, One Life: The fate of Geraldine's blue-eyed black cat foreshadows Pecola's own fate. In the same way that the cat is used, abused, and left for dead, Pecola is used by others and left in a deluded, disturbed state.

SPRING
Section 1

One spring day, Claudia comes home from playing outside and finds Frieda upstairs lying in bed, crying. Frieda tells her that Mr. Henry fondled her breasts. When Mr. Henry returns home later that day, Mr. MacTeer runs him off with a rifle. A neighbor wonders if Frieda needs to see a doctor to make sure she is not "ruined." Mrs. MacTeer berates the neighbor for this suggestion, but Frieda is terrified to think that she might become ruined like the prostitutes. She and Claudia imagine being ruined and fat (i.e., pregnant). They remember that the prostitutes drink a lot, and Claudia suggests that Frieda drink whiskey to avoid gaining weight.

Claudia and Frieda set out to the Breedloves' house because they know that Cholly has whiskey. They find no one home. Upstairs on the porch they see Maginot Line, who tells them that Pecola is at the white **Fisher** family's house, where Mrs. Breedlove works. The girls go to find her. On the way, they pass a whites-only park, a place they dream of.

Pauline invites them into the sparkling kitchen at the Fishers' house, but cautions them not to touch anything. When Pauline goes to retrieve some laundry, the blonde **Fisher daughter** walks into the kitchen and asks the girls where "Polly" (Pauline) has gone.

Pecola accidentally knocks a hot pan of blueberry cobbler all over the floor and her legs, scalding herself. Pauline returns and knocks Pecola to the floor for her clumsiness. When the Fisher daughter starts to cry, Pauline rushes to comfort her. The daughter asks Pauline who the other girls are, and Pauline says, "Don't worry none."

UNDERSTANDING AND INTERPRETING
Spring, Section 1

"Ruined": The incident with Mr. Henry is a reminder that Claudia and Frieda are still young. Claudia is wise beyond her years in matters of race, understanding the cruelty of Hollywood enough to reject Shirley Temple, but she knows little about sex. The neighbor who wonders if Frieda is "ruined" is wondering if Mr. Henry raped Frieda, but the girls do not understand this. They think, with some truth, that "ruined" means that Frieda is doomed to the sad life of a prostitute. The incident also reminds us that Mrs. MacTeer is a good, understanding mother. She lashes out at the neighbor for suggesting that her daughter is ruined. She esteems her daughter and seems determined to protect her from harsh words.

A Rose By Any Other Name: Pauline lives another life in the Fisher house, which is a place that gleams and shines, unlike the Breedloves' storefront abode. The Fishers' house is quiet, and Pauline is in her element there, baking and minding the house. She assumes a different name in this world and maintains composure and dignity. In the Fisher's house, at least, Pauline cares more about maintaining her role as competent maid than she does about being a good mother to her daughter. She immediately rushes to the crying Fisher daughter instead of helping her own injured Pecola, a betrayal that shows how much Pauline treasures her place in her employers' home.

Where the Girl Has No Name: Pecola sees herself through the eyes of the Fisher daughter, and when her mother declines to tell the white girl Pecola's name, Pecola becomes nameless. Pecola learns from her mother's behavior that the identity of black children is apparently unimportant and that in the presence of whites, her mother is no longer the stern, authoritative "Mrs. Breedlove," but the affectionate and submissive "Polly."

SPRING
Section 2: SEEMOTHER...

We learn Pauline's life story from an omniscient narrator and Pauline's first-person recollections. She is born Pauline Williams in Alabama, the ninth of eleven children. When Pauline is young, her family moves to Kentucky and lives in a five-room house with running water. As a teenager, Pauline takes care of her younger siblings, Chicken and Pie. Also, she begins to have romantic fantasies about men, love, and sex. She dreams of a "Presence" who would carry her off somewhere forever.

One day, this "Presence" arrives in the form of Cholly Breedlove, a sober, light-eyed, and fancy free man. Pauline and Cholly move north to Ohio, where Cholly hopes to find work in a steel mill.

In the North, Pauline feels alienated from other black women. She does not straighten her hair, wear the right shoes, or talk with the same refinement as these women. Cholly begins to spend all his money on drinking. He becomes meaner and begins picking fights with Pauline. Pauline finds a regular job in order to have her own money. Her relationship with Cholly begins to falter, and she feels lonelier than ever, especially after she gets pregnant.

To escape the loneliness, she goes to the movies, where her romantic dreams are rekindled by white actresses such as **Jean Harlow** (1911–1937). The movies introduce her to the concept of physical beauty. One day, while watching a movie, Pauline loses a tooth while chewing on candy. After seeing these movies, Pauline cannot look at other people without judging their beauty. The omniscient narrator says that physical beauty and romantic love are "probably the most destructive ideas in the history of human thought."

Pauline describes going into labor. When she goes to the hospital, an old white doctor and some medical students treat her as if she is an animal. The doctor says she will give birth quickly and with no pain, like a horse. When one of the medical students looks at her face, Pauline looks straight back at him, and the man blushes. When she gives birth to the child, she cries out in pain just to prove the doctor wrong. After Pecola's birth, Cholly continues drinking heavily. Pauline becomes the family's main breadwinner. She returns to church and tries to live virtuously to deepen the contrast between herself and Cholly, whom she now sees as a model of sin. Pauline sees her children as her cross to bear.

"In *The Bluest Eye*, [Morrison] has split open the person and made us watch the heart beat. We feel faint, helpless, and afraid—not knowing what to do to cover it up and keep it beating. We think of remedies past and remedies in progress to apply somehow while the thrashing heart still beats."

RUBY DEE

LIVING IN LORAIN

The Bluest Eye takes place in Lorain, Ohio, the real town where Toni Morrison grew up. Lorain is an ethnically mixed, small city about thirty miles west of Cleveland, on the shores of Lake Erie. The steel industry was the primary employer in the city until the 1970s, so Cholly Breedlove's search for a job in a steel mill is a realistic plot detail. Today, the steel industry is still a major part of the area's economy, as it is in much of the Great Lakes region. Oberlin College, not far from the city of Lorain, was the first American institution of higher education that admitted women, and it was one of the first to enroll African-Americans. Oberlin and other parts of surrounding Lorain County were important stops on the Underground Railroad, which shepherded fugitive slaves into Canada.

The job at the Fisher house becomes a source of great pride to Pauline. She is devoted to the Fisher daughter and plays with her as if she is a baby doll, brushing her hair and dressing her in baby clothes. She loves the Fishers' house, which is a model of cleanliness, order, and beauty, and begins to neglect her own house and family, which seem horrible in comparison. The Fishers call her an "ideal servant." Pauline enjoys their praise and their lifestyle. Occasionally, she dreams of the days when she and Cholly were happy. She chooses not to leave him because staying with him reminds her of their happier past.

UNDERSTANDING AND INTERPRETING
Spring, Section 2

Two Perspectives: The life story of Pauline Breedlove is told from two perspectives: the omniscient narrator's point of view and Pauline's first-person narration. With Pauline's narration, Morrison makes the novel's most direct homage to the oral tradition of storytelling. Pauline's narration is like a documentary interview in which she offers her memories and impressions of certain periods from her life, speaking in her own nonstandard English which sings with the rhythm and cadence of stories told aloud. By speaking like this, Pauline reclaims her identity. She felt out of place in Ohio, surrounded by women like Geraldine with their straightened hair and college-inflected voices. Pauline speaks in her own way, and her act of storytelling is respected as an important one. It does not matter that she did not go to college; her story should be heard.

At the Movies: Pauline's visits to the movie theater awaken her to the standards of physical beauty as espoused by white people—standards that remain with her for the rest of her life. When she sees beautiful white movie stars like Jean Harlow, she realizes that according to the movies, she is not beautiful.

Beauty Without a Bite: The tooth Pauline loses symbolizes the disintegration and decay of her own notions of beauty. It also shows how the movies hurt moviegoers. As a result of going to the movies, Pauline loses a tooth, which makes her less attractive. Just as surely, as a result of going to the movies, Pauline loses her ability to see her own beauty. After the tooth is out, Pauline sits in the theater, starkly different from the beautiful Jean Harlow: Pauline is black, pregnant, missing a tooth, and married to a drunk. Meanwhile, the gorgeous Jean Harlow leads a romantic, carefree onscreen existence.

Treated Like an Animal: Pauline's experience in the hospital dehumanizes her once again. The doctor discusses her as if she is a horse, talking about her condition as if she cannot understand what he is saying. Only one of the medical students looks into her eyes, and when he does, he realizes that that they are mistreating her. Pauline forces the student to understand how she sees him as inhumane, just as she has been forced to understand that the students see her as an animal.

Pauline Becomes Polly: Pauline's alternate life at the Fisher home becomes her only source of pride. Morrison shows us how sad it is that Pauline can only thrive and be happy when she is serving white people. Like every human, Pauline craves peace and order and happiness, and in her life, such things are impossible. Only in the house of her white employers can she feel peaceful and happy. She does not aspire to be white. On the contrary, she is pleased to be identified as Polly, the ideal black servant. When she lets herself be called "Polly," it shows not only her affection for this alternate life, but her willing subservience to whites.

A Doll's House: Pauline's devotion to the Fisher daughter is similar to a girl's devotion to a baby doll. The Fisher daughter reminds us of the white baby doll that Claudia tore to pieces. Pauline plays with her doll-girl in a different way, loving it and embracing it. Both doll and real girl force their black owners to make a difficult choice about how to relate to them. No easy, thoughtless play is possible. Claudia chooses to reject white beauty, Pecola chooses to long for it, and Pauline chooses to embrace it.

SPRING

Section 3: SEEFATHER...

The omniscient narrator describes the life of Cholly Breedlove. When Cholly is four days old, his mother leaves him in a junk heap near the railroad tracks. Cholly's **Great Aunt Jimmy** finds Cholly and raises him herself. She tells Cholly that his father is **Samson Fuller**. Cholly quits school after six years and takes a job at a feed store. One of his coworkers is an old man named **Blue Jack** who has stories about slavery, women, and a time when he escaped a lynching.

When his Aunt Jimmy dies, Cholly meets distant members of his family at her funeral. Cholly goes into the woods with his girl, **Darlene**. On a bed of pine needles, they awkwardly figure out the mechanics of sex, but they are interrupted when two white men come upon them by accident. The men laugh and order Cholly to finish while they watch. Cholly simulates completing the sex act. Cholly feels nothing but hatred, not for the men but for Darlene.

Cholly irrationally fears Darlene might be pregnant, so he decides to leave town. He runs off to Macon, Georgia, where he hopes to find his father, Samson Fuller. He finds Fuller, who shows nothing but contempt when he finds out that Cholly is his son. He angrily shoos Cholly away. Traumatized, Cholly soils himself and jumps in the river to get clean.

Cholly soon realizes that he has nothing to lose. He begins to live according to his immediate needs and sensations. He wanders from job to job, sleeps in doorways, beds and beats many women, and serves time in jail and on a chain gang. It is hinted that he murders a few white men. When he marries Pauline, Cholly sinks into a routine that is novel for him in its steadiness. Only by drinking can he escape the boredom of this new life. He reacts to his children "based on what he felt at the moment."

Cholly comes home drunk one day and sees Pecola washing dishes. She is scratching her leg with her foot, a gesture that reminds him of the day he first met Pauline. He rushes forward and catches Pecola's foot, and she falls to the floor. He is filled with a strange desire for "what is forbidden and wild" and rapes Pecola on the kitchen floor, filled with a mixture of hatred and love.

UNDERSTANDING AND INTERPRETING Spring, Section 3

Cholly's Tragedy: Cholly has led a life of rejection, abandonment, and humiliation. His violated sex with Darlene is the most haunting experience from his past. What began as a harmless frolic turns into a degrading humiliation. When the white hunters watch him, treating him like a prostitute or an amusing animal in heat, Cholly suffers shame and loss of manhood. Although he might not be able to articulate the precise meaning of the violence the men inflict on him, his sense of their contempt and cruelty wounds him. Instead of losing his virginity, which would have been a step toward manhood, he becomes a sideshow. Like Pecola will years later, Cholly sees himself through the hunters' eyes. He becomes an animal, a clown, a half-naked black boy lying in the dirt, humiliated. Because the white men command that the sex act occur, it is as if they are raping Darlene. Cholly begins to hate Darlene perhaps because he senses that hating white men would be pointless, since they are so powerful. Hatred of black women, however, is something Cholly can indulge in and put into practice. Or perhaps he begins to hate Darlene because he sees her through the white men's disgusted, demeaning eyes.

River Deep, Mountain High: After being rejected by his father, Cholly goes to the river and washes himself. Water typically symbolizes renewal in literature, as it does here. Cholly renews himself and then realizes that he is free from the bonds of obligation to others. After he realizes that he has nothing to lose, Cholly begins to pursue a new, carefree life. This turns out to be a disastrous realization and approach to life, which suggests that not all renewals are happy ones.

Ironic Freedom: Cholly's newly free life soon becomes meaningless. He cares only about his own "perceptions and appetites" and lives according to no moral code. He sleeps wherever he wants, with whoever he wants. He is violent and murderous and takes the consequences of prison and the chain gang in stride. In his viler moments, Cholly violates his own family. He has no idea how to be a father or care for a family. After having lived according to his own whims, Cholly finds family life intolerably boring, and he hides in drunkenness and carelessness. Cholly lives the freest life of anyone in the novel, which makes us think that perhaps we should desire the constant fetters of family and responsibility. He knows there is no meaning in his life, and tries to take advantage of this absence by indulging in bad behavior. His pursuit of personal satisfaction makes him completely useless to anyone but himself.

SPRING

Section 4: SEETHEDOG...

A few months after being raped, Pecola seeks out one of Lorain's old eccentrics, a man nicknamed **Soaphead Church** who is a faith healer, fortune-teller, and believer in the supernatural. Descended in part from British nobility, Soaphead is born Elihue Micah Whitcomb in the Caribbean. The family's skin is light enough that most of them can pass for white, and Soaphead's Anglophile (English-loving) ancestors have learned to separate themselves from everything Africa-related.

The family excels in academics, and Soaphead lives immersed in books. He falls into a deep melancholy that causes the one love of his life, a woman named **Velma**, to leave him. He comes to America and eventually settles in Lorain, Ohio, where he poses as a minister, rejects all women, and lives a celibate life, except for occasional dalliances with young girls. He is given the nickname "Soaphead" because he soaps his hair to make it shiny and wavy.

Soaphead has become contemptuous of decay and disorder, but he believes that all the disorder in the world is part of God's cosmic plan. Disorder tests people and helps them strive for success and happiness. Soaphead believes that he might have done a better job with the universe than God did.

Pecola asks Soaphead to make her eyes blue. Soaphead first feels affection for the girl, whom he sees as "a little black girl who wanted to rise up out of the pit of her own blackness and see the world with blue eyes." But then he becomes frustrated because he knows he cannot help her. Soaphead suggests she ask the Lord to help her. He decides offering up his landlord's revolting dog, **Bob**, will do the trick. Soaphead cannot stand to watch Bob suffer. He has bought poison to put the dog out of its misery, but has not yet been able to bring himself to use it.

Soaphead gives Pecola a piece of meat dipped in poison and instructs her to feed it to Bob. If Bob eats it and nothing happens, he says, God will not grant her wish. But if Bob eats the meat and behaves strangely, her wish will be granted. She feeds the dog, and it quickly gags and collapses. Pecola runs off in fear and bafflement. Soaphead sits down and writes a long letter to God, complaining about the disorder in the world, disorder that sends a girl like Pecola to seek out his services. He informs God that he (Soaphead) granted Pecola's wish and gave her "cobalt blue" eyes, which no one will see but her.

UNDERSTANDING AND INTERPRETING
Spring, Section 4

God's Shoddy Work: Soaphead's family rejects its African roots in order to gain acceptance in British colonial life. As a result, Soaphead seems to lack a firm identity. He is neither black nor white, and he does not strive to be either. This lack of identity worsens his melancholy and unhappiness with the world. He believes that the world is disorderly because of God's mistakes, and he prefers to rely on his own judgment, however skewed it may be. He thinks of Bob the dog, for example, as a mistake that needs to be put out of its misery. When Pecola comes to him, he thinks he has a chance to set the world straight for both Pecola and the dog. Soaphead can understand Pecola and feel loving toward her, because he relates to her racial self-hatred. He is charmed by Pecola's desire to "rise up out of the pit of her own blackness," just as his family once did.

The Bleak Truth: Soaphead's philosophy, as revealed in his letter to God, is based on the idea that people's lives are predetermined. Soaphead and Pecola believe that their race is a determining factor in their lives. They both try to do what they can to change their race, since this seems like the only way to avoid doom. Soaphead and Pecola can seem almost certifiably insane at times, but Morrison does not suggest that they are all wrong in their assumptions. To a great extent, Pecola's life *is* determined by her race. Even if she was confident and happy, she would not magically win the respect of whites. She would not be treated well or escape the unhappy legacy of her family or be afforded good opportunities. In the end, she is right: in the world she has been given, in the atmosphere of racism that chokes her, Pecola could change her destiny only by changing her very race.

Blue-Eyed Understanding: Soaphead and Pecola understand that getting blue eyes means getting a new chance at life. Pecola wants to "see the world with blue eyes," which means she wants to see the world as white children do. Children with blue eyes, like Dick and Jane, see the world as a happy, benevolent, fair place where good people get the good things they deserve, and merit is rewarded. Getting blue eyes also means that people will see your eyes and treat you as white people are treated: with kindness and fairness.

SUMMER

Claudia, as narrator, remembers the summer as the "season of storms." She and Frieda sell marigold seeds door to door to save up for a new bicycle. During their trips around the neighborhood, they overhear people talking about a pregnant girl. Eventually, they figure out that Pecola has become pregnant by her father.

The girls feel embarrassed for Pecola and the Breedloves. Claudia longs for someone to want the baby. They overhear someone say that it would be a miracle if the baby lived, so they decide to encourage their own miracle. Instead of selling the seeds, they plant them, hoping that if the flowers grow, Pecola's baby will be healthy.

The novel's final section ("LOOKLOOKHERECOMESAFRIEND . . . ") is a dialogue between Pecola and an imaginary friend who sees her blue eyes. During the conversation, we learn that Cholly actually raped Pecola twice. Upon discovering Pecola's pregnancy, Pauline beats her daughter, since she assumes that Pecola is partly to blame for the rape.

Pecola loves her new blue eyes and wants them to be the bluest in the world. Even her imaginary friend threatens to run off because Pecola is being so silly about her eyes. Pecola asks the friend if she will come back when Pecola has the bluest eyes, and the girl says she will. Claudia, who

> "Much of writing might be described as mental pregnancy with successive difficult deliveries."
>
> J. B. PRIESTLEY

narrates the final passages, remembers that Pecola tried to flap her arms and fly into the blue sky. Claudia and Frieda never go to see Pecola again because they feel they failed her. The marigolds do not grow, and Pecola descends into madness.

In conclusion, Claudia remarks that the soil in their town is not good for flowers that year, and she thinks that perhaps the country itself is hostile. Certain seeds will never be nurtured there.

UNDERSTANDING AND INTERPRETING
Summer

Putting It Together: The story about Pecola becomes the stuff of gossip, and Claudia and Frieda learn about it after overhearing their mother and the neighbors talking. In keeping with the novel's various stories and narrations, the tale of Pecola's pregnancy comes to the girls in bits and pieces.

Longing to See: Pecola's conversation with her imaginary friend reflects her growing madness. Anxious that she does not have the bluest eyes possible, she is desperate to be seen and fraught with fear that the only friend who can see her blue eyes will leave her. She has never been able to see herself, and now the only way she can is to invent another person through hallucination.

Life is But a Dream: Claudia's final narration is ominous and mournful. She leaves the reader with the image of barren soil and the opinion that Pecola's madness and her baby's death were determined by her environment: her neglectful and abusive family, her race, and her violent, cruel world.

ON THE BRINK ✻ Pecola's story ends in the fall of 1941, an ominous time in history, when the United States was on the brink of entering World War II. After Japan's surprise bombing of Pearl Harbor Naval Base in Hawaii on December 7, 1941, President **Franklin Delano Roosevelt** (1882–1945) addressed Congress with a speech in which he called the date a "day of infamy." Soon thereafter, Congress formalized a declaration of war against the Axis Powers, Japan and Germany. In an alliance with England, France, and the Soviet Union, the United States tipped the war's balance in favor of the Allied Powers. Germany fell in May of 1945, and Japan surrendered after the United States decimated the cities of Hiroshima and Nagasaki with atomic bombs three months later.

Conclusions

The Bluest Eye explores white America's ideal of physical beauty and the ways in which this ideal ravages the identity of a young black girl. Pecola rejects any identity except the one she believes would make her beautiful. She longs to be white, as signified by her longing for blue eyes, and since this cannot be, she goes mad. With Pecola's story, Morrison suggests that physical beauty is the most devastating ideal of Western civilization.

Pecola, like other neglected, scorned people in *The Bluest Eye*, has difficulty separating her own sense of identity from the way other people see her. The narrative technique of using different voices throughout the novel reflects Pecola's disjointed identity. The distorted, mangled language of the *Dick and Jane* primers at the beginning of many chapters is a metaphor for this destruction of identity and for gruesome disconnect between idealized white America and Pecola's reality.

SULA

An Overview

Key Facts

Genre: novel of black identity

Date of First Publication: 1973

Setting: 1919–1941 and 1965 in the "Bottom" neighborhood in the hills above Medallion, Ohio

Narrator: Anonymous, third-person

Plot Overview: Two black girls grow up in a small town. One follows a traditional path to adulthood, one follows an unconventional path.

Style, Technique, and Language

Style—Narration and Fluid Time: A third-person omniscient (all-knowing) narrator tells the story of the characters, explaining their thoughts and feelings. Briefly, in Part Two, the narration shifts to first-person when Nel prays and Sula thinks. This switch to first-person allows the women to express their individual searches for identity.

The story unfolds chronologically, but each chapter scissors back and forth in time. We learn about Shadrack's and Eva's pasts, for example, through flashbacks. The story is circular. The short prologue at the beginning of the novel connects with the final chapter. Both prologue and final chapter are narrated in the 1960s.

Technique—Imagery and Metaphors

Water and Fire: Water and fire help characters achieve identities. Shadrack discovers his existence by seeing his reflection in water, and he later turns to fishing and living by the water. Nel and Sula discover their own mortality and capacity for good and evil after Chicken Little drowns in the river. The fire set by Eva and the one later that kills Hannah show how Eva approaches motherhood as a creator and destroyer.

Life as a House: The appearance of houses reflect the personalities of their inhabitants. The Wright house is repressively well-ordered and tidy, which reflects the conventional order that Helene Wright imposes on herself and her family. The home of the Peace family is chaotic. Boarders move in and move out, dishes sit in the sink, old newspapers pile up, and Hannah has sex in every nook and cranny. In keeping with Shadrack's calm, his shack by the river is neat and orderly.

> "Morrison's dialogue is so compressed and life-like that it sizzles."
>
> SARA BLACKBURN

Sula's Birthmark: Good and evil are not rigidly defined in this novel, an ambiguity that is reflected in Sula's birthmark, which everyone interprets differently. People see it, variously, as a stem and rose, a serpent, Hannah's ashes, and a tadpole. Depending on the person judging Sula, her "evil" takes on different meanings.

A Plague of Robins: The Bottom's residents' attitude toward the birds is typical of their general attitude toward evil. Instead of attempting to prevent the birds from taking over their town, the citizens sit back and let them run their course, just as they let Sula go about her life.

Language—Greek Chorus and Individual Voice: The townspeople of the Bottom generally speak with one voice, almost like a Greek chorus. Through gossip and rumors, they blame Sula for the strange happenings in town. Sula is an individual, which offends this town of conformists. Nel speaks for the town when she tells Sula, "You can't be walking around all independent-like, doing whatever you like, taking what you want, leaving what you don't."

Sula distinguishes herself by speaking tersely and directly. She does not mince words and she does not hide her beliefs. She is defiant and individualistic. As she says, "I got my mind. And what goes on in it. Which is to say, I got me." Ajax, another free spirit, speaks with his own brand of vulgar sensuality.

Characters in *Sula*

Ajax: The young man in town known for his "magnificently foul mouth." He mutters "pig meat" when young Sula and Nel walk by him. But time passes, and when he is thirty-eight, he and Sula become lovers. His real name is Albert Jacks (he got his nickname because "A. Jacks" sounds like "Ajax").

Betty: Teapot's careless mother. After Teapot falls down Sula's stairs, Betty gets sober and tries to be a better parent.

Boyboy: The husband of Eva Peace. A womanizer, he abandons Eva after five years, leaving her with three young children and no way to support them. He returns a few years later with a new, young companion, seeming flush with money.

Chicken Little: The young boy whom Sula and Nel accidentally drown in the river.

The Reverend Deal: The minister of the Bottom.

The Deweys: Three unrelated boys taken in by Eva Peace and each named "Dewey King" by her. The Deweys spend all their time together and appear to stop growing after age ten. They die in the tunnel collapse that occurs in the Bottom, although their bodies are never found.

Jude Greene: The husband of Nel Wright, with whom he has two children. Jude has an affair with Sula and leaves his family.

Mrs. Jackson: A neighbor of Eva Peace. She likes to eat ice. A frail woman, Mrs. Jackson dies in the tunnel collapse.

Henri Martin: Cecile Sabat's friend in New Orleans.

Eva Peace: The matriarch of the Peace family. Eva is mother to Hannah, Pearl, and Plum, and owner of the large boarding house on Carpenter Road in the Bottom. She has only one leg.

Hannah Peace: Sula's mother. She never remarries after her husband, Rekus, dies. Hannah dies in an accidental fire in the backyard.

Pearl Peace: Eva Peace's middle child. She married at fourteen and moved to Flint, Michigan.

Plum (Ralph) Peace: Eva Peace's youngest child. He fought in World War I and returned to Medallion addicted to heroin.

Sul Peace: The novel's protagonist and the best friend of Nel Wright. Sula is a free spirit who leaves the Bottom at seventeen to attend college and returns to wreak havoc on her small hometown.

Mr. Buckland Reed: The proprietor of the Bottom's lottery.

Rekus: The late husband of Hannah Peace and father of Sula.

Cecile Sabat: The strict, religious grandmother of Helene Wright. Cecile raised Helene and eventually set her up with Wiley Wright, Cecile's great nephew. When Cecile dies, Helene and Nel go to New Orleans by train for her funeral.

Rochelle Sabat: The forty-eight-year-old mother of Helene Wright. She is a Creole-speaking prostitute in the Sundown House of New Orleans.

Shadrack: A half-crazed veteran of World War I. He returns shell-shocked from the war and founds National Suicide Day in 1920. He supports himself by fishing, but is usually seen walking around town drunk, yelling insults at people, and urinating in public. Shadrack lives on the outskirts of town in a well-kept shack.

Mr. and Mrs. Sugs: Eva Peace's closest neighbors in the Bottom.

"Extravagantly beautiful, Morrison's characters are locked in a world where hope for the future is a foreign commodity, yet they are enormously, achingly alive."

SARA BLACKBURN

Tar Baby: One of Eva Peace's boarders. Tar Baby is rumored to be white. He is jailed for causing an auto accident while walking in the street.

Teapot: The little boy who lives across the street from Sula. He accidentally falls down Sula's stairs, and she is accused of intentionally hurting him. After the incident, Teapot's mother stops drinking and resolves to be a better parent.

Helene Wright: Nel Wright's mother and Wiley Wright's wife. She is a beautiful woman with presence and conviction that give her authority. She runs a stern, upright household.

Nel Wright: The best friend of Sula and the daughter of Helene and Wiley Wright. She marries Jude Greene and is abandoned by him.

Wiley Wright: Nel's father and Helene's husband. He is a ship's cook on a Great Lakes steamer and is often away from home for months at a time.

Reading *Sula*

PART ONE
Prologue and Chapter 1: 1919

Until the 1960s, the black residents of Medallion, Ohio, lived above the town in the hills in a place known as "the Bottom." The Bottom, once a vibrant neighborhood in which there was much dancing, music, and laughter, is no longer a pretty place. Now stripped-down, faded buildings front its empty streets.

There was an old joke about how the Bottom got its name. Before Medallion became a town, a white farmer hoodwinked his emancipated slave into believing that the land in the hills was more fertile than the rich valley below. He told him the hills were "the bottom of heaven." The slave took possession of the hills, which were neither fertile nor easy to farm. So while the whites lived down in the valley, the blacks lived in the Bottom, where they literally looked down on the whites. The hills had a beautiful vista and large, shady trees, and occasionally whites would visit and wonder if the blacks actually did get the better bargain.

In the Bottom, on January 3, 1920, a young man named **Shadrack** institutes a new holiday he calls National Suicide Day. During World War I, Shadrack fought in horrific battles in France. Once, he watched a shell blow the head off the soldier next to him. Shadrack fell unconscious and was hospitalized for shell shock. When he woke up in the hospital, he saw food on his tray, neat and ordered in compartments, and it comforted him.

The half-crazed Shadrack comes back to America and goes to an institution near Medallion. After he is released, he sees the people on the street as "thin slips, like paper dolls floating down the walks." He realizes that he is twenty-two years old, but he knows nothing, has no possessions, and has nothing to do. He becomes a vagrant and is taken to jail, where he stares at the walls and looks at his reflection in the toilet-bowl water. He sees his face and is astonished at its blackness. His own reflection proves to him that he exists, which he has been unsure about.

When he is released, Shadrack walks twenty-two miles to the Bottom. He invents Suicide Day, which he intends to be the one day each year when the townspeople have a chance to commit suicide or kill each other. This way, he thinks, people can live without fear of death during the rest of the year.

Shadrack lives as a hermit near the river, selling fish a couple of days a week and the rest of the time getting drunk and yelling obscenities around town. When the townspeople discover that he is generally harmless, they learn to live with his eccentricities. Most people hide in their houses on Suicide Day, when Shadrack parades through town banging a cowbell and shouting insults. Still, the Day becomes a town tradition and part of the fabric of life.

UNDERSTANDING AND INTERPRETING Prologue and Chapter 1

As Time Goes By: *Sula* is divided into two parts that chronicle two different periods in the lives of the major characters, Nel Wright and Sula Peace. The narration moves chronologically, beginning when the girls are ten and moving forward to their adult years and Nel's middle age. Chapters that have titles containing a date or year (e.g., "1919") are generally centered around events that occur during that year. Frequently, however, the timeline departs from the year in question so that Morrison can describe past events. For instance, in "1919," much of the action takes place during Shadrack's tour of duty in France, which occurred in December of 1917. The narrator then follows his subsequent institutionalization in 1918–1919 and his return to the Bottom in late 1919. The inaugural parade of National Suicide Day, mentioned in the opening sentences of the chapter, actually takes place in 1920. So, in a manner that sets the pace for the rest of the novel, the year of the chapter's title, 1919, is used simply as a focal point for the chapter.

Bottoms Up: The untitled prologue gives us the picture of a once-thriving neighborhood that is now gradually deteriorating. The Bottom, ironically named since it is up in the hills, is now dotted with shacks and rutted roads. The residents of the Bottom laugh at the way they were tricked, according to an old story, into taking the bad land of the hills, but they suspect they got the better end of the

WORLD WAR I

Shadrack's experience in World War I is typical of the brutality of the so-called Great War fought in Europe between 1914 and 1918. The Allies (France, Britain, Russia, and later the United States) defeated the Central Powers (Germany, Austria-Hungary, and Turkey) after years without a single decisive battle. More than 10 million soldiers were killed and twice that number wounded in what came to be known as trench warfare. Armies fired rounds of machine-gun fire and shells at each other's dug-in front lines, separated by "No Man's Land," the ground between the enemies. After the war ended, harsh penalties and reparations were imposed on Germany, humiliating the country and contributing to the rise of Hitler and the Nazis only fifteen years later. The war, which was the bloodiest century of fighting in world history, is considered the defining event of the twentieth century. It led to new views on alienation and life's meaninglessness.

deal. Years after giving the Bottom to the blacks, the whites take it back and turn it into a golf course and, we find out later, a terrain of neat suburban homes with a view of the valley below. The Bottom, it seems, is not the bottom of anything. The white farmer of the story was right to say that it is desirable land.

Out of Many, One: As the novel progresses, the community of the Bottom takes on the features of one character with one set of attitudes and reactions. Morrison explores how outsiders such as Shadrack and, later, Sula, reveal the way the community thinks as a group and passes judgment as a collective chorus of voices.

The Self-Aware Shadrack: The war leaves Shadrack shell shocked. He has a new outlook on life, which he now believes to be full of incomprehensible disorder. He emerges from the institution completely blank, with no memory of his past and nothing to guide him in any direction. It seems that he is coming loose from the moorings of reality, wondering if he even exists. Only the reflection of his black face proves to him that he is real. In a sense, Shadrack's blackness saves him. When he sees his face reflected in the water, he sees an identity. Shadrack's twenty-two-mile walk back to Medallion—one mile for each of his years—suggests that Medallion and the Bottom are an extension of his self. Shadrack is an integral part of the community, even if he lives in a shack on the outskirts of town and is greeted with wariness when he walks around town screaming at people. Shadrack is a pariah and an outcast, but has a definite sense of self and his place in the community.

Order from Chaos: The order of Shadrack's new life, forged from the chaos of the war, is unique. Upon his release from the institution, Shadrack does not know which way to go. He is directionless and bewildered by his war-born realization that the world is brutal and illogical. National Suicide Day is his way of giving order to the universe. The Day is both absurd and completely logical. Creating it is a gesture of humanity and kindness on Shadrack's part, because he wants people to compartmentalize their fear of death and confine it to a single day. He reasons that since we must fear death, we might as well fear it on our own terms. Confining the fear to one day theoretically allows people to live the other 364 days of the year free from the fear of death. Despite this orderliness, however, the rest of the town views Shadrack as an element of chaos, walking around "drunk, loud, obscene, funny, outrageous." Other characters have more mundane ways of ordering their lives, and they do not understand Shadrack's attempt at existential order.

The Safety of Shapes: Triangles are a mathematical entity, precise and well-defined. They bring to mind a divine order, the trinity. Shadrack's hospital food tray is the first clue that he will be able to achieve a new order in his life. The triangular compartments of the tray hold the different-colored food in a way that comforts Shadrack. Their order makes him feel restful.

PART ONE
Chapter 2: 1920

Helene Wright is born in New Orleans to a Creole mother who works as a prostitute in the Sundown House. She is raised by her grandmother, **Cecile Sabat**, who keeps Helene as far away from her mother and the Sundown House as possible. When Helene is a teenager, Cecile matches her up with one of her great-nephews, **Wiley Wright**. Wiley and Helene are married and move to his home in Medallion, where he works on Lake Erie as a ship's cook.

Nine years later, in 1910, Helene Wright gives birth to her only child, a daughter named **Nel**. Under Helene's stern upbringing, Nel becomes obedient and polite. Helene takes it upon herself to drive "her daughter's imagination underground" and quiet Nel's enthusiasm. Helene thinks of her life as "satisfactory." She feels she has gotten far enough away from Sundown House. She is an impressive woman, with an imposing, authoritative air. She wears her hair in a tight bun, keeps an eye on other people's manners, and attends a black conservative church.

In November, 1920, when Nel is ten, Helene learns that Cecile is ill. She takes Nel on a long railroad trip to Louisiana. They are forced to sit in the "Colored Only" cars of the trains. Many of the stops along the way do not have bathrooms for black people. At one point, Nel wets her pants. When they finally arrive in New Orleans, Cecile has already passed away. Helene's mother, **Rochelle**, is at Cecile's house waiting for them. Helene reluctantly introduces Nel to Rochelle, and Rochelle tries to be friendly to the girl. She speaks Creole, and Nel cannot understand her. Helene can barely hide her contempt for her mother. Later, she gives Nel a bath.

When they return to Medallion, Nel concludes that the trip was exciting and scary. She looks at herself in the mirror and whispers, "I'm me. I'm not their daughter. I'm not Nel. I'm me. Me . . . I want to be wonderful." She imagines taking trips away from Medallion in the future. We learn that the trip to New Orleans is the first and last she ever makes.

Still, Nel's newfound sense of herself gives her the strength to cultivate a new friendship with a girl named **Sula Peace**. Sula is charming and polite, and she is soon welcomed into the Wright home, despite Helene's initial misgivings about Sula's mother, who has a spotty reputation. Nel prefers to visit Sula at Sula's house, since it is a rowdy abode. Sula's mother, **Hannah Peace**, is less strict than Helene, and Sula's one-legged grandmother, **Eva Peace**, tells stories and gives Nel candy. All sorts of people drop by to chat, and dirty dishes are left stacked in the sink for hours. It is a welcome change from Nel's own home.

> "The purest treasure mortal times afford
> Is spotless reputation."
>
> WILLIAM SHAKESPEARE

UNDERSTANDING AND INTERPRETING

Chapter 2

The Upright Wright Woman: The creator of her own secure, middle-class existence, Helene has spent her life trying to escape the Sundown House, the embarrassing location of her earthy, unseemly roots. She cringes when she must come near her mother, Rochelle, as if Rochelle's values and lifestyle are somehow contagious. She even gives Nel a bath upon reaching New Orleans, as if to wash off Rochelle's corrupting influence. Even the Creole language that Rochelle speaks is a symbol of grime and commonness to Helene, and she refuses to translate the words for Nel. Helene is happy to have escaped her past and moved up in the world. Cecile raised Helene with religion and strictness, an ethos Helene follows in raising her own daughter. Besides Cecile's influence, Helene judges other parts of her New Orleans heritage not worth remembering or passing on to Nel. Her married name, "Wright," echoes "right," which she has strived to do and be.

First Exposure: When she is ten, Nel is exposed for the first time to a life outside the conventions of the structured universe that Helene has created for her. The railroad trip is one of discovery, and it fills her with both exhilaration and fear, feelings brought on by the newness of the experience. In Rochelle, she sees the inverse of her mother in her grandmother, who is a gritty, candid, friendly woman who even speaks a different language than Helene does. Nel might not understand that her grandmother was, or still is, a prostitute, but she senses that Rochelle has a starkly different life than she and her own mother have. Nel realizes that just because Rochelle is different, she is not necessarily bad. In many ways, Nel reacts to Rochelle in a more mature, wise way than her mother does.

She is beginning to pull away from her mother and form her own moral sense. After the trip, she realizes that she can be herself, not simply the daughter of Helene. She begins to yearn for a different life than the one her mother has lived, a yearning that takes the immediate form of planning more trips. Nel begins to see the possibilities of the world, and they appear endless.

Sooty Sula: Nel's friendship with Sula opens her to a world that resembles New Orleans more than Medallion. The Peace house is in constant flux. Boarders move in and out, dirty dishes lie about, and stories are told. It is a place of lively activity that contrasts with the placid quiet of her own house. Hannah Peace is not authoritarian or rigid, and Eva Peace is a fantastic one-legged wonder. The house reminds Nel of the exhilaration she experienced in New Orleans. It is "woolly" and "sooty" and full of women who show their "me-ness."

Peace versus (W)right: The second chapter of *Sula* is a study in order versus chaos. It pits the traditional values of Helene Wright against the unconventional paths taken by Rochelle and the Peaces. The narrative begins in the neat and tidy Wright household, moves south to the roughness and disorder of Rochelle, and returns north to Nel and Sula, both of whom discover, at the other girl's house, what they are missing in their everyday lives. Morrison does not suggest that order is better than chaos, or vice versa. We can easily understand Helene's impulse to separate herself from prostitution and seek out respectability, and we can also see the appeal of Sula's happy-go-lucky household. Morrison may mean that elements of both order and chaos are necessary for a happy life. Sula needs the peace and quiet of the Wright's house, and Nel needs the ease of the Peaces' house. Neither girl has the proper mixture of elements in her life.

PART ONE
Chapter 3: 1921

The narrator tells us Eva's story. Eva marries a man named **BoyBoy** and has three children: **Hannah**, **Pearl**, and **Plum**. BoyBoy abandons her after the children are born, leaving Eva with no money. The neighbors, **Mr. and Mrs. Suggs** and **Mrs. Jackson**, who likes ice cream, try to help out, but Eva knows she cannot not rely on them forever.

When Plum is still an infant, he stops having bowel movements. In desperation, Eva finally reaches inside his bowels with her lard-greased finger to save his life. Eva realizes she needs to do something to assist her family. She entrusts the children to Mr. and Mrs. Suggs and leaves town, saying she will be gone for a couple of days. Eighteen months later, she comes home with a big wad of money, missing her leg.

BoyBoy returns for a visit a few years later, wearing a new suit and accompanied by a young, well-dressed companion. Eva treats him cordially, but after he leaves, she feels great hatred for him. She retreats to her bedroom on the third floor and rarely sets foot on the stairs again. Eva takes many cast-off children into the house and raises them. She welcomes three such boys in 1921 and names each of them "Dewey." Thereafter the boys are collectively called the **Deweys**, and they live in the house all their lives.

Another resident of the house is **Tar Baby**, a "beautiful, slight, quiet" man who never speaks above a whisper. He is rumored to be half-white, although Eva thinks he is all white. He lives quietly, drinking a lot and getting work when he can. He and the Deweys are the first to join Shadrack in his observances of National Suicide Day. Eva's oldest child is Hannah, the mother of Sula, who lives at the house with Eva and helps with the boarders. The Peace women love men. Hannah flirts with every man she meets, even newlyweds. She is always having sex in some corner of the house. She never settles down with anyone other than Sula's father, **Rekus**, who died when Sula was very young. Sula learns that "sex [is] pleasant and frequent, but otherwise unremarkable."

Eva hopes to bequeath her estate to her youngest child, Plum. He goes off to fight in World War I and returns home a heroin addict. He hides in his room and steals from the family and boarders to pay for his habit. One night in 1921, Eva leaves the third floor for the first time in years. She visits Plum's room and finds him in a drug-induced sleep. She spreads kerosene on him, lights a newspaper, and sets him on fire. The household wakes up and Hannah yells to Eva that Plum is burning. Eva looks knowingly into Hannah's eyes, and Hannah instantly understands the horror of what is happening.

HARLEM RENAISSANCE

In the 1920s, far from Medallion, Ohio, African-American literature and culture were alive and thriving in Harlem. Literary giants such as **Langston Hughes** (1902–1967), **Countee Cullen** (1903–1946), **Arna Bontemps** (1902–1973), and **Jean Toomer** (1894–1967) began to find an international audience during this era. The political and literary magazine *Crisis* was published by **W.E.B. Du Bois** (1868–1963), the noted activist and founder of what would become the NAACP. Jazz flourished with the music of **Duke Ellington** (1899–1974) and **Jelly Roll Morton** (1890–1941). Toni Morrison later captured the vibrancy of the era in her novel, *Jazz* (1993).

UNDERSTANDING AND INTERPRETING

Chapter 3

7 Carpenter's Road: The Peace house is an organic place, growing and stretching to fit the needs and demands placed on it. Eva presides over the matriarchy (female-run family) of the place, with Hannah functioning as her second-in-command. The Peace family is held together by the dynamics of action and reaction, as opposed to the Wrights, who live a placid, static, unchanging family life.

Sacrifices of Eva Peace: Like the biblical Eve, Eva is a mother figure. She offers a portrait of self-sacrificing motherhood. When BoyBoy abandons the family, Eva takes control of its fate and finds a way to support the children, even losing a limb in the process. We do not learn precisely what happened, but the implication is that she sold the limb, or lost it somehow in her quest for money. She is generous to those who lack the structure and support of stable families, as evidenced by her adoption of children like the Deweys. The house at 7 Carpenter's Road is her own creation, as if she were the carpenter herself. Her role as creator is symbolized in Christian terms by the number 7 (God created the world in seven days) and by name "Carpenter" (Jesus was a carpenter).

Dewey, Dewey, and Dewey: The Deweys talk alike and look alike, and people treat them as if they are three parts of the same being. Their interconnectedness mimics and foreshadows the ways in which Sula and Nel begin to coalesce in the next chapter.

Love and Sex: Different manifestations of love and lovemaking appear throughout the novel. Eva's love for Plum is one of the most vivid examples. When Plum is an infant, Eva shows that she will do anything to protect him, including lose a leg. But when he returns from the war a drug addict, Eva feels, rightly or wrongly, that taking his life is the most merciful action she can perform as his mother. Love is a complex and multifaceted entity for the Peaces. Their ways of loving are unconventional. They do not feel, as Helen Wright does, that love means only marriage, children, and fidelity. Sex in the Peace house is similarly unconventional. It has less to do with love than with affection and physical pleasure. Hannah sleeps with whomever she pleases and asks nothing from the men

> "Morrison's work is sensuality combined with an intrigue that only a piercing intellect could create."
>
> BARBARA CHRISTIAN

except simple pleasure. She stays with one man long enough to have a child, but once he is gone, she is not interested in finding another special man. Sula is loved by her own mother, and she absorbs the conflicting, unconventional notions of love that dominate her house.

PART ONE
Chapter 4: 1922

By the time Sula and Nel are twelve, they share a deep friendship. They luxuriate in their collective loneliness, spending all of their time together. Their personalities complement each other. Nel is strong and steady, Sula is capricious and unpredictable. Four white Irish boys occasionally harass the girls on their walks home from school, prompting them to find other ways home. One day, Sula suggests they take their usual route home. They run into the hooligans, and Sula pulls out a paring knife. The boys look eager for a better-than-usual fight. But instead of attacking them with the knife, Sula slashes off the tip of one of her fingers. She says to them, "If I can do that to myself, what you suppose I'll do to you?" The boys back off and scatter.

In time, the girls turn their attention toward grown men. Often, they walk down the main drag of the Bottom and subject themselves to the ogles of the men, both young and old. One of the men, a twenty-one-year-old named **Ajax**, is a man of "sinister beauty." He is also known as a man of few words. As Sula and Nel walk by him, he mutters "pig meat" in their general direction. The girls take his words as a compliment and hide their delight.

One summer day, Sula overhears her mother talking with some friends. Hannah says that all mothers love their children, but she adds, "I love Sula. I just don't like her. That's the difference." The girls wander over to the river and lie on the ground. A young boy, **Chicken Little**, joins them, and Sula offers to teach him how to climb a tree. After they climb a birch, Sula swings Chicken Little around. He slips from her hands into the water and sinks like a stone. The girls watch the stillness of the water. Chicken Little does not come back up to the surface.

Shadrack lives on the other side of the river, and Nel wonders if he saw what happened. Sula runs over to the house and knocks, but gets no answer. She goes inside and is surprised to find the house very orderly and peaceful. Shadrack appears at the door. She walks out without asking him anything. Shadrack says "always," as if to answer her unasked question. Nel comforts Sula and says she is not to blame for Chicken's death.

Chicken Little's body is found later that day by a bargeman. The girls never tell anyone that they are responsible for the drowning. At the funeral, there is a distance between Nel and Sula. Nel feels as if the rest of the mourners have "convicted and hanged her right there in the pew," even though she also feels blameless. Sula sobs without heaving or gasping. At the cemetery, Nel and Sula stand with their hands entwined, their separateness gone, as butterflies fly in and out of the flowers around the grave.

UNDERSTANDING AND INTERPRETING
Chapter 4

An Odd Couple: After less than a year of friendship, Nel and Sula are inseparable, as if parts of the same being. Just as their households are opposites, Nel and Sula have opposite personalities that, put together, form one complete person. Nel is dependable, and Sula is fickle. Their contrasting personalities complement each other, and they each derive something different from their friendship. Sula provides Nel with a way to cut loose—to get away from the oppressive orderliness of the Wright house—as when the girls go out and invite the attention of grown men. In Nel, Sula finds a type of love that she feels unable to get at home from her mother. Nel also inspires Sula to assert herself more in her daily life, as when Sula terrifies the four boys who have been tormenting the girls.

Revised Jekyll and Hyde: Nel is responsible, Sula is unreliable. Nel is loyal, Sula is unfaithful. Nel is, generally, good, and Sula is, generally, evil. But we begin to see that Sula and Nel may not be as different as they first appear to be.

As is the case with Eva Peace's brand of love, the definitions of good and evil take on an ambiguous meaning. For example, although Sula is most responsible for Chicken Little's death, Nel is complicit in it. Even though Sula physically throws Chicken into the river, which seems to make her the more evil of the pair, neither girl has the instinct to leap into the water and try to save Chicken Little. Both girls try to hide the deed from other people. In fact, Nel's first impulse is to find out if Shadrack has seen anything. At the funeral, the girls have separate but similar reactions. Nel secretly feels as if she's been convicted by the moral authority of the town, but at the same time she feels blameless for Chicken's death. On the other hand, Sula cries quietly and seems to feel guilty. The behavior at the funeral seems to make Nel the more evil of the two.

> "Good and evil appear to be joined in every culture at the spine."
>
> FLANNERY O'CONNOR

The Sky Has Fallen: When Chicken Little drowns, the girls' childhoods come to an end. They must now begin to question their own mortality and think about people's capacity for destruction and evil. Their existence as children had started to wane even before Chicken Little's death, however. When Sula cuts off the tip of her finger, she shows that childhood fun and rivalries have given way to the violence of adulthood. When the girls enjoy the insulting, sexual words of Ajax, it shows that their sexuality is beginning to emerge. The seeds of Sula's adult experience are planted, and she foreshadows her own future when she plays with Chicken Little. By tempting him into the tree, spinning him around, and letting go, she is symbolically enacting her eventual pattern of seducing men, sleeping with them, and then hurting them by discarding them.

THE TALE OF CHICKEN LITTLE ❦ Just as Sula tempts Chicken Little to climb a tree, a fox in the Chicken Little fairy tale tempts Chicken Little. The simple story begins when Chicken Little is hit on the head by an acorn falling from a tree. He fearfully screams out his famous refrain, "the sky is falling," rushing to warn his friends, Ducky-Lucky, Goosey-Loosey, Cockey-Lockey, and Turkey-Lurkey. The birds decide to go the king and warn him, but before they get to the palace, their enemy Foxy-Loxy tricks them into entering his lair, where he devours them one by one. The story is often cited in contemporary politics as a metaphor for the way in which some activists make dire predictions based on dubious information.

Messy Outside, Tidy Inside: The location of Shadrack's home isolates him from the town, but his tidy shack also shows that his mind is orderly, even if his behavior is chaotic. The neatness and serenity of his home reflect Shadrack's comfort with his own identity. Sula expects the place to be messy, a natural expectation that reflects the human tendency to judge others by external appearances.

Carefree Ajax: The foul-mouthed Ajax, who makes a brief appearance in this chapter and then disappears from the story for seventeen years, adopts a free-spirited approach to the world. He is a man who is comfortable in his own skin. His "graceful and economical" moves and words seem perfectly in sync with his personality. He cares little for what others think of him, which makes men admire him and women lust after him.

PART ONE

Chapter 5: 1923

One year later, during an extraordinarily hot summer, odd things begin to happen around the Bottom and the Peace house. A strong wind blows through town, bringing lightning, but no rain. Hannah asks her mother, "Mamma, did you ever love us?" Taken aback, Eva reminds Hannah that times were tough during Hannah's childhood, and love came in the form of helping the family survive. Hannah finally asks Eva why she killed Plum. Eva explains that Plum had come back from the war as needy as he was when he was a baby boy, saying, "I had room enough in my heart, but not in my womb, not no more."

ON THE INTERPRETATION OF DREAMS ✠ Eva and Hannah use their own supernatural system to interpret Hannah's dream. It is this system that makes them decide on the number 522. Numerology, the occult study of numbers, is an ancient superstition. The related practice of interpreting dreams dates back to biblical times. Dreams and visions play an important role in the Book of Daniel, the book in which we find Shadrack's namesake. Interpreters of dreams keep records of recurring themes in dream books. Dreams and other events can be translated into numbers according to a series of arcane equations and devices. Toni Morrison's grandmother kept such a dream book and believed in the hidden meaning of numbers.

Hannah dreams of a wedding in which she is wearing a red bridal gown. The next morning, both she and Eva interpret the dream as an indication that they should play the number 522 in the town lottery run by **Mr. Buckland Reed**. Sula becomes more sullen in her thirteenth year. She has a well-defined birthmark above her eye that resembles a stem and rose. As she gets older, the birthmark gets darker.

Eva looks for her missing comb. From her third-floor window, she sees Hannah lighting a brush fire in the backyard. Eva finds the comb and looks outside again. This time, she sees Hannah on fire. Eva lifts herself up on her one good leg, breaks the window, and jumps to the ground below in an attempt to save Hannah. Mr. and Mrs. Suggs rush over and douse Hannah with a tub of water, but Hannah is already severely burned. Eva and Hannah go to the hospital in an ambulance, but Hannah dies on the way.

At the hospital, Eva reflects that Hannah may have foretold her own death in her dream, since the color red indicates fire. She remembers seeing Sula standing on the back porch, watching Hannah and doing nothing to help her. Most people ascribe Sula's inaction to fear, but Eva thinks Sula did nothing and watched "because she was interested."

UNDERSTANDING AND INTERPRETING Chapter 5

Strange Happenings: The strange events that occur in this chapter create a sense of foreboding, leaving us to wonder what will result from the charged atmosphere. The first strange event, the wind, becomes all-important. Although it is not explicitly stated in the novel, we can conclude that the wind is what spreads the fire to Hannah. The list of odd happenings that begin the chapter also has the effect of imposing order on the disordered series of events that lead up to Hannah's death.

Eva's Unending Love: Eva's love for her children gives her two goals: to help them survive, and to treat them with mercy. She kills Plum to save him from suffering, and in this chapter it is suggested that she may have killed Hannah in the ambulance to save *her* from suffering. Another interpretation, however, is that Eva loses Hannah to the fire because of some literary or universal force for justice that says since Eva burned Plum alive, killing him with fire, now she must watch helplessly as Hannah burns herself alive, killing herself with fire. Eva's unending love is apparent, but such a strong love can sometimes be destructive.

A Mysterious Birthmark: Sula's birthmark is interpreted differently throughout the novel according to what people see in her. Sometimes it is interpreted as a sign of Sula's evil, sometimes just the opposite. Eva notices that the birthmark, which is in the shape of a rose and stem, seems to be getting darker as Sula moves into adolescence. The birthmark is a symbol that indicates Sula's growing sense of self, and perhaps her growing darkness of spirit.

Witness to a Death: When Sula stands on the back porch, watching Hannah burn, it is reminiscent of the way that she and Nel stood and watched Chicken Little drown. Eva cites Sula's inaction as one of the reason's for Hannah's death. Perhaps this is true, but it is also true that people tend to ascribe evilness to Sula simply because they need someone to blame for the evil and disorder of the world.

PART ONE
Chapter 6: 1927

A few years later, the Bottom celebrates the marriage of Nel to **Jude Greene**, a waiter and singer in the Mount Zion's Men's Quartet. Jude is handsome and suave. Recently, Jude has been frustrated in his efforts to get a job working on the New River Road. He does not really want to get married, but he is furious about his failure to get the job. So, determined to take on a man's role somehow, he decides to settle down. He feels that marriage to the sympathetic Nel will make him complete.

Nel and Sula are still so close that sometimes they have "difficulty distinguishing one's thoughts from the other's." Only when she is with Sula does Nel show any aggression or assertiveness, qualities that her parents have discouraged. The two girls still share everything. Sula encouraged the romance between Jude and Nel as if it were something the girls could share. However, Nel is flattered by Jude's attention because he sees her "singly," not as Sula's other half. Sula is happy about Nel's marriage to Jude. She helps plan the ceremony and reception. After the wedding, Sula leaves town, not to return for ten years.

UNDERSTANDING AND INTERPRETING
Chapter 6

Conformist Nel and Nonconformist Sula: By the time Nel and Sula are in their late teens, they have begun to make different decisions about the course of their lives. Although they fed from each other's exotic qualities, both women end up following the paths already cleared for them by their families. Despite her earlier impulses to step out of her mother's shadow, Nel follows the same path her mother did by marrying young, choosing as her spouse a responsible man much like her own father. Sula, however, follows the Peace family tradition and goes her own way.

Growing Apart: For the first time since becoming friends, Nel and Sula are physically separated. This separation marks the division between the two parts of the book, and it also foreshadows the ways in which the definitions of good and evil change with the girls' separation. Nel will go on to become a model housewife and mother, all good and right, and Sula will return to town, bringing back the chaos of her individualistic way of life.

PART TWO
Chapter 7: 1937

Sula returns to Medallion ten years after Nel's marriage, at the same time that a "plague of robins" victimizes the town. The birds cover the town with droppings. Eventually, their dead carcasses are scattered everywhere.

The town dislikes the idea that something as irritating as the robins can take over its thoughts. Despite their fears and annoyance, they almost welcome the oddity of the situation. Instead of finding ways to rid themselves of the birds, they let the plague run its course. This is not laziness, but instead a realization that bad forces, as well as good, are legitimate.

Sula walks through town dressed like a movie star, attracting attention. She stops by Eva's house, where Eva says, "I might have knowed them birds meant something." An argument ensues. Eva calls Sula selfish for not having a husband. Sula tells her grandmother to shut up and reminds her that neither she nor Hannah had husbands. Sula flaunts her independence, saying "Whatever's burning in me is mine . . . And I'll split this town in two and everything in it before I'll let you put it out!" Sula idly threatens to burn down Eva's house, just as Eva burned Plum. Soon afterward, Sula commits Eva to an old-age home.

Nel notices a new vibrancy in town after Sula arrives. It is spring, and Sula and Nel have a joyful reunion. Nel is horrified that Sula put Eva in the Beechnut home, which is an institution populated by poor people and invalids, but Sula says she only did it because Eva scared her and she did not know what else to do. Nel remembers that Sula always had trouble making even the most trivial decisions.

Jude arrives home after a bad day and says that the life of a black man is a hard one. Sula prevents Nel from comforting him and says that life for black people is not so bad. She says that white people love black men, which is why they obsess about their penises and indulge in rape fantasies. Jude and Nel have a good laugh at Sula's ideas.

An undetermined amount of time later, Nel discovers Jude and Sula sleeping together. Jude gets dressed and walks off. When he returns for his belongings, he takes everything, although he inadvertently leaves a tie behind. Sula says nothing. Nel is heartbroken and depressed. She hunches down in a small bathroom and remembers that Sula once said Hell is doing the same thing over and over. Nel thinks, to the contrary, that "hell is change." She knows her grief and misery will be gone one day. She yearns for Sula's companionship, but realizes that she has lost both her husband and her best friend. Nel prays, saying she would willingly be a mule if only she could have a man between her legs again.

MULES AND MEN

Nel's reference to mules makes an oblique allusion to *Mules and Men* (1935), a landmark collection of folktales by novelist and folklorist Zora Neale Hurston (1903–1960). Morrison's work is often compared to that of Hurston because both writers use folklore and dialect and vividly depict an African-American life that is portrayed as separate from the larger world. Hurston's landmark novel *Their Eyes Were Watching God* (1937) tells the story of Janie Crawford, who learns that every person "got tuh find out about livin' fuh theyselves." Janie's first husband forced her to do all the backbreaking physical labor on his farm, and her second husband, Jody Starks, forced her to be a decorative object. Janie determines not to be any man's mule. She finds happiness only with Tea Cake, her third husband. Hurston died before her work had received any serious recognition, but her work was revived in the 1970s in part thanks to the efforts of author Alice Walker (b. 1944). Today, Zora Neale Hurston's work is popular and widely read.

UNDERSTANDING AND INTERPRETING
Chapter 7

The Perils of Sula: Upon her return to the Bottom, Sula flaunts her new self to her old neighbors. She walks down the street in her nice clothes, wrangles with her own grandmother, and snatches her best friend's husband. She wears her nonconformity on her sleeve, but nothing she does is forced or affected or studiously rebellious. Her actions seem like a natural extension of her personality and upbringing. Fiercely independent, she never considers leading the kind of life that Nel has chosen, a disavowal of marriage and domesticity that is an inheritance from her mother and grandmother. The friction Sula creates is first interpreted by Nel as "magic," since Sula breathes new life into the town. But it's not long before Nel and others turn on Sula. Sula still shows an indecisiveness carried over from her youth. She is not prepared to make big decisions. Her flightiness becomes apparent when she first steals Jude away from Nel and then drops her feelings for him immediately when he leaves town.

Plague of Robins: The Bottom usually accepts evil things in its midst, and it almost welcomes the plague of robins and Sula. The robins are not inherently evil; they are more of a nuisance than anything else. People step in their droppings, and children throw stones at them. The robins become part of the Bottom's daily life, just as Sula's misbehavior does.

The Biggest Part of Me: The devastation Nel feels after Jude's departure shows how she has completely taken on the new identity of good wife and mother, the same identity against which she rebelled as a child. Her marriage to Jude, as described in the last chapter of Part One, is one that makes her feel complete as a person. As the narrator says, "[s]he didn't even know she had a neck until Jude remarked on it." After Jude leaves, Nel's body expresses the loss that she feels. Her thighs ache and she feels "naked." Nel gathers herself in the cramped bathroom and wants to feel small. Her self-esteem has disappeared with her husband, who had become a defining feature of her identity.

A Pondering Prayer: After Jude leaves, the narrative style shifts from a third-person omniscient narrator to Nel's first-person testimonial. This shift enables us to experience the personal devastation that Nel suffers. Hearing Nel express her sadness in her own voice forces us to feel her pain. She conceives of Jude's forgotten tie as a relic of his existence in her life. It prompts her to think back over their lives together and consider what her life will be like without him. She ends by addressing God angrily, asking how she can be expected to live a sexless, barren life.

> "The elegant craft and intense emotional power of *Sula* remind us that our search [for truth and freedom] is not new; it is part of the continuum of self-discovery we must know before we come to the greatest of all freedoms: the understanding of human frailty and the understanding of other equally universal laws."
>
> ROSEANN P. BELL

Lamentation and Loss: During Nel's lament, her thoughts turn to Sula, and she takes comfort in the conversations she used to have with Sula when they were younger. But she scolds herself for these thoughts, knowing that she has lost Sula's friendship. Having lost both her husband and her best friend, Nel is no longer the free spirit she once was in her friendship with Sula, nor is she any longer the "respectable" woman she was with Jude. She is now nothing, or at least she feels like nothing.

Inevitable Evil: The Bottom's conception of evil as a natural part of the world explains the way in which its reaction to Sula develops over time. The townspeople do nothing to kick her out or repress her; instead, they learn to live with her as they do with the plague of robins. In their view, evil cannot be annihilated, and must be accepted. To some extent, they are right. Sula's perceived "evil" will cause them to change and become better people. This redemptive element inherent in evil emphasizes the notion that the line between good and evil is a blurry one.

PART TWO

Chapter 8: 1939

After placing Eva in the old-age home, Sula becomes an unwelcome sight in town. When the townspeople learn that she stole Jude away from Nel, they begin calling her a bitch. The men begin to despise her because of rumors that she has slept with white men. The fact that most of them are of mixed-race heritage does not change their opinion, since their ancestors were raped by white men.

However, they let Sula's evil run its course. **Teapot**, a young boy, accidentally falls down Sula's steps one day. Teapot's drunken and neglectful mother, **Betty**, witnesses him fall and assumes that Sula pushed him. Betty resolves to get sober and be a better mother.

A man in town chokes to death on a chicken bone one day when Sula walks by. People begin to believe that the rose-and-stem birthmark over Sula's eye is "Hannah's ashes marking her." Sula attends church suppers wearing no underwear and does not compliment people's cooking. The women in town remember that Hannah's lust for their husbands was a compliment in some way, because Hannah found the men desirable. But Sula is different. She uses men and then discards them. The women begin to cherish their husbands more, which soothes the men's pride and vanity.

One woman saw Shadrack, who is never civil to anyone, tip an imaginary hat at Sula on the street. Sula smiled back at him. On this evidence, the town concludes that the two are "devils." Sula knows the town despises her. She has no ambition, no greed, and no ego. Because Hannah didn't like Sula, Sula learned to count only on herself. And when Chicken Little drowned, she learned she had "no self" to count on either.

Nel is the closest thing to a self that Sula has ever had. Sula did not realize that bedding Jude would hurt Nel. She and Nel shared everything, so why not share Nel's husband? The aftermath of the affair makes Sula realize that she and Nel are not one person. Nel's jealousy surprises Sula, and she begins to see Nel as one of the conventional wives she and Nel used to mock.

Sula sleeps with men frequently, since in sex she finds "the ability to feel deep sorrow," which she craves. During sex, she feels stronger and empathetic. At the age of twenty-nine, Sula begins an intense affair with Ajax, who is now thirty-eight. Ajax's only two loves are Sula and airplanes. He takes long trips to cities just to sit at an airport and watch the planes.

Ajax treats Sula well. He brings her gifts, such as a jar full of butterflies. Still, Sula feels a "creeping disorder" during their lovemaking. In an italicized interior monologue, she imagines how she might rub his skin and find, underneath it, gold leaf, then alabaster, then fertile loam. Soon, Sula becomes possessive of Ajax. One night, she prepares a candlelit table before he comes over. When Ajax arrives, he tells her that Tar Baby has been put in jail for causing a traffic accident and that Ajax and a few other black men were arrested for making a fuss at the police station about it.

When Ajax sees what Sula has done to prepare for his visit, he begins to sense her possessiveness and to regret their relationship. He spends the night with her and then leaves for an air show, never to return to her. All Ajax leaves behind is his driver's license, which Sula keeps. She discovers that his real name is Albert Jacks. As she holds his license, she thinks back to the way she made paper dolls with Nel. She thought her own head would fall off as easily as a paper doll's. Nel told her otherwise, but now she feels her head falling off again.

UNDERSTANDING AND INTERPRETING

Chapter 8

An Evil Presence: When strange things begin to occur, the people of the Bottom ascribe them to Sula's evil presence. They blame her for Teapot falling down the stairs and a man choking to death on a chicken bone. By blaming Sula, the townspeople bring some kind of supernatural order to their lives. It is reassuring to imagine that you are not at the mercy of chance, and that some entity is responsible for all of the bad things that happen in the world.

A Blessing in Disguise: Sula's perceived evils actually bring the people of Bottom a sense of purpose and redemption. Betty becomes a better mother, and women become better wives to their scorned husbands. People dig out the best in themselves in order to show that they are better than Sula. As the townspeople unify against Sula, their efforts to be virtuous bring them a new kind of order.

"When I wrote *Sula*, I knew I was going to write a book about good and evil and about friendship. Seemed to me that black women have friends in the old-fashioned sense of the word."

TONI MORRISON

Sleeping with the Enemy: The townspeople are disgusted by Sula's suspected affairs with white men. To the townspeople, nothing is worse than sleeping with white men. In their minds, the sexual attention of white men is something akin to rape.

Birds of a Feather: The brief interaction on the street between Sula and Shadrack becomes very significant to the people of the Bottom. Both characters shape the town's consciousness by their individual acts of nonconformity. The townspeople are unnerved by the prospect of Sula and Shadrack, two explosive, dangerous forces, in league with each other. The meeting on the street also foreshadows the way in which Shadrack will draw out the townspeople's goodness after Sula has departed.

Love for Lust: Sula returns to Medallion in search of comradeship, having missed the feeling of wholeness that her friendship with Nel once brought her. But Nel and Sula no longer share a common bond. In Sula's eyes, Nel has become one of "them," one of the masses of conventional people Sula saw in Medallion as a girl and elsewhere in the country as a woman. The only person Sula knows who has the potential to be different is Nel, but she realizes that Nel no longer holds that promise. Thus, Sula becomes an "artist with no art form" who turns her attention to other people, namely men, to satisfy her need for a bond. In Ajax, she finds another free spirit like herself. She tries to form a bond with him as tight as the one she once shared with Nel, but she mistakes him for someone who needs her as much as she needs him.

A Flimsy Paper Doll: Sula attempts to don the identity of loving wife in her efforts to claim Ajax. Her life of chaos, learned at the Peace house, becomes briefly ordered. She keeps the place neat and tidy, and the boarders have left, taking their mess with them. Proving that personality often follows where outward appearances lead, Sula's new order leads to a new possessiveness and weakness. The way she imagines pulling away the layers of Ajax's skin reveals the depth of her possessive feelings. She wants to penetrate to his core. When Ajax leaves her, Sula is devastated in the same way that Nel was when Jude abandoned her. Discovering that Ajax's real name is "Albert Jacks" makes Sula realize that she could never have had a man whose real name she did not even know. His true identity was a mystery to her, and her own has now become a mystery. Her head, her self, feels liable to fall off like a paper doll's.

Creeping Introspection: Throughout this chapter, Sula reflects on her possessive, intense feelings for Ajax. She confronts the "creeping disorder" that their relationship brings to her, along with her need for the security he offers. After Ajax leaves, Sula thinks of Nel again and of how Nel is the one who "told her the truth."

PART TWO

Chapter 9: 1940

A year later, Sula falls ill and becomes bedridden with incapacitating pain. Nel visits her for the first time since Jude's departure. A few minutes after Nel arrives, Sula sends her on an errand to pick up medicine. When she comes back, Nel tells Sula she needs someone to take care of her. Sula maintains that she likes being alone. Nel tells her she cannot have everything, and Sula asks why not.

Sula says that all black women are dying just like her, but they are dying "like a stump," whereas she is falling like a redwood. She tells Nel, "I got my mind. And what goes on in it. Which is to say, I got me." Her loneliness is her own, she says, not the "secondhand lonely" from which Nel suffers.

Nel asks her why she stole Jude away and how she could have hurt her best friend. Sula reminds Nel that Jude left, and she merely initiated something that would have happened anyway. Sula continues, saying that being good is just as risky as being bad, but you never get anything by being good. She asks why Nel cannot get over the loss of Jude for the sake of their friendship. Nel asks how Sula can expect people to love her after all she has done.

Sula replies, "Oh, they'll love me all right. It will take time, but they'll love me."

After Nel leaves, Sula has a dream of the Clabber Girl Baking Powder lady. The woman smiles and beckons to Sula, but when Sula comes closer, the woman disintegrates into dust. Sula tries to stuff the dust into her pockets, but it billows around, choking her. She wakes and sees the boarded-up window that Eva had jumped out of to save Hannah. She thinks to herself that she is, for the first time, completely alone and free. She feels a smile come across her face, and she dies.

UNDERSTANDING AND INTERPRETING Chapter 9

Refusing to Feel Guilty: Nel arrives at Sula's feeling morally superior to her. Sula stole Nel's husband away, so it seems obvious that Nel is the wronged party. Now, Nel once again seems like a better person because she is the first to initiate contact with her old friend after three years of estrangement. Even Nel's errand to the pharmacy shows an attempt to claim moral superiority. But Sula inconveniently refuses to take blame for the past. She points out that Jude left Nel, and that she, Sula, merely facilitated a process that would have happened anyway. Sula's claim does not sound entirely illogical, either.

Unyielding to the End: Even on her deathbed, Sula refuses to repent for anything she has done in her life. She has felt entitled to have it all, and considers it a triumph that she always refused to conform to the Bottom's rules. She has felt responsible only to herself, and she finds virtue in this attitude. Sula knows that there are negative consequences to her actions, but ultimately she possesses her own mind and thoughts, and that is the only important thing. Perhaps she is lonely, but only because she made a choice to be lonely. Nel, on other hand, is defined as "secondhand lonely," lonely because she placed her identity in the hands of another person. Nel gives up her feistiness in order to take on the socially acceptable community virtues: marriage, children, and family. Sula is not simply judging Nel and condemning her. Sula let go of her own identity when she was with Ajax, and she induced her own downfall. Now, seeing the error of her ways, and seeing Nel make the same mistake that she did, Sula wrangles with Nel to the very end.

Women As Trees: Sula's comparison of all women as "stumps" to her "redwood" is condescending, but it drives home her point. Unlike Nel, Sula refuses to let herself become a stump after Jude chops her down. Instead, Sula stands tall. She insists on her own legacy when she tells Nel, "It will take time, but they'll love me."

A Handful of Dust: Sula does not fear death. In the Clabber Girl dream, she feels herself turning into dust, and when she tries to stuff the dust into her pockets, she can't. This moment signals Sula's acceptance of death. The dust symbolizes herself and her life; her very existence slips through her fingers like the dust. Her thoughts turn back to Nel, as if she could share this final image with the one person who might appreciate it. Sula never lets go of the part of her that Nel once represented, and she still feels some measure of unity with her old friend. She knows that Nel also retains part of Sula, and that in time, Nel will realize this.

PART TWO
Chapter 10: 1941

After Sula dies, the town receives two signs that Sula's death will bring them good things. First, they learn that Medallion's new tunnel project may use black workers, unlike the road project before it, which used only white labor. Second, a new senior-citizens home for black people is going to be built. Eva Peace is one of the first to move there.

One day in October, freezing rain falls, followed by a brutal cold spell. For days, everyone remains housebound. Thanksgiving comes and goes with paltry meals, and most of the children come down with scarlet fever. Even before the ice or the illness, it was clear that something is wrong in the Bottom. Without Sula around, restlessness and insolence takes hold of everyone. Teapot's mother beats him, daughters complain about taking care of their mothers-in-law, and wives stop coddling their husbands.

On New Year's Day, the temperature shoots up and the ice melts. By January 3, the sun is shining and Shadrack is preparing for National Suicide Day. Shadrack has recently cut back on his drinking, realizing that he no longer remembers the war that he drank to forget. He begins to miss the presence of other people. The only indication that anyone has ever visited Shadrack's house is Sula's belt, which Shadrack has kept for nearly twenty years. Shadrack vividly remembers their encounter. When Sula came to him after drowning Chicken Little, he said "always" as a way to comfort her. Over the years, he has remembered her as the only pleasant visitor to his house.

THE BIBLICAL SHADRACH

The Shadrach (alternately spelled Shadrack) of the Old Testament is, like the Shadrack of *Sula*, a nonconformist. In *Daniel* 1:3–3:30, Babylonians and their King, Nebuchadnezzar, sack the land of Judah. The king orders Shadrach and his associates Meshach and Abednego brought into the palace and fed royal food and wine, so that in three years' time, they can become part of the king's court. Daniel, who has been sent with them, resolves that he will not eat the royal rations. After ten days, God rewards the men by giving them complete knowledge of literature and wisdom. Nonetheless, the men are made part of the Babylonian king's court. Later, when the king forges a golden idol for everyone to worship, Shadrach and the others refuse to comply. They are sentenced to die in a fiery furnace, but their bodies will not burn. The king sees the awesome power of God and converts to Judaism, proclaiming it the religion of the land.

After Sula's death, Shadrack sees her body at the funeral home and realizes that her life is not permanent, not "always." He begins to suspect that all his years of commemorating Suicide Day have been for naught. When January 3 arrives, he wants to sit inside his house with Sula's belt, but instead he gathers his bell and goes out for his annual ritual.

People laugh at Shadrack as he marches down the street. The contrast between the warm weather and Shadrack's gloom makes people confront death and feel unafraid. Soon, much of the town is dancing along behind him. They call to others to come and join them "as though there really [is] hope." The crowd makes its way toward the tunnel construction site. They leap over the fence and destroy all the building materials with glee. But people begin to slip down the muddy slope. The tunnel collapses and traps them inside. Many are crushed and drowned, including Tar Baby and the Deweys. Shadrack stands above the scene, ringing his bell.

> "For all her selfishness and cruelty, Sula's presence elicits the best in people, diluting their usual meanness and small-spirtedness. Indeed, with Sula's death the 'Bottom' dies, its black people rushing heedlessly in a comi-tragedy of communal suicide."
>
> JERRY H. BRYANT

UNDERSTANDING AND INTERPRETING Chapter 10

Salvation through Sula: Shadrack reinforces his own connection with Sula by recalling their interaction when she was a girl. He viewed her birthmark as a tadpole, which is a harmless creature with potential for growth, and a symbol of water. Shadrack mourns Sula's passing. He keeps her lost belt with him for years because it reminds him of Sula's potential. It is his only shred of human companionship. After that first encounter, Shadrack did not see Sula in the flesh, but by holding onto her belt, he saw her in memory. When Sula is truly gone, he realizes he has lost this speck of companionship, and without it begins to miss the presence of other people. He finally realizes that there is no permanency in life, and this helps him confront his fear of death.

Ice Storms and Irony: Although the people of the Bottom celebrate Sula's death, their own lives fall apart after she is gone. The absence of a scapegoat, a focal point for blame, makes them less willing to be virtuous. The ice storm blows into town and freezes their growth, a metaphor for the emotional freeze Sula's death casts over the town. When the ice melts, their resolve breaks and disorder takes over.

Collective Suicide: In the parade, the people of the Bottom lose their collective identity as good people. Without precisely meaning to, they give literal meaning to the "Suicide Day" ritual they used to mock as a sign of Shadrack's peculiar eccentricity. Their one attempt at following Shadrack and thumbing their noses at death backfires. As soon as they stop fearing death, death overtakes them and sucks them under.

PART TWO

Chapter 11: 1965

By 1965, change has occurred. Black people work in the shops in downtown Medallion, and there is a black teacher in the schools. The young people remind Nel, now fifty-five, of the Deweys. She wonders if perhaps the Deweys survived the tunnel collapse after all and raised the children she now sees. The Bottom disappeared after white people began moving into the hills. The hill land became more valuable and black people were gradually pushed out. Nel is sad to think the Bottom is gone. It was a "real place."

One day, Nel visits the old-age home, where there are now more whites than blacks. She visits Eva and realizes that Eva is suffering from dementia. Eva asks Nel how she threw Chicken Little in the water. Nel says Sula did it. Eva replies, "You. Sula. What's the difference? You watched, didn't you?" Nel gets upset and leaves. As she walks down the street, Nel remembers having a "good feeling" as she watched Chicken's hands slip from Sula's. Nel was calm and composed about the whole incident while Sula was uncontrollable. Now, Nel realizes that her calm was the natural "tranquility that follows a joyful stimulation."

Nel walks to the cemetery and finds the Peace family plots where Sula is buried. She realizes that she always thought highly of Eva. She believed Eva refused to attend Sula's funeral for the same reason the other townspeople refused—they thought it beneath them to pay respect to someone who had caused so much pain. Now Nel realizes that Eva was nothing more than mean and spiteful.

Nel was the only one in town to make funeral arrangements for Sula. Nel was also the only black person at the funeral ceremony, although she saw a group of people from the Bottom on the outskirts of the cemetery. Only after the whites had left did the black people walk over to Sula's grave and sing a hymn, "Shall We Gather at the River?"

Nel leaves the cemetery in sadness. She walks past Shadrack on the road, and he stops to look at her as if he remembers her face from the past. He cannot place her and moves on. Nel suddenly stops in her tracks and whispers Sula's name. She realizes that during all the years she mourned the loss of Jude, she was really missing Sula. She lets loose a long fit of crying.

UNDERSTANDING AND INTERPRETING

Chapter 11

Both Evil, Both Good: After her visit with Eva, Nel realizes two things that bring clarity to her life and to the themes of the novel. She admits to herself that she enjoyed watching Chicken Little float through the air and into the water, and she even enjoyed it when he did not come up for air. She always blamed Sula for Chicken's death, but now she finally comes to terms with the fact that she was as much to blame, and perhaps more to blame, than Sula. Sula may have let go of Chicken Little's hands, but she was frantic about it. Nel may have only watched, but she enjoyed the drowning. Sula was not more immoral than Nel, or vice versa. The two women were just halves of the same whole, complementing each other, different sides of the same moral fabric. Nel has the same capacity for evil that Sula had, and Sula had the capacity to evoke good in others that Nel has.

> "Sula's rebellion both derives from and coheres with the author's own rebellion from certain black novelistic traditions that decree, and enforce upon readers the expectation, that all black texts must be politically determinate, amenable to some ideological translation be it 'black protest' or 'radical feminist.' "
>
> ROBERT GRANT

Secondhand Lonely: Nel also realizes that she misses Sula, not Jude. When she admits that Sula was never a bad person, or at least no worse than Nel herself, she realizes that she has held a grudge for no reason. Sula's goodness lay in her stubbornness, in her recalcitrance, in her rebellion against social norms. Nel could have been a redwood with Sula, but the comfortable appeal of respectability lured her in and landed her in "secondhand lonely."

If Nel had been as strong-willed as Sula, she might have been able to put Jude's abandonment behind her. But she lost the part of her identity that Sula gave her when they were friends. At the end, thinking of Sula's grave, Nel finally understands why Sula was so important to her own life and finally lets herself grieve for the loss of her best friend.

Hymns and Prophecies: The townspeople's hymn at Sula's funeral shows a new ambivalence about the legacy of Sula. Without her, they fall into chaos. The way they hang back from the funeral and eventually join in the mourning perhaps foreshadows the way Sula's legacy will initially be one of ill-will and eventually one of respect. The question asked in the hymn—"Shall we gather at the river?"—tragically foreshadows the way the townspeople's chaos will lead them to drown at the river's edge. They need Sula, the subversive element against which they can define themselves as good. Without her, they stumble.

Sula's Legacy: The nonconformity and chaos that Sula represents will be remembered after her death. She allowed herself to be a pariah and to be equated with evil in order to prove that individualism is worth more than the numbing sameness of the community's so-called virtues. Her feeling that spirit is worth more than conformity is confirmed when the foundation of the community, the very land it is built on, is later turned into a golf course and suburban subdivisions. Conformity is useless if, in the end, it makes a community weak and breakable. Sula's lasting legacy is her power over her self and her insistence on self-determination. To echo Shadrack, Sula's permanence is a state of mind. She held fast to her convictions.

Conclusions

Sula examines the conventions of a black community confronted with the question of good and evil. Sula refuses to conform to what she sees as a numbing sameness among her neighbors. The community considers her an evil presence, but over the course of the novel we see that evil can be a force for good, and the distinction between good and evil is blurred.

The ambiguity of good and evil is symbolized by the friendship and strain between Nel and Sula. While Sula is regarded as evil by the town and by Nel herself, Nel eventually confronts her own evil impulses and realizes that neither she nor Sula can be defined by either label. Sula defiantly imposes her individualism on the residents of the Bottom and refuses to conform to their values. Her nonconformity is frowned upon, but Nel finally realizes that Sula's path was the most fulfilling.

SONG OF SOLOMON

Song of Solomon

An Overview

Key Facts

Genre: novel of personal and cultural identity; coming-of-age novel

Date of First Publication: 1977

Setting: 1931–1963 in Michigan, Pennsylvania, and Virginia

Narrator: Anonymous, omniscient, third-person

Plot Overview: A young man lives an aimless life until he sets off in search of lost treasure. Along the way, he finds his family's history in the lyrics of an old children's song.

Style, Technique, and Language

Style—Music and the Oral Tradition: In *Song of Solomon*, Toni Morrison utilizes songs and storytelling, giving the prose the rhythms and refrains of music. Music and storytelling are legacies of Morrison's childhood, legacies she honors by using them herself and by showing, through her characters, the importance of passing on family history and tradition to future generations.

Technique—Milkman's Quest: The novel's two-part structure updates the structure used in ancient epics to tell the stories of heroes such as Odysseus and Achilles. Our hero is Milkman. Part One focuses on his beginnings: his family, his relationships, and his uneasy feeling that something important is missing. Part Two tracks the odyssey prompted by that uneasiness.

An omniscient (all-knowing) narrator tells Milkman's story in "close third-person" narrative, following Milkman's thoughts and actions while still explaining what other characters are thinking. In addition, characters such as Pilate, Macon, and Ruth narrate stories of their pasts, filling in gaps in our knowledge of the family history.

Language—Symbols and Metaphors

Flight: As the central metaphor of the novel, flight represents both personal freedom and abandonment of responsibility. Milkman's flight to Pennsylvania and then to Virginia is selfish. He wants to find gold and to shirk the responsibility of dealing with Hagar. Solomon's flight to Africa is an escape from oppression, but it is also an abandonment of Ryna and his children. Leaving is not always irresponsible, however; Milkman's final flight combines the personal and the communal.

> "*Song of Solomon* is the product of a skilled artisan who has grounded her work in the lore of two traditions, both gospel and barcarole, to achieve a surprisingly eloquent synthesis. It moves at its own pace, ultimately to invade the consciousness in force."
>
> SAMUEL ALLEN

Names: Names signify identity and empowerment in *Song of Solomon*. The black residents of the city express themselves by naming and renaming places. They call one street "No Doctor Street," for example, and protest their exclusion from the all-white Mercy Hospital by renaming it "No Mercy Hospital." People's nicknames are also significant. Milkman's nickname sticks because he does nothing to shed it, which reflects his passivity and aimlessness. Jake's name becomes Macon Dead because of a mistake made by a white man. The name Dead is fitting for Jake's descendents, who have no family legacy and live blank lives.

Peacocks: The two peacocks symbolize Milkman's increasing maturity. The first peacock cannot fly very well because its tail feathers, symbolic of vanity, weigh it down. In Part Two, once Milkman sheds his pride and vanity, the peacock "soars."

Pilate's House: Pilate is the connection between the Dead family and its rural past in Virginia. Her house in Michigan, set back in the trees and lacking in modern conveniences, reflects her love of the earth. The house is a site of singing and storytelling—signs of life and family traditions.

> "Music—songs and numerous similes—resonates throughout *Song of Solomon*, sustaining an exquisite intermingling of prose and poetry."
>
> JOYCE IRENE MIDDLETON

Songs: The songs of Pilate and the children in Shalimar represent the importance of the oral tradition and the ways people devise to remember the past without written records. Pilate's songs reflect her love and are one of the few legacies she has brought with her from her past, which is a legacy that Milkman inherits.

Characters in *Song of Solomon*

Guitar Bains: Milkman's best friend. Guitar is a few years older than Milkman. He becomes political and joins the secret Seven Days group. He later hunts down Milkman and accidentally shoots Pilate.

Mrs. Bains: Guitar's grandmother and guardian. She is a poor tenant of one of Macon Dead's houses in Southside. When Guitar is a young boy, Mrs. Bains has trouble paying her rent, and they are evicted.

Calvin Breakstone: A congenial member of the Shalimar hunting party, he is paired up with Milkman during a hunt.

Crowell Byrd: The brother of Sing Byrd (Singing Bird) and father of Susan Byrd. His original Native American name was Crow.

Sing: Wife of Jake, mother of Macon and Pilate Dead, and grandmother of Milkman. Sing dies giving birth to Pilate. Her Native American name was Singing Bird.

Susan Byrd: An old resident of Shalimar who reveals Milkman's family history. He is one of Milkman's distant cousins.

Circe: An ageless woman, more than 100 years old, who lives at the old Butler house. Golden-eyed Weimaraner dogs, which she breeds, surround her at all times. A midwife, Circe delivers both Macon and Pilate and later takes them in.

Reverend Cooper: An old resident of Danville who lets Milkman stay at his house.

First Corinthians Dead: The oldest child of Macon and Ruth. Although First Corinthians went to college and lived in Europe, she can only get a job as a maid to Miss Michael-Mary Graham. She has a secret affair with Henry Porter and eventually moves in with him.

Macon Dead (Jr.): The hardhearted, money-loving patriarch of the Dead family. Macon is a spiteful husband to Ruth, a stern father to Milkman, Lena, and Corinthians, and an unforgiving brother to Pilate. Macon allegedly kills a white man and leaves the man's gold in a cave.

Macon (Jake) Dead Sr.: The original Macon Dead. He is Macon's father and Milkman's grandfather. He got his name, "Macon Dead," because of an error by a white man at the Freedmen's Bureau. Jake marries Sing and points a wagon toward Boston, but gets lost and ends up settling in Danville, Pennsylvania. The white Butler family shoots Jake dead in order to protect property they stole from him.

Macon (Milkman) Dead III: The aimless protagonist of the novel. Milkman is the son of Ruth and Macon II. After living a directionless life, he sets off to find his father's lost gold and stumbles upon his family history.

Magdalene (Lena) Dead: The middle child of Macon and Ruth.

Pilate Dead: The sister of Macon, mother of Reba, and grandmother of Hagar. She lives with Reba and Hagar in a Southside shack with no modern conveniences. Rumors have it that Pilate practices black magic. She helps Ruth sneakily conceive a baby and prevents Macon from forcing Ruth to abort.

Ruth Foster Dead: Milkman's long-suffering mother. Ruth is the daughter of the wealthy Dr. Foster. She was close to her deceased father, and periodically visits his grave in the outer suburbs. Ruth, desperate to conceive a son, drugs Macon so that he will impregnate her.

Empire State: A mute member of the Seven Days and a janitor in Tommy's Barber Shop. Empire State marries a white woman he met in Europe while fighting in World War I. After he finds her sleeping with another black man and learns that she loves "the whole race," he becomes mute.

Dr. Foster: Ruth's father, a wealthy physician and the man for whom "Doctor Street" is named (after his death, it is called "No Doctor Street"). Ruth's worshipful affection makes Dr. Foster uncomfortable. Macon believes that Ruth and her father had an incestuous affair.

Freddie: The skinny, gold-toothed "town crier" and gossip of the Southside. He is the janitor at the local department store and a follower and tenant of Macon Dead. He spies on Ruth nursing her young son, Macon Dead III. He tells people about what he saw, which is how Macon Dead III gets the nickname "Milkman."

Miss Michael-Mary Graham: The Poet Laureate of Michigan and employer of Corinthians Dead. She takes pride in the fact that Corinthians is literate, and gives her books.

Hagar: Reba's daughter. When Hagar is seventeen and Milkman is twelve, they begin an affair that lasts for years. Milkman eventually ends the affair, which decimates Hagar. She stalks Milkman, intent on killing him.

Heddy: Sing's mother and Milkman's great-grandmother. A Native American, Heddy finds Jake when he is an infant and raises him as her own.

Hospital Tommy: Co-owner of the Southside barbershop and member of the Seven Days. He uses highfalutin language and tells stories about World War I.

Grace Long: A gossipy resident of Shalimar whom Milkman meets at Susan Byrd's house. Grace takes Milkman's gold watch and writes her address on a napkin in hopes that he will visit her privately.

Omar: A resident of Shalimar. He invites Milkman to join the hunting party.

Nephew: The thirteen-year-old nephew of the Reverend Cooper. He drives Milkman to the old Butler house on the outskirts of Danville.

Henry Porter: A tenant of Macon Dead's on the Southside and a member of the Seven Days group. In 1936, he gets drunk and threatens everyone with a shotgun. After flirting with Corinthians Dead on a city bus, he has a secret affair with her.

Railroad Tommy: Co-owner of the barbershop and member of the Seven Days.

Reba: Pilate's daughter. Reba has a knack for winning prizes, such as a diamond ring from Sears, but she always gives away everything she wins.

Ryna: Solomon's wife. Ryna is the mother of twenty-one children, including Jake, which makes her Milkman's great-grandmother. A gulch in Shalimar is named Ryna's Gulch because the echoes of the water sound like a woman crying for her lost husband.

Saul: A toothless resident of Shalimar who picks a fight with Milkman.

Small Boy: A member of the Shalimar hunting party. He starts the hunt by clapping his hands and letting loose the dogs.

Robert Smith: An insurance agent for North Carolina Mutual Life. At the beginning of the novel, Robert posts a notice saying he will fly away by jumping from the top of No Mercy Hospital. He is a former member of the Seven Days.

Solomon: Jake's father and Milkman's great-grandfather. A slave, he is also called Shalimar and is the namesake of the town in Virginia. He was the father of twenty-one children, including Jake. According to the legend and the children's song, he "flew off" from slavery with baby Jake and left behind his wife and the twenty remaining children.

Luther Solomon: A member of the Shalimar hunting party. (He is not related to the Solomon family that owns the General Store in Shalimar.)

Mr. Solomon: Owner of the Solomon's General Store in Shalimar. He tries to help Milkman, but becomes weary of Milkman's city-boy manner.

Sweet: A pretty young resident of Shalimar. At Omar's suggestion, Milkman stays with her while in town. Sweet bathes Milkman, feeds him, and makes love to him.

Vernell: Calvin's wife. She makes breakfast for the hunting party and is the first to identify Sing as a former resident of Shalimar.

King Walker: The small, bald, tobacco-chewing owner of a gas station turned clubhouse in Shalimar. He is a member of the hunting party. Earlier in life, he was a star pitcher in baseball's Negro League.

Song of Solomon

Reading Song *of Solomon*

PART ONE

Chapter 1

The narrator recounts that on February, 18, 1931, **Robert Smith**, a man well known to the black residents of town as a quiet, diligent insurance agent from North Carolina Mutual Life Company, straps a pair of blue silk wings to his shoulders and leaps to his death from the roof of Mercy Hospital. Two days earlier, Smith had posted a notice announcing that he would "fly away on [his] own wings" from the roof to the other side of Lake Superior, and a small crowd gathers to see what the notice is about.

Before Smith jumps, the mood is cheery. The crowd is a cross-section of the black population in town. A woman sings, "O Sugarman done fly / O Sugarman done gone / Sugarman cut across the sky / Sugarman gone home." Two girls gather velvet rose petals dropped by their pregnant mother. To the employees of the hospital, the scene outside looks like a religious gathering.

The black residents of the city live mainly in a dilapidated neighborhood known as Southside. The nearby hospital is nicknamed No Mercy Hospital, since black people have never been welcome there. **Dr. Foster**, now deceased, was the only black physician in town. When he was alive, the street he lived on was called Doctor Street. Now that he is dead, it is called No Doctor Street.

Dr. Foster's daughter, **Ruth Foster Dead**, goes into labor while watching Robert Smith leap from the roof of the hospital. The next day, she gives birth to **Macon Dead III**, the first black baby ever delivered at the hospital. The narrator says that Smith's silk wings must have marked the boy, because when he is four, he discovers that only birds and airplanes can fly, and he loses "all interest in himself."

Ruth had a very close relationship with her father. Even when she was a teenager, she insisted that he tuck her in and kiss her goodnight, a ritual that gave her a certain "ecstasy." Dr. Foster secretly found his daughter's behavior worrisome and was glad when she got married.

Ruth has two daughters by her husband, **Macon Dead**: **Lena** (short for Magdalene) and **Corinthians** (short for First Corinthians). The girls spend most of their time making velvet roses that they sell to the local department store. **Freddie**, the janitor at the store and Macon's helper, often drops by to pick up a new batch of roses. Macon Dead is an uncompromising, fearful presence in his family. He despises Ruth. His daughters' lack of ambition disappoints him. Macon expresses his spite in bursts of yelling and insults that are the family's only excitement. The Deads live in Dr. Foster's old house, a large, comfortable place on No Doctor Street.

One of the few rituals Ruth enjoys is nursing her young son. She breast-feeds him until he is about seven or eight years old. One day, Freddie arrives at the house to pay his rent. He peers through the window and sees Ruth nursing her son. Ruth drops the boy and rushes to cover herself, but it is too late. Freddie is amused at what he has seen, and spreads the news around town. Macon Dead III gets a nickname, **Milkman**, which sticks to him for life.

Macon Dead does not like his son's nickname. He knows only that it has something to do with his wife, which disgusts him. The narrator adds that Macon was not pleased by Milkman's unexpected birth. Macon has a sister named **Pilate Dead**. When Pilate was born, her father wrote her name on a piece of brown paper. When she was twelve, Pilate put the paper in a small brass box and wore the box on a string as an earring.

Macon has not seen Pilate for sixteen years or spoken to her since Milkman was born. He dislikes her independent ways and unfeminine dress. The narrator implies that Pilate was the woman singing "O Sugarman" before Robert Smith's jump. Macon also dislikes the fact that the unmarried Pilate has a daughter, **Reba**, and that the unmarried Reba has a daughter, **Hagar**. The three women live alone in Pilate's house.

One day, a few years after Smith's jump from the hospital, Macon walks to his office in Southside. The office is called "Sonny's Shop" after a company that once occupied the building. As he walks, Macon thinks of people's names. His father was also called **Macon Dead**, a name given to him because of the mistake of "a drunken Yankee in the Union Army." Macon Dead, Sr., passed his name along to his son, Macon Dead, Jr., who passed the name along to his own son, Macon Dead III. Macon, Jr. wonders if one of his ancestors had "a name given to him at birth with love and seriousness . . . not a joke, nor a disguise, nor a brand name."

When Macon arrives at his office, he finds the elderly **Mrs. Bains** waiting for him, accompanied by her two young grandsons. Old Mrs. Bains tells Macon that she cannot afford to pay her rent. Macon, unsympathetic, says she must pay rent within a few days or face eviction. Macon thinks about the extent of his wealth. When he was twenty-five and first courting Ruth, he had only two houses for rent. He thought his property was the only reason the wealthy Dr. Foster allowed him to court Ruth.

Freddie arrives at the office and announces that one of Macon's tenants, **Henry Porter**, is drunk and waving a shotgun from his window, threatening to kill people. The two men walk over to the house and watch Porter until he finally slumps into a deep sleep. Macon sends Freddie inside to get the rent from the sleeping man's pocket. While Freddie is inside, Macon looks out over the neighborhood. He sees his rental houses scattered around "like squat ghosts with hooded eyes" and feels lonely.

He decides to go back to the office via a shortcut that leads past Pilate's house, a one-room shack with no electricity or gas. When Pilate was born, the strain of the labor killed their mother. Pilate was born without a navel. As Macon walks by the house, he hears Pilate, Reba, and Hagar singing together.

UNDERSTANDING AND INTERPRETING
Chapter 1

A Hero's Birth: The two-part structure of *Song of Solomon* borrows from ancient epic style. The first part of the novel focuses on the relationships among the characters, and the second part recounts the travels of the central character, Milkman. As if Milkman is a mythic hero, his birth is mystical and heavy with significance. Amazingly, his birth begins just as another man dies, which suggests the kinship of spirits, or the tight link between death and life. Almost pagan accoutrements accompany the birth. The singing crowd outside the hospital seems worshipful, and rose petals are scattered on the ground. Everyone watches the skies, waiting for something to happen, and Robert Smith's jump arrives like a divine proclamation.

Time Flies: From the first page of the novel, Morrison begins to show how strongly the past influences the lives of her characters. The first chapter of the novel floats between different time periods, from Robert Smith's jump and Milkman's birth (1931) to Dr. Foster's prominence as the city's most respected black person (1910s–1920s), to Pilate Dead's birth and naming (around 1900–1910). People living in the present constantly think about the past. Morrison's fluid movement between time periods reflects the mental time travel we undertake by remembering and by telling stories.

> "*Song of Solomon* is a brilliant, compelling achievement. It demands to be discussed, if only to force the reader to wrench himself free from a prose which spins a relentless web of conjure."
>
> MELVIN DIXON

Neighborhoods of the North: The city in which Part I of *Song of Solomon* takes place is never mentioned by name. We learn only that it is near Lake Superior, which places it in northern Michigan. However, the name of the city is not particularly important. What is important is that the city is located in the North. The Great Migration of black Americans in the late nineteenth and early twentieth centuries from the rural South to urban areas of the North is a key element in the novel and will shed light on the family history of the Deads. Also crucial are the neighborhoods within the Michigan city. Characters' neighborhoods and houses are physical expressions of personality. Most of the black people in town live in Southside, a neighborhood of dark houses, many of which are owned by Macon Dead. Pilate lives in a house that reflects her earthiness and independence. It is set back among pine trees and has no electricity or gas. The Dead house, which once belonged to Dr. Foster, shows how Dr. Foster still permeates the consciousness of the Dead family. The house also represents Macon's grasping ways. It stands on the far edge of Southside, nearer to the more affluent, white sections of the city.

Flights of Fancy: Flight is a central theme in the novel. Morrison explores how flight can be simultaneously a literal journey through space, a grab at freedom, and an act of running away. Pilate sings, "O Sugarman done fly . . . Sugarman done gone," which captures the idea that flight is both physical flying and running away. The novel begins with Robert Smith's flight from the hospital roof, a moment that neatly lays out the complexities of flying. Smith, perhaps deranged, intended to truly fly. In one way, his flight, which ended in death, was a tragedy.

At the same time, however, it was an escape, for Smith ended his desperation by flying from the roof. When Milkman finds out that people cannot fly, he is dismayed. Milkman realizes that people, including himself, lack a crucial power he thought they possessed. This realization makes Milkman, a flightless human, uninterested in himself.

> "In *Song of Solomon*, Morrison has captured our sometimes painful search to discover our names and articulate their meaning. And she named the myths that linger after the nightmare to tell us we have survived."
>
> MELVIN DIXON

The Importance of Naming: Naming and renaming fills the first chapter, setting up a series of questions the novel will raise. Morrison wants us to wonder who is in charge of naming, how names evolve, and what naming has to do with staking a claim and grabbing power. In this chapter, renaming is a way of calling attention to unjustness, or of exerting a small bit of power. For example, Mercy Hospital, an important institution in the city that caters mainly to white people, is dubbed "No Mercy Hospital" by the black residents who are barred from the hospital. No Doctor Street, formerly Doctor Street, shows the pride the black community takes in Dr. Foster, the city's only black physician. Morrison suggests that naming is a powerful tool for the disenfranchised. Naming or renaming costs no money and requires no particular power, and by creating a name that sticks, the downtrodden can override officialdom. For example, No Doctor Street becomes the widely used name for what is officially called Main Avenue. Whites also exercise the power of naming, as when a drunk soldier names Milkman's grandfather Macon Dead. The name Macon Dead persists through the generations, which means the white soldier has left a ghostly thumbprint on generations of Dead men.

Singing and the Oral Tradition: Songs, as we can gather from the novel's title, play a key role in *Song of Solomon*. Morrison draws inspiration from the oral tradition of storytelling, folklore, and songs that she learned from her extended family. Songs appear twice in the first chapter, when Pilate sings before and during Robert Smith's jump and again when she sings as Macon walks by her house.

The Deadly Macon Dead: Wrathful Macon Dead is overpowering. He terrorizes his family, hates his wife, merely endures his son, scorns his sister, and threatens to evict a poor old woman. Macon's exchange with Mrs. Bains makes him out to be a villainous, stingy character. He is proud of his accomplishments, which include making an advantageous marriage to the wealthy Dr. Foster's daughter. Obsessed with making money, Macon is a pursuer of the American dream in its purest form, but he is disconnected from the rest of the black community.

The Suffering Ruth Foster Dead: Ruth is a model of the long-suffering wife. She is the daughter of the "most important Negro in the city," Dr. Foster, and the wife of the richest black man in the city, Macon. Most people identify Ruth by the men in her life, thinking of her as Dr. Foster's daughter or Macon's wife. Ruth on her own has no defined existence in the minds of the city's residents. Ruth's father and husband are rich, which means she does not want for money, but she suffers from emotional poverty. She had her son, Milkman, against Macon's wishes, which alienated her husband. Bereft of her husband's attention, Ruth seeks the love of her son. Perhaps because Ruth's identity has always been filtered through one man or other, she instinctively seeks closeness with Milkman. Just as she cuddled with her father past a seemly age, she nurses her son past an appropriate age, as if she is replicating the physical closeness she had with her father. Ruth scrounges everything she can from the men who will return her affection.

The Strange Pilate Dead: Pilate is one of many female social pariahs in Toni Morrison's novels. Her literary sisters include Pecola Breedlove in *The Bluest Eye*, and Sula Peace in *Sula*. Unlike her brother Macon, Pilate shuns wealth and modern conveniences, lives in a primitive house tucked away behind trees, and makes a connection to the rural past of African-Americans who migrated to the North to escape slavery and sharecropping in the rural South. She remains connected to her own family's past by keeping her name in her brass-box earring. Her name is a legacy from her father who gave it to her, and she keeps a tie to him by keeping her earring. Pilate, who mysteriously lacks a navel, is like an earthy witch living in the woods with her coven, Reba and Hagar.

PART ONE
Chapter 2

The Dead family frequently takes Sunday afternoon drives in Macon's shiny new Dodge. These drives are a rare pleasure for Corinthians and Lena. Milkman is too small to see out the windows and can only look out the back. This creates a feeling that the narrator likens to "flying blind." Looking to the back becomes a habit of Milkman's, "[a]lmost as if there were no future to be had." Macon keeps his car in mint condition. He likes to show it off to the black people in town, since few of them can afford a nice car. The townsfolk smirk at the car, noting that there is "no real lived life" inside the vehicle. They call the Dodge a hearse.

When Milkman is twelve, he becomes best friends with **Guitar Bains**, one of Mrs. Bains's grandchildren. Macon has forbidden Milkman to visit Pilate, but one day Guitar takes Milkman to her house. When Milkman sees Pilate, he knows that nothing can keep him from her. Pilate kids with the boys for a while. Guitar asks her about her navel, and Pilate admits that she was born without one. Milkman realizes that Pilate is not dirty or drunk, as his schoolmates claim. She lives in poverty, but with a certain natural grace.

Pilate says only "three Deads" are still alive. Milkman gets defensive and furious. He shouts that there are more than three. Pilate considers Milkman's complaint for a moment, and then pleasantly invites Milkman and Guitar inside, where she cooks them some eggs. Pilate tells them her family history. Her father, Macon Dead, Sr., was shot dead while guarding their farm home. She and Macon, Jr. ran away. At first they stayed with their friend, a servant named **Circe**. They lived in the dark woods for a while. Their father returned to them as a ghost, which frightened them. Guitar asks questions about the ghost, but Pilate remembers nothing else besides the deep blue sky.

Pilate hears Reba and Hagar coming. Pilate introduces Milkman to Hagar as her "brother." Reba says that Milkman is actually Hagar's cousin, but Pilate says there is no real difference. Reba has lighter skin than her mother or daughter, and she has the "simple eyes of an infant." She has a knack for winning prizes without even trying. Most recently, she walked into Sears and Roebuck to use their bathroom and won a diamond ring for being their half-millionth customer. Hagar and Pilate joke that Reba usually gives away her winnings to men she dates.

Hagar's beauty mesmerizes Milkman. Surrounded by this group of women, he realizes that this is the first time he has felt completely happy. The women seem to enjoy him, and they love to laugh. It is all very unlike Milkman's life at home. The women talk about their latest batch of homemade wine, which they sell to make ends meet, since they have no other source of income. Hagar says that if Reba had not won a bundle of groceries, they might have starved over the past winter. The three women sing the Sugarman song.

When Milkman returns home that night, Macon has already heard through the grapevine of his son's visit to Pilate. He scolds Milkman, but eventually calms down. Macon tells a story about his childhood. He remembers working with his father on their farm in Montour County, Pennsylvania. They lived a happy life, and after sixteen years the farm was actually turning a profit. Then, someone tricked his illiterate father into signing a document giving away the title of the farm.

Macon explains the origin of the family name. In 1869, former slaves like Macon's father were obliged to register their names when they wanted to move north. The Freedmen's Bureau mixed up Macon's father's name, pulling words out of context. He said he was born in Macon and his own father was dead, and the drunken soldier working at the Freedmen's Bureau decided that his name was Macon Dead.

Macon's father was illiterate, so did not know they had recorded his name incorrectly until his wife told him. He met his wife on a wagon trip to the North. She liked the name Macon Dead because it "would wipe out the past."

Milkman never knew that his grandfather was a slave. He peppers Macon with questions, but Macon does not know his father's real name and will not say who shot him. He does not remember his mother too well, since she died when he was four. All he can say is that she was a pretty woman and light-skinned, in contrast to his dark-skinned father. Macon says again that he does not want Milkman to visit Pilate. He tells Milkman that it is time to start helping him at the office after school, and that only he can teach Milkman about the real world. He advises Milkman to "own things. And let the things you own own other things. Then you'll own yourself and other people, too."

UNDERSTANDING AND INTERPRETING
Chapter 2

Hearse versus House: The Dead family name is an apt representation of their life. Their trips in Macon's "hearse" are their only source of excitement, apart from occasional fits of yelling. Macon does not enjoy the car rides that his family looks forward to, because for him, the car is a status symbol, not a way to have fun. On the car rides, everyone sits in silence. In contrast to the deadening atmosphere of the Dead family, Pilate's house is a place where stories are told, eggs cooked (Morrison uses eggs as a symbol of life), and songs sung. Pilate, Reba, and Hagar are entirely different from Ruth, Lena, and Corinthians. There is life in the Deads, but not in Milkman's household.

Milkman's Passivity: Milkman is "flying blind" when he is in the car, impotent and trapped. He is physically trapped by his family, squashed in the car with his parents and sisters, and literally trapped in his life, oppressed by a gloomy household. Despite this stifling life, however, Milkman seems uninterested in making his escape. He obeys his father's commands until Guitar takes him to meet Pilate. It probably does not occur to Milkman that he could go to his aunt's house on his own. When Pilate tells her story, Milkman asks no questions. He sits in a silent stupor during the entire visit. Passivity is a central element of Milkman's character. Unless someone forces change upon him, he remains static.

Curious Guitar: Guitar, who can be interpreted as Milkman's alter ego, is adventurous and inquisitive. In contrast to Milkman, who sits in stunned silence at Pilate's house, Guitar asks cheeky, inquisitive questions, even daring to ask Pilate about her navel. In contrast to Milkman's vagueness, Guitar exhibits quick-wittedness, pinpointing elements of Pilate's story and asking questions.

A Supernatural Woman: Mysticism and earthiness both cling to Pilate. She admits that she has no navel, and she shows an almost supernatural intuition when she hears her daughter and granddaughter approach the house. She has seen her father's ghost. Despite her otherworldliness, however, Pilate is connected to natural, earthy things. Her house is like a little farm, brimming with life. She tells the boys that they call to her as if she is a pig or a sheep. She remembers only the blue sky and dark woods of her past—only the physical and natural sights—and cannot summon up more manmade details like names and dates.

A Family Song: When Pilate, Reba, and Hagar reach a point of melancholy silence, they begin singing. The song, which they sang in the previous chapter, has a resonance and harmony that captivates Milkman. Unbeknownst to any of them, the song has roots in the Dead family history. But for the moment, it is a simple means of bringing together the family, the three singing and the one listening.

Two Dead Families, One Alive: Milkman feels comfortable at Pilate's house, where he is treated like a close brother instead of a more distant cousin. When Pilate implies that there are only three Deads, Milkman feels excluded from the family that has only just started to seem interesting and warm. At Pilate's, Milkman seems to have found a family where he feels accepted and loved. Being in her house is soothing and freeing.

One Story, Two Memories: Memories of the Dead family history have a calming effect even on the raging Macon. He tells the same story that Pilate tells Milkman, but he tells a completely different version than his sister told. His is specific, and full of precise names and dates. It becomes apparent that Milkman has never known much about his family's past. He does not know, for example, that his grandfather was a slave. This time, however, he asks questions when confronted

FREEDMEN'S BUREAU

In March 1865, Congress created the Bureau of Refugees, Freedmen, and Abandoned Lands, better known as the Freedmen's Bureau, with the intent of helping freed slaves after the Civil War. The agency registered the names of free blacks, provided them with food, shelter, and abandoned land, and supervised work contracts between former slaves and their employers. The Bureau also helped coordinate northern charity groups that financed the construction of hundreds of hospitals and more than 1,000 schools for blacks, including Toni Morrison's alma mater, Howard University. However, the Bureau became the victim of political infighting. President Andrew Johnson, a southerner who took office after President Lincoln was assassinated, called the Bureau's work unconstitutional meddling in the affairs of Southern states. Congress succeeded in expanding the Bureau's powers in 1866, but the Bureau was decommissioned in 1872, a symbolic moment in the brutal period of Reconstruction following the Civil War.

with Pilate's and Macon's stories. (These questions may be evidence not of Milkman's lessening passivity, but of his annoyance with his father. After Macon forbids him to visit Pilate again, Milkman asks questions partly as a way of getting back at Mason.) Macon's and Pilate's stories are different not only in tone, but in intent. Pilate tells her story for the sake of telling it, but Macon has an ulterior motive. He hopes to teach Milkman the value of hard work, which the original Macon Dead instilled in him. Macon finishes his story with a credo typical of him: "Own things." The two contrasting stories illuminate the vast difference between Macon, the northern entrepreneur, and Pilate, the rural storyteller.

PART ONE
Chapter 3

Life improves for Milkman after he begins working after school for Macon. The job, which entails collecting rent, gives him the chance to visit Pilate's house. Once in a while, Milkman and Guitar skip school and hang out in the meanest part of Southside, the Blood Bank. One such day, when Milkman is twelve, he and Guitar try to get a beer at a pool hall. The place is full of Air Force pilots who seem amused by the two boys. The owner of the pool hall shoos them away, so they visit a barbershop owned by **Railroad Tommy** and **Hospital Tommy**. Railroad Tommy laughs when the boys complain about not getting a beer. Then he lists a number of other luxury items that they will never get to enjoy.

As the years go by, Milkman continues working for his father. The business thrives, even during World War II. By 1953, when Milkman is twenty-two, Macon is doing very well. He still feels spiteful toward Ruth, who spends the occasional night away from the house. He finds it unlikely that she has a lover now that she is more than fifty years old. He considers slapping her, but the last time he struck Ruth, Milkman struck back at him to defend her.

When Milkman hit Macon, he felt "infinite possibilities and enormous responsibilities" that he was not prepared to accept. He realizes that his action will not change anything in the house. His mother and sisters begin treating him with "vaguely alarmed blandness." After the fight, Milkman takes stock of his life. For the past few years, he has had an on-again, off-again affair with his cousin Hagar. He has not had to go to war because Macon arranged a draft deferment for him. He has not gone to college, either, since Macon did not see the point.

> "The comfortable smell of friendly fingers,
> Hair's fragrance, and the musty reek that lingers
> About dead leaves and last year's ferns. . . ."
>
> RUPERT BROOKE

Milkman casually decides to talk to Macon about their fight. Macon stops his son before he can begin talking and tells Milkman the history of his marriage to Ruth. Macon married Ruth when she was sixteen. Her father was not only the most powerful black man in the city, but the biggest hypocrite Macon had ever known. Dr. Foster insisted on delivering Ruth's babies himself. Macon saw Ruth's father leaning over Ruth's spread legs and found it indecent. He already suspected that they might have an incestuous relationship.

A few years later, Macon tried and failed to get Dr. Foster to invest some money in a railroad deal. Macon still maintains that the deal would have made them rich. He blames Dr. Foster's illness, which eventually killed him, on his addiction to ether. The night Foster died, Macon discovered Ruth naked in her father's bed, sucking the corpse's fingers. This confirmed Macon's suspicions that Ruth and Dr. Foster were sexual deviants.

Milkman listens, but feels removed from his father's story. He has sympathy for Macon, but still believes he was right to hit him. Milkman realizes he has never thought of his mother as a person. Milkman leaves the house and heads toward the Southside to find Guitar. He notices that everyone is walking by him in the other direction. He suddenly has a flashback to his mother breastfeeding him and Freddie laughing at them. He also thinks of his visits to Pilate's house, where the women love him with such ease. He does not know which parent is in the right. His confusion makes him yearn to find Guitar, who always feels clear.

Milkman finds Guitar at Tommy's Barbershop, where a large group of men are listening to a news report on the radio. In Mississippi, a young black man named **Till**, a northerner visiting the South, has been murdered for whistling at a white woman. Among the group listening is **Empire State**, a man who never speaks. The men speak of personal atrocities and humiliations they have suffered.

Milkman and Guitar go to a bar. Milkman wonders how he got his own nickname, but Guitar deflects the question. They discuss Milkman's fight with Macon. To shed light on the incident, Guitar tells a story about his own past. He grew up in Florida, where he often hunted. Once, he killed a doe, which made him feel guilty. He compares Ruth to the doe, and explains that Milkman struck Macon out of sympathy for her. Milkman later returns to the question of his nickname and says he dislikes it. Guitar replies, "Niggers get their names the way they get everything else—the best way they can."

UNDERSTANDING AND INTERPRETING Chapter 3

Going to the Southside: Aside from Macon's story about Ruth, this chapter takes place in Southside, a place alive with boisterous conversation, beer drinking, and camaraderie. Like Pilate's house, the neighborhood is brimming with energy and history. Railroad Tommy can list all of the things that Milkman and Guitar will never have because he has struggled through a lifetime of discrimination, and he knows about racism firsthand. He speaks for an entire deprived, mistreated population, the black people of the South in the 1950s. The Southside is a place full of pain, fear, and bitterness, but also a place full of vitality. The "blood" of the Blood Bank nourishes a living population. Milkman comes here to escape the bland deadness of his life at home, where only a fistfight with Macon breaks up the monotony, and after the fight ends, life returns to its normal boredom. Southside offers Macon emotional vibrancy, just as Pilate's house does. Both places have a past, a future, and a present liveliness.

Swaddled in Childhood: Milkman's passivity, always part of his character, has worsened and made him feel removed from himself and his family. He lacks life experience, having known nothing but family life and the Southside. Neither military duty nor college have toughened him up or breathed intellectual curiosity into him, since he has escaped both. Even Milkman's love affair does not break any new ground, for his relationship is with a family member instead of a stranger. Milkman swathes himself in memories of the past. His sudden flashback to breastfeeding as a young boy suggests Milkman's continued childishness. Fighting with Macon seems encouraging, since at least it shows spirit and principles. However, Milkman has a discouraging reaction to the fight, realizing that he is unprepared for the responsibilities and possibilities that present themselves to a man who takes a stand. Milkman looks to Guitar to explain things to him and point him in the right direction. Milkman feels unformed and isolated, as evidenced by his sense that everyone is walking in the opposite direction from him.

Milkman's Search for Self: Despite his stasis, Milkman at least realizes that he has a problem. He knows that something is missing from his life, although he cannot put his finger on what. He understands that others feel an intensity and

A BRUTAL HATE CRIME

The murder of Emmett Till, in August of 1955, was one of the earliest defining moments of the Civil Rights movement. That summer, Till, a fourteen-year-old Chicago native, was visiting relatives near Money, Mississippi. Although he had experienced segregation at home, there in the South he became a victim of the distinct, horrifically violent brand of hostility to which black people living in the Deep South had long been subjected. When some local boys dared Till to talk to a white girl in a grocery store, he accepted their challenge. He entered the store and bought some candy, and, as he left, he said "Bye, baby" to the wife of the store owner. A few days later, two men—including Ron Bryant, the owner—came to the cabin of Mose Wright, Till's uncle, in the middle of the night. The men drove off with Till. Three days later, his mangled corpse was found in the Tallahatchie River, an eye gouged out and a "bullet in the skull. The incident attracted national media attention. It sparked racial violence and galvanized activists. In 1986, Morrison wrote *Emmett Dreaming*, an award-winning play about the episode.

conviction that he lacks. The men in the barbershop listen carefully to the news accounts of the attack in Mississippi and react passionately. They feel a gravity that Milkman cannot possibly feel, since he has been sheltered his entire life. Milkman visits Southside, but he goes there almost as a tourist, playing at escaping his comfortable routine. For residents like the Tommys, Guitar, and Empire State, Southside is a real place, fraught with real problems. After they listen to the news on the radio, the men share stories of similar horrors they have endured or witnessed. Milkman, as usual, can only listen, since he has not had these sorts of direct experiences himself.

Rural Background: In this chapter, we learn more about Guitar's background. His stories about hunting in Florida reveal something important about his character. He describes himself as a "natural-born hunter" with catlike senses. When he moves to the North, he brings his predilection for hunting with him. Guitar's nature fits in with the grittiness of the Southside and allies him with Pilate, who has connections to rural life. Later, Guitar's rural instincts will come to dominate his character.

The Best of a Bad Lot: Guitar's comment that black people must scrounge for names and hope for the best presents another interpretation of naming and renaming. Guitar believes that naming, for black people, does not mean seizing power or announcing identity, but trying to collect the best of a bad lot. He does not explain to Milkman where the nickname "Milkman" came from, but his ideas about names echo in Milkman's head. Milkman begins to wonder about other people's names, a wonder that will come to consume him.

PART ONE
Chapter 4

It is Christmastime, and Milkman is now thirty-one. He wonders whether he should break off his affair with Hagar. They have been involved, on and off, for fourteen years. Milkman remembers the first time they slept together. He went to Pilate's house one day and found a domestic crisis. A man Reba had been dating had come over and demanded that she lend him money. When she said there was no money to lend, the man got violent. Pilate held a knife to the man's throat until he promised to leave. Milkman was left alone with Hagar, who lured him into her bedroom. Milkman hit his head on a green sack full of Pilate's belongings, which Pilate called her "inheritance."

> "A stunningly beautiful book .... I would call the book poetry, but that would seem to be denying its considerable power as a story. Whatever name you give it, it's full of magnificent people, each of them complex and multi-layered, even the narrowest of them narrow in extravagant ways. They are still haunting my house. I suspect they will be with me forever."
>
> ANNE TYLER

Milkman decides to break it off with Hagar. He writes a letter to her and sends her some money as a Christmas gift. When Hagar receives the letter, she dashes out in search of Milkman. A few days later, Milkman sits in his father's office, looking over the accounting books. He is distracted by thoughts of Hagar's distress over their breakup and by the recent killings of some white people. The murders have been blamed on a serial killer who supposedly roams the region, but after listening closely to conversations at Tommy's Barbershop, Milkman suspects that his friends know something about the murders. The men describe details about the crime that Milkman had never heard before, and they laugh nervously about the murders.

Milkman asked Guitar about the murders, but Guitar lashed out at Milkman and said he is not a "serious person." He said it must look to Milkman like he is the only one going in the right direction. Milkman insisted he knows where he's going—"wherever the party is." Milkman now reflects on Guitar's words. He thinks that Guitar is partly right, that his life is "pointless, aimless." At the same time, though, Guitar's talk of politics, especially racial issues, bores him. Also, Guitar resents Milkman's family for having money, which offends Milkman.

Later, Milkman runs into Freddie, who tells him that a lot is going on in town. When Milkman prods him for more information, Freddie tells him that Guitar and Empire State act like Empire State is guilty of the murders. Freddie also says that Corinthians might know about everything.

UNDERSTANDING AND INTERPRETING

Chapter 4

Self-Absorbed and Immature: Milkman continues his gradual process of thinking about himself. As usual, Guitar provides the impetus for Milkman's self-reflection, and uses brutal honesty to snap Milkman out of his daze. As Guitar rightly says, Milkman is not a serious person. Ten years pass, and almost nothing about Milkman changes. He floats through life at thirty-one as he did when he was twenty-two. The only big decision he manages to make is to break off an unhealthy fourteen-year relationship with Hagar. However, although he succeeds in making a decision, he fails to carry it out maturely. Instead, he breaks off the relationship in an impersonal letter, adding insult to injury by including money, the most impersonal of gifts. By giving Hagar some money, which is something his father might do, Milkman thinks he is cushioning the blow of the breakup, when actually he is insulting Hagar. Further evidence of Milkman's immaturity is his unwillingness to have political discussions with Guitar. Talk of race and discrimination bores him, even though these issues apply directly to him and his friends and should fascinate him.

The Absence of Fire: Milkman thinks only of his immediate needs and his sensory pleasure. Surrounding him are people like Guitar and Freddie, who think daily about the racial issues of the community and feel passionate about defending their dignity. Money shelters Milkman, so he does not bother to care about the issues that consume his friends. None of their passion rubs off on him. Even Guitar's painfully honest remarks do little to change Milkman's attitude. He watches passively as the world goes by, content with his risk-free life.

Guitar's Reality: Guitar, like the other men at the barbershop, feels a sense of community, a connection to others that eludes Milkman. The racial politics he discusses are not just a pastime or an intellectual exercise. Unlike Milkman, he lives in Southside. The rough neighborhood is not a theme park to him, it is home. He lives with the prospect of discrimination and hate crimes, unsheltered by money. He and the other black men in the barbershop must constantly fear being picked up by the police, especially during times of crisis or violence.

PART ONE
Chapter 5

Six months later, Hagar is still devastated by the breakup with Milkman. Regularly—once a month—she tries to kill him. One night, when Milkman expects Hagar to come after him, he hides at Guitar's apartment. The two friends argue companionably. Guitar politicizes everything, even the tea Milkman is drinking.

Guitar leaves for the night, and Milkman begins to think about an event from a week earlier. He saw his mother walking down the street one night and followed her onto a train, which took them to the remote suburbs. He trailed her to a cemetery, where she lay down on her father's grave. When she left the cemetery a few hours later, he confronted her.

> "Morrison draws from a rich store of black oral tradition as well as from her own imaginative angle of vision to illuminate the potentialities for both annihilation and transcendence within the black experience."
>
> **ROBERTA RUBENSTEIN**

Ruth told him that she goes to the cemetery every so often to talk to her father. Ruth's father was the only person who took her seriously. Ruth told Milkman that she believes Macon killed her father. Dr. Foster was already sick, but Ruth thinks Macon took away his medicine to hasten his death. She also tells Milkman how he was conceived. Macon had stopped sleeping with Ruth years before Milkman was born, so Ruth went to Pilate for help. Pilate gave Ruth an aphrodisiac to put in Macon's food. The drug worked, and Macon slept with Ruth a few times. When Macon found out that Ruth was pregnant, he suspected Pilate's involvement and demanded that Ruth get an abortion. He assaulted her several times to force a miscarriage. Pilate tended Ruth and protected her from Macon until Milkman was born.

As Milkman sits in Guitar's house, Hagar arrives and holds a knife to his throat. But when she sees Milkman, she remembers how much she loves him. Milkman sarcastically suggests she kill herself by plunging the knife into her vagina.

The narrative shifts back to Ruth, who realizes she knows nothing about her own son. Milkman's birth was her one success in life, and it pains her to think that he might be killed. Ruth walks over to Pilate's house and finds Hagar there alone. She quietly threatens to hurt Hagar if she tries to kill Milkman, but Hagar is defiant. Pilate comes home and defuses the situation by telling them the story of her life prior to her arrival in Michigan.

After Pilate's father was murdered, Pilate and Macon wandered in the woods for a few days, then argued and separated. Pilate headed toward Virginia because she had heard she had family there. She walked for seven days until a preacher's family took her in and sent her to school. Things soured there eventually, so she left, taking only a geography book with her. She roamed the country with some migrant workers, picking up rocks as souvenirs. The migrants shooed her away after discovering she had no navel. When she finally reached Virginia, Pilate realized that she did not know which town her family was from. She eventually made her way to an island off the coast, where she became pregnant with Reba by a man on the island.

Her father's ghost appeared to her again and said, "Sing. Sing. You can't just fly on off and leave a body." Pilate took his words as a suggestion, and sang to the infant Reba. She traveled back to Pennsylvania and collected the bones of a man Macon murdered years before, when they were running from their father's murderers. A month later, she returned to Virginia with a sack containing the bones, her rocks, and her geography book.

Pilate soon felt restless. She wandered around the country for twenty years until she realized she missed her family. Reba now had Hagar. Pilate tracked down her brother in Michigan, but found him "truculent, inhospitable, embarrassed, and unforgiving." She stayed only after learning that Ruth needed her help in conceiving Milkman.

UNDERSTANDING AND INTERPRETING Chapter 5

Not Ruth, but Milkman's Mother: Ruth's story of Milkman's conception further illuminates her continuing battle for self-worth. Her visits to her father's grave are reminiscent of those of the biblical Ruth, who shows utter devotion and loyalty to her mother-in-law, Naomi, after Naomi's family suffers from terrible famine (Ruth 1:16–17). In the Bible, Ruth says, "Where you die, I will die—there will I be buried. May the Lord do thus and so to me, and more as well, if even death parts me from you!" In Morrison's story, Ruth has no identity of her own. She clings to her father's memory, which comforts her. Her father treated her as if she was an individual, and listened to what she had to say. Visiting Dr. Foster's grave is Ruth's only indulgence now that she can no longer nurse Milkman. She did not want Milkman to grow up, and she nursed him like a doll to banish the idea that he could survive independent of her. Now, Ruth regards Milkman as the one triumph in her life—a triumph over Macon and her father's absence. By being Milkman's mother, Ruth has an identity. Milkman's possible death, then, threatens Ruth's own existence. Ruth begins to realize, however, that the son she loves no longer exists, except in her imagination. Her actual son, as opposed to the baby enshrined in her memory, is now an immature, cruel, passive man.

Stories in Circles: Most of the chapters in *Song of Solomon* include flashbacks. In this chapter, we get Pilate's life story, a flashback to a scene that explains part of the family history. Pilate successfully uses the story as a device to soothe Ruth's vengeful anger toward Hagar. The story describes a perfect circle. It starts as a means to prevent Ruth and Hagar from fighting over Milkman, and it ends with the conception of Milkman, who indirectly caused Pilate to stay in Michigan.

Piloting Pilate: "Pilate" is a homonym for "pilot," an apt similarity. Pilate pilots herself through life, dragging her few possessions with her, finding her way toward family. She pilots other people's lives, too, providing help to Ruth and more or less bringing Milkman into being. Pilate's flights around the country are a search for identity, and when the search fails in one place, she simply picks up and moves on. She thinks she might find herself by finding her family in Virginia, and when she cannot, she keeps moving. For a while, Pilate lacks real family ties, sometimes by chance and sometimes by choice. In the beginning, a ghost and an unstable brother are her only companions. Later, she leaves her daughter. Only when Reba gives birth to Hagar does Pilate begin to crave time with her family.

Scheming for a Baby: Pilate seems to share equal responsibility for Milkman's birth with his biological mother, Ruth. Without Pilate's scheming, Ruth never could have lured her husband into bed or prevented him from forcing a miscarriage. After the revelation of Pilate's heavy involvement in Milkman's conception, we understand why Milkman feels so instantly happy in Pilate's house. Pilate's guidance, direct and indirect, will point Milkman in new directions.

The Geography Book: Like Guitar, Pilate seems preoccupied with geography. The geography book was her guide for roaming the country, although it did not help her locate her family. Pilate seems to have absorbed the expanses represented in her book. Her wanderlust frequently overtakes her and demands that she pick up and move somewhere new.

A Murder Mystery: In her flashbacks, Pilate reveals that Macon murdered a man in Pennsylvania, something neither she nor Macon have mentioned before, even though they both told Milkman the story of their years in Pennsylvania. We have not heard the last of the mysterious murder Macon committed.

PART ONE
Chapter 6

Guitar finds Hagar frozen to the spot where Milkman left her the night before, and worries that Hagar has totally lost her mind. Later that day, Guitar accuses Milkman of driving Hagar mad. Milkman says he only broke up with her, and lashes back by asking Guitar why he was hiding Empire State. Guitar finally admits everything. He explains that he is a member of the **Seven Days Society**, a clandestine group dedicated to revenging the racially motivated murders of black people by whites. The group has seven members, one for each day of the week. If the murder of a black person occurs on a Monday, then the "Monday man" is responsible for the corresponding murder of a white person. Their revenge killings take the same form as the original murders.

Milkman says Guitar is as evil as the white murderers. He argues that the Seven Days are doing nothing but murdering innocent people. Guitar argues there are no innocent white people, because all whites are potential killers. He believes that the murders committed by the Seven Days maintain a natural equilibrium.

Guitar admits that Seven Days members do get anxious. Robert Smith, the man who jumped from the roof of the Hospital, had been a member and could not take it anymore. **Henry Porter**, a current member, got drunk one day and waved his shotgun around. Empire State is a member, as is Guitar, who is the "Sunday man." None of the Seven Days can marry or have children. Milkman says they have no love in their lives, but Guitar disagrees, saying, "It's about loving us. About loving you. My whole life is love."

Milkman remarks that Guitar should change his name from Guitar Bains to Guitar X. Guitar says he does not care about slave names, but about " slave status," and that the Seven Days fights the oppression of black people in America. Milkman is unconvinced. He worries that the Seven Days could begin to murder regularly and that the group might kill someone like him. Guitar reassures him that the group does not kill black people. Milkman tells Guitar he is scared for him, and Guitar replies that he is scared for Milkman.

UNDERSTANDING AND INTERPRETING
Chapter 6

Murder to Restore the Balance: Guitar justifies the Seven Days' murders with natural and mathematical ideas. For him, the world is about equilibrium and equalization. If a black person dies a victim of hate, a white person must die in order to restore the equilibrium. Any moral qualms or laws, such as the ones Milkman raises, are irrelevant. We see that Guitar's past in Florida, where he hunted, probably informs his actions now. But to members of the Seven Days, including Guitar, retributive murders are not about sport or hunting. They are a performance of justice that someone must undertake, since the American judicial system will never do justice to black Americans.

Guitar X: Milkman cannot comprehend Guitar's views or his membership in Seven Days. He jokes to Guitar that he should change his name to "Guitar X," in the same way that Malcolm X dropped his last name to wipe away the name his

MALCOLM X

Malcolm X (1925–1965), who was born Malcolm Little in Omaha, Nebraska, rose from a life of petty crime to become one of the great black leaders of the twentieth century. While in prison, he converted to the Muslim faith of the Nation of Islam. Upon his release, Malcolm X became a powerful and charismatic spokesman for black separatism and nationalism. In 1964, political differences between Malcolm X and Nation of Islam leader Elijah Muhammad caused X to split off from the group, at which point he converted to orthodox Islam and founded his own highly successful Organization for Afro-American Unity. His political and racial philosophy gradually changed from militant black separatism to interracial coexistence. His ascendance was tragically cut short by his assassination in 1965. It has been suspected, but never proven, that Malcolm X was murdered by members of the Nation of Islam.

enslaved ancestors inherited from their master. For Guitar, though, names are not that important. Actual status matters far more than the symbolic value of names. If Guitar changed his name, it would not change anything about his life. He believes that only willful action can change things. Milkman, a man of no action, forever worries about his own nickname. His worries have nothing to do with race, however, and everything to do with vanity—he simply dislikes the name Milkman.

PART ONE
Chapter 7

The narrator explains that people from the Great Lakes region feel they have a shoreline because of the five lakes, but when they realize they are actually landlocked, they feel the need to escape their homes. Milkman is struck with wanderlust and asks his father if he can leave. Macon tells him if he stays, he will inherit all of the money, and "money is freedom." Milkman tells Macon not to be like Pilate, who keeps her fortune in a green sack hung from a wall.

Macon freezes. He presses Milkman for a description of the sack, and Milkman tells him Pilate calls the sack her "inheritance." Agitated, Macon tells Milkman more about the past in Pennsylvania. Macon's father was murdered when Macon was sixteen and Pilate was twelve. Macon and Pilate could not stay with Circe long, because she worked for the people who had killed their father.

After two weeks with Circe, they set out into the woods. On their third day there, they both saw their father's ghost motioning them toward a cave. They followed him into the cave, but he disappeared. They slept in the cave that night, and when Macon awoke he found an **old white man** sleeping there too. The man woke up, and Macon struck him with a rock and stabbed him with a knife. The man fell down, presumably dead. Macon found a green tarpaulin and some gray bags filled with gold under the man's body. He awakened Pilate. Their father appeared to them again, saying, "Sing. Sing." Macon gathered the gold, but Pilate thought they should not take it.

They quarreled about the gold until Pilate pulled a knife on Macon. Macon left the cave and Pilate did not come out for one day and night. Macon heard dogs and hunters approaching and ran off. Two days later, he returned to the cave and found the dead man's body, but no gold, no green tarpaulin, and no Pilate. To this day, Macon believes that Pilate escaped with the gold, which is why he dislikes her. He thinks she spent all the money before showing up in

Michigan without a penny. It delights Macon that Pilate has a green sack at her house. He thinks she may still have the money. Macon says that if Milkman steals the sack, they can split the gold in half. That way, Milkman will have the money he needs to leave town.

UNDERSTANDING AND INTERPRETING
Chapter 7

Landlocked by the Great Lakes: The chapter's opening paragraph contains a vivid description of restlessness. Living by the Great Lakes gives people a false sense of living on a coastline, when in fact they are landlocked, trapped in Michigan. Milkman is similarly trapped in his own existence. Morrison uses the image of landlocked people to suggest the restlessness that can come of living in the same town for one's whole life. Just as the literally landlocked long for the ocean, the emotionally landlocked long for new experiences. Milkman, so passive and motionless for so long, finally feels a need for action. He decides he needs to roam, to fly away. Geography now fascinates Milkman, just as it fascinates Guitar and Pilate.

Money Lust: Macon is a truly static, unchanging character. His love of money is an almost monomaniacal pursuit. He grabs at every chance to make a buck, no matter how cold or calculating he must be in order to succeed. The origin of his grudge against Pilate has never been clear, and now we learn that he dislikes her solely because he suspects her of taking money. This seems like a forgivable offense, especially since the money was not Macon's, he is not even sure Pilate took it, and the whole incident transpired when both siblings were nearly delirious with grief and fear and the shock of seeing their dead father. Underlining his own stasis, Macon ends his story of the past in the same way that he ended his story in Chapter 2, saying, "Get the gold."

Fill in the Blanks: Macon's story fills in the blanks about Macon and Pilate's escape from Pennsylvania. However, while it solves one mystery, it creates another—the question of the gold and of Pilate's "inheritance." Pilate says the sack contains bones, a book, and rocks, but Macon believes it holds gold. We do not yet know which sibling is right.

PART ONE
Chapter 8

Back in Southside, Guitar gets his first assignment as Sunday man of the Seven Days. Four black girls were killed in a church bombing on Sunday, and Guitar must retaliate. He needs money to buy explosives. That day, Milkman approaches Guitar to ask for his help in getting Pilate's gold.

Milkman wonders if Guitar has actually murdered anyone yet. In Guitar, Milkman sees a changed, dangerous man. Milkman realizes he has always thrived next to fear-inspiring people like Guitar, Macon, and Pilate. As Milkman and Guitar plot their theft, they see a white peacock trying to fly. Guitar sees its "tail full of jewelry" and concludes it is male. The peacock flies away and lands on a nearby Buick. It can't fly very well, and Guitar remarks, "Too much tail . . . Like vanity. Can't nobody fly with all that shit."

They fantasize about what they might buy with the gold. Guitar dreams of buying nice things for his poor relatives, especially his grandmother. He imagines buying a marker for his father's grave. Most importantly, he wants to buy dynamite. Milkman dreams of boats, cars, and airplanes—vehicles that would take him to new places. Milkman realizes that he does not want to feel much or know much. He wants to be cautious about stealing the sack, but Guitar is impatient. Guitar's conviction begins to affect Milkman. He feels his tentativeness replaced by resolve, and "a self inside him emerge, a clean-lined definite self." They decide to rob Pilate the following night.

When they enter Pilate's house, they find it dark and cold. They cut down the sack, which feels much lighter than they expected. As they exit through a window, Milkman swears he sees the figure of a man standing right behind Guitar. Pilate, looking out at them as they leave, wonders what they want with the sack.

UNDERSTANDING AND INTERPRETING
Chapter 8

Dreams of Gold: The disparity between Guitar's dreams and Milkman's dreams further illuminates their differences. Guitar secretly dreams of dynamite. He longs to fulfill his duty, revenge deaths, and create an explosion of action. He also dreams of providing for his family and honoring their dead, of getting gifts for his relatives, especially the grandmother who raised him, and of buying a gravestone for his father. Guitar thinks about his family, his roots, and his responsibilities. Milkman, on the other hand, thinks only of himself.

FOUR LITTLE GIRLS

The killing of the four black girls in a church bombing was another pivotal event of the Civil Rights movement. The Sixteenth Avenue Baptist Church in Birmingham, Alabama, was the center of civil rights activism in the city. It was a gathering place for marches, rallies, and organizational meetings. On the morning of Sunday, September 15, 1963, just before the 11:00 A.M. service, while Sunday School classes were still in session in the basement, a dynamite bomb was detonated. It destroyed part of the building and injured scores of parishioners who had just arrived. It also killed four young girls. Three of them, Cynthia Wesley, Carole Robertson, and Addie Mae Collins, were fourteen years old. The fourth, Denise McNair, was eleven. White racists Thomas Blanton and Bobby Frank Cherry were later indicted in the bombing. Blanton was found guilty. Cherry, who maintained his innocence, was only recently retried and found guilty of first-degree murder. While the bombers intended the explosion to hinder the activist efforts of the church, their act of violence had the opposite effect. The bombing received international media attention and quickly drew many moderate southern whites into the Civil Rights movement. In 1997, filmmaker Spike Lee revisited the bombing and its aftermath in the Academy Award-nominated documentary *Four Little Girls*.

His unconscious self-absorption leads him to long only for his escape. He lusts for cars, boats, and airplanes—anything that will help him get away. He never thinks of helping his suffering mother or his angry father.

Milkman Wakes Up: Chapter 8 marks a pivotal moment for Milkman. When Guitar scoffs at Milkman's pleas for caution, Milkman wakes up. He has realized that he flourishes in the presence of big, terrifying personalities, and now he finally feels alert and ambitious. No longer stupefied, Milkman feels driven to rob Pilate's house. This decision is of questionable moral worth, but at least Milkman is no longer drifting.

Returning to Rural Roots: It is no coincidence that Milkman's decision to take action guides him toward Pilate, the woman who made his own birth possible. Prodded by Guitar, and by Guitar's connection to his rural Florida upbringing, Milkman is headed toward a new geography, toward Pilate's green sack—her "inheritance." The green sack is the physical manifestation of Pilate's legacy. Milkman will seek it out, and it will lead him to seek out her legacy elsewhere, back in the rural roots of the Dead family.

Vanity Tail: The peacock that can barely fly is a metaphor for Milkman's own inability to succeed. Like the peacock, Milkman is weighed down by vanity. Milkman's self-absorption and lack of aspiration are his "tail feathers." As Guitar says, one cannot fly dragged down by the weight of vanity. The biggest influence on Milkman, even if he will not admit it, is Macon, who has seduced his son into a life of comfort and complacence. But when Guitar tells Milkman to shun reason, suddenly Milkman has the urge to fly away from Michigan and toward a new life. For now, Milkman sees flight as a means of freedom and escape. He does not yet understand that true flight will mean shedding his vanity and finding a new identity that will allow him to embrace his freedom in an unselfish way.

> "Vanity—has brought more virtues to an untimely end than any other vice."
>
> ANONYMOUS

Flying High: The peacock metaphor also alludes to the ancient Greek myth of Icarus and Daedalus, in which the prideful Icarus flies too close to the sun and falls to his death. Like Icarus, Milkman's attempts to fly are stunted by his selfish, prideful ways. When he tries too hard to show off his wings, Milkman falls directly to the ground and is caught.

ON WAX WINGS

Morrison draws on Greek mythology to tell her characters' stories. According to ancient myth, Daedalus was the greatest craftsman and inventor on the island of Crete, the center of Minoan civilization, an ancient culture predating ancient Greece. After hearing of Daedalus's skills, King Minos asked him to build a great labyrinth so that he could imprison the minotaur, a half-man, half-bull monster the gods had cursed to lust after Minos's wife. Daedalus and his son Icarus did as the king requested, but when they finished, Minos did not allow them to leave the labyrinth. The clever Daedalus contrived a way to escape: he built wings out of wax and feathers so that he and his son could fly away. When father and son flew up into the air, Icarus was so proud of his wings that he flew higher and higher toward the sun. His wax wings melted, and he fell to his death in the sea below.

PART ONE
Chapter 9

Milkman's sister, Corinthians, is now forty-four. She has been unhappy for some time. When she was younger, she went to Bryn Mawr College and took a trip to Europe on the *Queen Mary*. Still, she failed to find a suitable job or a suitable husband. She waited for years, but she lacked drive and confidence. All she did was help her sister make red velvet roses. She now works as a maid for **Miss Michael-Mary Graham**, the state's Poet Laureate, a gentle, bohemian woman who is overjoyed that she can employ a literate black woman, since it suits her liberal ideals. The rest of the Dead family believes that Corinthians is a secretary. Ruth boasts to her friends about Corinthians' job, calling her an "amanuensis" (someone hired to write from dictation).

Corinthians flourishes in her own way, gaining confidence through her job. She takes the bus to Miss Graham's house, and every day for a month, a man sits down next to her and smiles at her. One morning, he leaves her a card entitled "Friendship" that she takes home and reads. Soon enough, they begin to talk and flirt. The man's name is **Henry Porter**. Corinthians and Porter begin dating, but she never goes home with him. He secretly shames her, so she keeps him a secret from her family. She blames her hesitation on her strict father. The same night that Milkman robs Pilate, Porter, frustrated, breaks off his relationship with Corinthians, saying, "I don't want a doll baby. I want a . . . grown-up woman that's not scared of her daddy." As Porter drives away, Corinthians chases him down and bangs on his car window. Her vanity disappears, replaced with a new self-esteem.

She spends most of the night with Porter. He drops her off very late. Corinthians hears Macon talking to Milkman. After Milkman and Guitar stole the sack from Pilate's, the police picked them up. The sack contained no gold, just bones, rocks, and the geography book. Pilate helped Milkman and Guitar, telling the police they were playing a joke on her. She says the bones are those of her dead husband.

Milkman remembers how Pilate spoke in a high, silly voice and looked small in front of the police, but spoke normally and looked tall as soon as they left the station. Macon picked them up at the police station, acting deferential to the police officers. In the car on the way home, Pilate tells them that three years after the incident in the cave, she went back to Pennsylvania to get the bones of the white man Macon had killed. She had interpreted her dead father's message as a command to sing and take responsibility for the murder. She found the bones at the front of the cave and assumed that a wolf had dragged out the dead body.

Milkman awakens the next day feeling ashamed of his actions and of seeing his father and Pilate cringe in front of the policemen. He feels guilty because he stole something from Pilate and even more guilty because he would have knocked her down if she had tried to stop them. Pilate has done everything for him, "told him stories, sung him songs, fed him." She does not deserve his violence, Guitar's contempt, or the policemen's disrespect.

Milkman goes looking for Guitar and sees him in Henry Porter's car. Milkman remembers seeing the same car pick up Corinthians, and realizes that she has been dating Porter. Milkman tells Macon about Corinthians' affair, and Macon forbids Corinthians to leave the house or work at Miss Graham's. This incites the wrath of Milkman's other sister, **Lena,** who blames Milkman for ruining Corinthians' happiness. She tells him that Macon shows off his daughters like prizes, while privately keeping them submissive and humiliated. He parades them "through Babylon and humiliat[es them] like whores in Babylon." Milkman leaves home.

UNDERSTANDING AND INTERPRETING
Chapter 9

Two Separate Sisters: Before this chapter, Milkman's two sisters have seemed almost interchangeable. Now, however, we learn more about them, and they become individuals. Lena understands how Macon treats his daughters, and she resents it. A smart woman, she sees how Macon's public pride in them is not the true pride of a loving parent, but the pride a car owner might take in his car. Macon's true feelings for his daughters come out in private, where he treats them like whores, humiliating them. Corinthians emerges as a beaten down, meek woman, who has nevertheless managed to retain a bit of spirit. When finally motivated to fly to Porter, she breaks out of her submissiveness and becomes strong.

Milkman's Shame: Milkman is gripped by shame—a totally new emotion for him—after robbing Pilate and encountering the police. Not only is it the first time he has seen the police in action, it is also the first time, as far as we know, that he has seen his father and Pilate interact with white authorities. Watching the adults he loves bow and scrape before the police humiliates Milkman. He also feels deep shame for his attitude toward Pilate. He cannot justify greed at the expense of all else, which his father encouraged, when Pilate has always shown him affection and love. She did not deserve to be insulted or offended, let alone robbed or physically attacked. Most of all, Milkman is shamed by the sight of what he calls Pilate's "Aunt Jemima act." For Milkman's sake, Pilate debases herself, putting on an act in order to talk their way out of the police station. As Pilate talks to the police, she becomes diminished in Milkman's eyes. She does not seem to be the same tall, admirable, strong woman he has known in the past. The shame Milkman feels on her behalf marks the first time he has felt a visceral emotion for another person.

Flight to Part Two: Just as Guitar's words incited Milkman to action in the previous chapter, here Porter's words inspire Corinthians to jump headlong into their relationship, to fly in a new direction. By the end of the chapter, Milkman has taken a different kind of flight, abandoning Hagar, his family, and all responsibility.

PART TWO
Chapter 10

Milkman sets off on a journey, hoping to find the cave and the lost gold. Before departing, he agrees to split the gold with Guitar if he finds it. He tells Guitar he needs to get away from his family for awhile, saying, "Everybody wants something from me." Guitar says whites want the black man dead or quiet, and black women want all of their black man.

Guitar worries that Milkman might find the gold and not come back. They shake hands limply and part company. Milkman flies from Michigan to Pittsburgh, an experience that excites him and also makes him feel vulnerable. From Pittsburgh, he takes a bus to Danville, Pennsylvania. When he arrives there, he realizes that he does not know where to go. A stranger directs him to **the Reverend Cooper**, who might know Circe. Milkman introduces himself to Cooper as "Macon Dead," and Cooper, overjoyed, says he knows Milkman's people. Milkman feels less like a stranger. Milkman and Cooper have drinks together, and Cooper says his father, a blacksmith, once made an earring for Pilate.

He knows Circe, but assumes she has been dead for years. Circe used to live with and work for the Butlers, the white family that shot and killed Milkman's grandfather. Cooper arranges for his **nephew** to take Milkman to the Butler house when his car is fixed. Milkman stays with the Coopers for four days, until the Reverend's car is ready. All of Cooper's friends remember Milkman's father and grandfather as extraordinary men. They describe his grandmother as light-skinned and black-haired, maybe Native American.

Milkman learns that his family's farm outside Danville was called "Lincoln's Heaven" and was a model of success. He tells them that his father is now a prosperous businessman, married to a doctor's daughter, with lots of property, new cars, and money. They cheer this news, and Milkman beams with pride. He echoes his father's words, saying, "I worked right alongside my father. Right alongside him."

Cooper's nephew drives Milkman out to the old Butler house, which is huge and terribly rundown. It looks like a murderer's house to Milkman. He knocks on the door, but the place seems abandoned. Milkman closes his eyes and remembers a recurring childhood dream about witches. He reopens his eyes and realizes a pack of golden-eyed, beautiful dogs surrounds him. The dogs are accompanied by the woman in his childhood dreams. She is a disheveled mess with crazy eyes, in contrast to the elegant, groomed dogs.

The woman motions to Milkman to follow her inside. From what she says, Milkman realizes she has mistaken him for his father. He corrects her. The woman says she is Circe. Circe tells him that the last Butler descendent, a woman, used to breed dogs. She killed herself years earlier when all the family money was gone. Now Circe breeds dogs and lives there alone. Circe was a midwife to nearly everyone in Danville and the surrounding county, and she lost only one person, Macon's grandmother.

Circe tells Milkman that his grandmother was a mixed-race Native American named **Sing**. Sing and Milkman's grandfather met on a wagon full of ex-slaves leaving Virginia. Milkman mentions the cave, which Circe identifies as Hunter's Cave. It was in Hunter's Cave that some fisherman dumped the corpse of Macon Dead, Sr. Macon and Pilate had buried the body, but it floated up in a heavy rain.

"As much as any novel that stands before it.... *Song of Solomon* lays out a whole world made from the wrack and cinders of an unimaginable waste and loss—from the all-top imaginable centuries of the cruel enslavement of untold millions."

REYNOLDS PRICE

Circe tells Milkman how to find the cave. Before he leaves, she tells him that his grandfather's real name was **Jake**. Milkman makes his way into the woods and eventually finds the cave, but it is empty. Discouraged, he hitches a ride into Danville, where he decides to get out of town as quickly as possible. As he leaves town, Milkman realizes that he wanted the gold as much for himself as for anyone else. It occurs to him that Pilate might have brought the gold to Virginia. He decides to hunt for it there.

UNDERSTANDING AND INTERPRETING
Chapter 10

Hero's Quest: In Part Two, Milkman undertakes a quest, a modern update of the kind of journey portrayed in Homer's *Odyssey*. As Milkman travels great distances on his odyssey, he meets new characters who help or hinder him. The original goal of his quest is to find gold, but as he travels and learns more about his family's past, he undergoes a transformation. He begins to look not for gold, but for his family heritage. Milkman's travels have a tinge of the mystical, as when he encounters Circe and her dogs. In Homer's *Odyssey*, Circe is a goddess who drugs men and turns them into pigs. Unlike her namesake, the Circe of *Song of Solomon* helps Milkman.

Family Pride: The Reverend Cooper quickly reminds Milkman that he has an identity as a member of the Dead family. Now that Milkman is separated from his Michigan home, he can look back on his immediate family with a measure of detachment, and he sees them in a new light. The Danville men hang on every word of Milkman's stories about Macon Dead, the boy who grew up in their neck of the woods. Milkman feels a pride in his family name that he has never felt before. Just as Macon enjoyed saying he works next to his son, Milkman now, for the first time, takes pride in saying he works at his father's side. He also realizes that Macon took a great deal of pride in his own father, the original Macon. Macon's boasting about Jake's farm in Pennsylvania was not empty bragging, but genuine recollections of admiration and love. Aside from his childhood visits to Pilate's house, this is the first time Milkman enjoys being part of a family.

KING SOLOMON'S MINES
Milkman's search for gold brings to mind *King Solomon's Mines*, the 1885 "book for boys" by H. Rider Haggard. It was a page-turner modeled on another popular adventure novel of the era, Robert Louis Stevenson's *Treasure Island*. Both novels are constructed around the theme of buried treasure. In *King Solomon's Mines*, the treasure is supposed to be buried deep in the mountains of southern Africa, in what the fortune hunters believed to be the lost city of Ophir, where Israel's wise and wealthy King Solomon (970–928 B.C.) mined diamonds for his kingdom.

THE BIBLICAL "SONG OF SOLOMON"

Also called the "Song of Songs" or the "Canticle of Canticles," the Song of Solomon is the twenty-second book of the Old Testament, thought to have been written by the wise King Solomon. It is one of the Bible's books of poetry and is grouped with Psalms and Lamentations as well as with the books of wisdom (Job, Proverbs, and Ecclesiastes). The Song of Solomon is a series of love poems told from the perspective of a bride and bridegroom, but it can also be read as an allegory of God's love for Israel and the Jewish people. The poems famously include the refrain repeated by black churchgoers everywhere: "I am black and beautiful / O daughters of Jerusalem . . . Do not gaze at me because I am dark / Because the sun has gazed on me."

Lincoln's Heaven: For Reverend Cooper and his friends, the Dead family farm stood for the idea that black people could succeed. Milkman does not immediately recognize it, but the farm also shows his family's rural heritage and vitality. Pigs and cows, peach orchards, and rows of crops fill the farm, which bustles with life. The business of the farm contrasts with the deadness of the Deads in Michigan and shows how far they have wandered, in spirit, from their roots.

The Shadowy Circe: The nature of Circe's ghostly appearance makes us wonder if she is a real woman or a vision. She arrives like a mythical enchantress, accompanied by a pack of hounds. She is reputed to be at least 150 years old. No one has seen Circe in years, although she claims that occasionally someone brings food for her dogs. It may be that Circe appears only to Milkman, or that he conjures her up. Pilate and Macon have told stories about Circe, depicting her as a healer and a wise, gentle soul. Upon meeting the old woman, Milkman sees that she is just as Pilate and Macon described. A midwife extraordinaire, Circe helped at the births of Macon, Pilate, and "just about everybody in the county." Now, she gives life to Milkman's quest by providing the names of his long-lost grandparents. Circe also brings Milkman closer to understanding his cultural and racial legacy by explaining how she has survived since the death of the last Butler. The Butler woman committed suicide rather than continue to live in the poverty that Circe endured for her entire life.

New Names, New Life: When Milkman learns that his grandparents' real names were Jake and Sing, he peels back a layer of white gloss and gets closer to uncovering his family history. His grandfather's name, Jake, erases the arbitrary name Dead, and his grandmother's name, Sing, is sonorant and vibrant. Milkman begins to imagine his grandparents as real people with real names, filling some of his empty soul with life.

PART TWO
Chapter 11

Milkman buys a decrepit used car and drives to Shalimar, Virginia, a collection of a few buildings and shotgun houses. The general store proprietor, **Mr. Solomon,** tells Milkman that Milkman's friend had been there looking for him. The friend left a message: "Your day is coming," the phrase uttered to the victims of the Seven Days.

Milkman thinks the message must be from Guitar. He worries that the phrase is a warning, but concludes that Guitar is fleeing Michigan because of his murders. Outside, Milkman notices that the people of Shalimar look alike. A group of children sings, "Jay the only son of Solomon / Come booba yalle, come booba tambee /Whirl about and touch the sun / Come booba yalle, come booba tambee." The song ends, "Twenty-one children the last one *Jay!*" A boy doing an imitation of an airplane drops to the ground on the last word, "Jay." Milkman remembers discovering, at the age of four, that humans cannot fly.

When Milkman remarks that the women in town are very pretty, Solomon and some other men respond with awkward silence. Milkman says he might have to buy a new car and then realizes that remark probably annoyed those listening. He feels like a "city Negro" whose fancy clothes and brusque manners appall these men. A young man, **Saul**, picks a fight with Milkman. The two slash at each other with a knife and a broken bottle until Mr. Solomon and others break it up.

An older man named **Omar** invites Milkman to go hunting with a group later that night. Omar tells Milkman to meet them at King Walker's gas station at sundown. Milkman feels disoriented in Shalimar. He thought it would feel homey, but instead people treat him with grudging respect and without love. At King Walker's gas station, a makeshift clubhouse for men, Milkman meets **Luther Solomon**, **Small Boy**, and **Calvin Breakstone**. Breakstone will be Milkman's hunting partner. Luther releases a pack of hunting dogs, and the men split up.

In the woods, Milkman hears what sounds like a woman crying in the distance. Calvin tells him it is Ryna's Gulch. The dogs bark furiously, and Calvin realizes the dogs are on a bobcat's trail. Milkman cannot keep up with Calvin, and finally sits down. He thinks he does not deserve this treatment. Then he considers the word "deserve" and realizes that he uses it often. He does not "deserve" his family's dependence. He did not "deserve" to hear about his mother's and father's sad pasts. He did not "deserve" Hagar's vengeance. He realizes that he thought he deserved only love and pleasant stories.

The sounds of the hunting party remind him of communication in a "time when men and animals did talk to one another." He thinks of Guitar's hunting stories, and feels that he finally understands Guitar. Suddenly, he senses someone behind him. He raises his hands just fast enough to get a hand on the wire with which his assailant was about to strangle him. The wire cuts into his neck, and Milkman hears the man say, "Your day has come." He realizes it is Guitar. The two men struggle, and Guitar finally runs off after Milkman fires his gun twice. Milkman hears the barking dogs and knows the hunters have treed the bobcat.

The hunting party meets back at King Walker's at dawn. Milkman jokes with the others, admitting that he was "scared to death" in the woods. The man who dismembers the bobcat asks Milkman if he wants the bobcat's heart, and Milkman accepts. The men are going to eat the carcass. A peacock soars over them and lands on the hood of a Buick. Later, a woman named **Vernell** cooks breakfast for the men. Milkman mentions Sing's name. Vernell remembers hearing about a Sing who was a Native American playmate of her grandmother's. Sing was one of **Heddy**'s children, from the **Byrd** family, who lived near a place called Solomon's Leap. **Susan Byrd** still lives there. Milkman realizes that he feels comfortable with the "elders" of Shalimar.

That night, at Omar's suggestion, Milkman spends the night with a pretty young woman in town named **Sweet**. She feeds him, bathes him, massages him, and makes love to him. The next morning, he gives her fifty dollars and says he will be back that night.

UNDERSTANDING AND INTERPRETING
Chapter 11

City Mouse: As Milkman moves further into his family's past, he moves further south, backtracking over the path that Jake and Sing supposedly took when they went North. He arrives in Shalimar almost by chance, perhaps repeating his ancestors' chance arrival in Pennsylvania years before. Milkman feels less at home in Virginia than he did in Pennsylvania. His northern city manners alienate him from the people he meets. Sheltered all his life, Milkman is not used to exercising tact when discussing money. He realizes too late that it offends people to hear wealth carelessly flaunted. Later, in the woods, Milkman realizes that he is clueless about hunting and cannot keep up with his rural hunting partners. In fact, hunting so stymies Milkman that although he thinks he is the hunter, he is actually the hunted, tracked down and pounced upon by Guitar.

A Wanderer's Troubles: Milkman's travels continue to mimic an epic hero's wanderings. Like Odysseus in Homer's *Odyssey*, Milkman must confront challenges to his safety and, sometimes, to his life. He must contend with the unfriendliness of Mr. Solomon and the others at the General Store, the fight with Saul, the skill of the hunting party, and the struggle with Guitar. Each incident transforms Milkman slightly and heightens his self-knowledge. Finally, after three decades of life, he begins to examine his own shortcomings. The episode at the General Store shows him that he is often rude, self-absorbed, and materialistic. He makes tasteless remarks about buying new cars and about the attractive women in town, and, for once, his own rudeness actually dawns on him.

Later, while hunting, he has an epiphany and realizes that all his life, he has fooled himself into believing he deserves only love and none of the pain of love. He has been unwilling to help the people he loves bear their burdens, and now he realizes that "not deserving" to hear about people's pain is not only impossible but undesirable. The dismemberment of the bobcat (another ritual that echoes the defeat of a mythical beast) makes Milkman reflect on his race and mortality. As Milkman grabs the bobcat's heart, his own heart fills with knowledge of his connection with others—with the brotherhood of his hunting partners, with his family, and with his race and roots.

Hunting for Bobcat: Just as Milkman hunts down his past, the men hunt their prey. The hunt also emphasizes the southern, rural roots of the Dead family, and shows how far the Deads have drifted from these roots. Hunting was a part of Guitar's old life in Florida, a ritual that brought him a feeling of unity with the earth. Now, performing the unfamiliar hunting ritual with older men, Milkman begins to feel a sense of harmony. Just as the men open the bobcat and sort through its body, Milkman opens himself up and examines himself. He pokes around in his head, thinking about responsibility, race, and selfishness. By the end of the hunt, Milkman has become part of a brotherhood. He once felt unwelcome among these men, but now he laughs easily with them and reflects on how comfortable he feels. It is as if they are his own ancestors. Milkman can even joke about his own cowardice in the woods, a sign that he feels comfortable enough to let down his guard around these men.

Learning to Fly: A peacock appears after the hunt, echoing the peacock that appeared in Chapter 8 of Part One. The first peacock had trouble flying, but this one sails over the men's heads. The progression of the peacocks suggests Milkman's progress. Milkman, like the first peacock, was weighed down by vanity and could not fly. Now, like the second peacock, he sheds his vanity and begins to take wing. The peacocks also symbolize the relationship between Guitar and Milkman. In Part One, Guitar said that he would eat the vain peacock if he caught it. Milkman was once the vain peacock, but now he is lighter. Without his vanity, he can elude Guitar in the woods.

Sweet the Baptist: Milkman strengthens his ties to Shalimar not only through hunting and fraternity, but through sex. The hunt was his blood ritual, and his night with Sweet is his baptism, a ritual cleansing, an act of love. Sweet provides further entrée into Shalimar society, as Milkman shakes loose his old identity and prepares for a new one.

PART TWO
Chapter 12

Milkman goes to Susan Byrd's house and asks if she will help him find out about his family. Susan's friend Grace Long is there. Over coffee and cookies, Milkman tells the women that his grandmother was Sing. Susan says Sing was her aunt, the sister of her father, **Crowell Byrd**. Sing was heading north on a wagon to Massachusetts the last time Crowell saw her. Evidently Sing went to a Quaker school in Boston, and after that, the family lost track of her.

Milkman leaves the Byrd house feeling tired and off center. He realizes that Pilate never lived in Shalimar and thinks that the Sing who lived in Shalimar is not his grandmother. Milkman feels like an outsider in his family and has no good friends other than Guitar. Still, finding his family has grown important to him. Milkman thinks about his grandfather's words to Pilate and Macon ("Sing. Sing. You just can't get up and fly away from a body") and wonders if the ghost was merely repeating his wife's name.

Milkman runs into Guitar, who confronts him about the gold. Milkman insists that he never found any. Guitar saw Milkman loading a crate onto a train and concluded that Milkman was running off with the gold. Milkman was just assisting the porter in the train station, but Guitar refuses to believe him. The two men part warily.

That night, Milkman sleeps cozily in Sweet's arms. He dreams in a relaxed position, as if lying on a sofa. The next morning, Milkman sets out to get his car fixed. He hears a group of children playing the same game he saw when he first arrived. Then they sing the old blues song Pilate used to sing—"O Sugarman don't leave me here"—except the children sing "Solomon" instead of "Sugarman."

Milkman recalls happier days when he and Pilate were close, a time when he hated his parents and his sisters. He now feels silly for having hated his own family. Milkman notices for the first time that everyone in the town seems to be called Solomon, which sounds vaguely like the name of the town, Shalimar. He suddenly comprehends a piece of the puzzle of his family history. The song goes, "*Jake* the only son of Solomon." He listens closely to the rest of the song and hears Heddy's name: "Heddy took him to a red man's house." He realizes that the children's song is actually about his family's genealogy. The song ends with the line, "Solomon done fly, Solomon done gone / Solomon cut across the sky, Solomon gone home."

Milkman deduces that Sing's name must have been **Singing Bird**, since she was brought up in Heddy's Native American home (the "red man's house").

She must have changed her name from "Singing Bird" to "Sing Byrd." Sing's brother, Crowell, must have been named "Crow." Excited, Milkman runs back to Solomon's store.

UNDERSTANDING AND INTERPRETING Chapter 12

Guitar's Dark Side: Guitar reveals a darker side of his character. He wants the gold so that he can perform the retaliatory bombing, but his means of getting the gold approach obsession. He goes all the way to Pennsylvania and then to Virginia to seek out Milkman, and he actually tries to murder his old friend in an attempt to get the money. Milkman originally argued that murder would become habitual for members of the Seven Days, and it seems he was right. Guitar's attempt on Milkman's life serves no real purpose. If Milkman truly had the money, Guitar could have held him up or threatened him with death, instead of immediately trying to kill him. Murdering Milkman fulfills no duty to the Seven Days, a group that allegedly refuses to kill black people, and it certainly does not get Guitar closer to money. Even if Milkman had the money hidden somewhere, by killing him, Guitar would permanently silence the one person who knew where it was hidden. Guitar attempts to kill Milkman carelessly, numbly, without even thinking it through. Once Milkman's guide, Guitar now seems less focused than Milkman.

Covered in Shame: Milkman is new at feeling shame, and it overwhelms him. When he first makes the connection between the children's song and Pilate, he once again feel shame, this time because he cannot believe he ever hated his parents and sisters. He suffers from the same kind of embarrassment and disbelief that dogged him after he stole Pilate's green sack.

Flying Lying Down: Previously, Morrison connected flight to pride. Icarus was the model, that prideful boy who soared too close to the sun. Now, however, we see a different model of flying. The night before Milkman hears the song, he dreams of flying not with wings proudly outspread, but lying down and relaxed. The comfortable sense of flying in his dream stays with him the next day, and he draws strength from it. This leads to the sudden realization that the children's song tells the story of his cultural and family legacy. He realizes that the answers in his life are not tied to his own desires, but to a commitment to the brotherhood that he discovered in the hunting party and to the family that he unearths in the songs.

The Song of Solomon: The children's song brings together all of the thematic and symbolic pieces of the novel. The singing echoes the songs of Pilate, who was previously Milkman's connection to his family's roots. She sung "O Sugarman" unwittingly, as if her family history, in slightly bastardized form, naturally sprung up from nowhere in a corner of her brain. Now that Milkman is closer to his roots, he can connect the Sugarman of Pilate's song to the Solomon of the children's song, especially when he hears the names "Heddy" and "Jake." Milkman does not yet understand how or why Solomon "cut across the sky," but he wants to understand.

PART TWO
Chapter 13

The narrative returns to Hagar. When Guitar finds her abandoned by Milkman, she cannot speak or move. Hagar is not as strong as Pilate or as simple as Reba. They cannot provide her with the strength and humor to get through life. Pilate and Reba sell off many of Reba's prizes and buy Hagar nice clothes, makeup, and a perm. Hagar wanders off with her new possessions and gets stuck in a rainstorm, dropping most of the nice things in the mud.

She finally makes her way home, where she dresses in her muddy new clothes and cakes her face with makeup. The looks on Pilate's and Reba's faces make Hagar realize she is in bad shape. Hagar sobs for hours, and then a fever grips her. The fever and madness eventually claim her life.

Aside from Ruth, only morticians, the church choir, and a few winos attend the funeral. Pilate finally enters singing and screaming for mercy. Reba arrives singing as well. Pilate says, "She was *loved!*"

UNDERSTANDING AND INTERPRETING
Chapter 13

The Consequences of Flight: This chapter reminds us that Milkman's flight from Michigan has had serious consequences. While he makes great strides, Hagar suffers. We can applaud his improvement, but we must condemn his selfishness. Milkman will come to understand that this kind of flight, this selfish escape, means leaving behind one's commitments to other people. Although Milkman did not love Hagar, he certainly could have let her down more gently, and he could have found a way to ease her pain and loss. Milkman treated

Hagar cruelly, even sarcastically suggesting she kill herself. Milkman was not obligated to stay with Hagar, but he was obligated to treat her with human decency, and he must share in some of the responsibility for her death.

Unappreciated Guides: The strong, formative influences in Milkman's life have been women: Ruth, Pilate, Hagar, and Circe. These women protect him, nourish him, love him, and guide him despite his relative indifference toward them.

PART TWO
Chapter 14

Milkman returns to Susan Byrd's house, where Susan tells him that Sing married Jake. Milkman, floored, asks why she did not tell him the day before. She says she could not talk about it in front of Grace, who is a gossip. Susan does not know Jake's last name and thinks he did not have one. He was a child of Solomon, also called **Shalimar**. Susan's grandmother, Heddy, an Native American woman, was Sing's mother. Susan's father, **Crowell**, was Sing's brother. Jake was an infant when Heddy found him one day. He grew up with Sing, and they ran off together. Sing's name comes from her original Indian name, Singing Bird. Susan's father changed his name from the Indian name "Crow."

Solomon was known as a "flying African" because of an old bit of folklore. According to legend, some of the Africans brought to America as slaves were able to fly back to Africa. Most people in present-day Shalimar claim some kinship to Solomon, which is why there are so many people named Solomon in town.

Milkman asks Susan if by flying she means running away, but she means literally flying. Solomon flew off, leaving his wife, **Ryna**, with their children. Ryna almost died of grief. Ryna's Gulch is named for her because of the sad noise it makes, and Solomon's Leap is named for the spot where Solomon took flight. Only one mystery remains: why is Jake called the "only son of Solomon" in the song? Susan guesses that Solomon took Jake with him when he flew away, but Jake slipped out of Solomon's arms and fell to the ground, where Heddy found him. Heddy must have discovered the baby was Ryna's, and decided to use his original name, Jake.

As Milkman takes his leave, Susan remarks on the dullness of the town, saying, "[t]here's absolutely nothing in the world going on here. Not a thing."

UNDERSTANDING AND INTERPRETING
Chapter 14

Mysteries Solved: Milkman's theories about the names "Sing" and "Crow" are proven correct. He lets the rest of the newly discovered story wash over him, amazed that Susan knows so much. The mystery has a supernatural, but satisfying, explanation: Solomon literally flew away, as a bird would fly. Rationally, this explanation should sound absurd. Susan admits that the story is hard to believe. Still, the narrator makes us see that a kernel of truth exists somewhere.

Free, but Irresponsible: Milkman demonstrates a new level of maturity when he asks Susan about Solomon's flight. Whether Solomon literally flew like a bird or metaphorically flew away by abdicating his responsibilities, he certainly abandoned his family of twenty-one children, leaving Ryna to weep, lose her mind, and nearly die of grief. Solomon's flight has a dual meaning. He gained his freedom by returning to Africa, but he also shouldered the guilt of abandoning his family. Milkman can easily see a lesson for himself in Solomon's flight, as his question to Susan reveals. He found his freedom by leaving Michigan and seeing the world, and he also found a sense of responsibility and family history. Perversely, however, he had to abandon his family and his old lover in order to fly.

Dull and Wildly Exciting: Susan's last words to Milkman are comically ironic. To Susan, and perhaps to the townspeople, Shalimar is a dull, sleepy little town where nothing goes on. To Milkman, however, Shalimar is a wildly exciting place. There, he has found everything important he ever needed, even if he did not know he needed it when he arrived. What Milkman finds in Shalimar replaces his feelings of emptiness and meaninglessness with a new resolve and sense of belonging.

PART TWO
Chapter 15

Overjoyed with the knowledge of his family history, Milkman races back to Shalimar and heads for Sweet's house. He sings the children's song about his family as they rush down to the river together. Milkman strips and jumps in, disregarding Sweet's warning that there are poisonous water moccasin snakes in the water. Tipsy with his new happiness, Milkman talks proudly about his "flying African" ancestors. Sweet does not think it significant that he is related to Solomon. Milkman keeps talking about flying.

WISE AND SUPERNATURAL

Song of Solomon makes several oblique references to the biblical **King Solomon** (970–928 B.C.) of Israel, son of David and Bathsheba. Not only was King Solomon the author of the biblical Song of Solomon, as well as of Ecclesiastes and Proverbs, but he was also reputed to have supernatural powers. In both the Bible and the Koran, God grants Solomon great wisdom and supernatural powers, allowing him to learn the languages of all creatures, animals, and birds. According to Talmudic legend, Solomon had dominion over the "beasts of the field" and the "birds of the air." He was also said to have fathered a son with the Queen of Sheba, whom present-day Ethiopian monarchs claim as an ancestor. King Solomon's many achievements included the construction of the first Temple of Israel, but he is perhaps best known for his part in the biblical story in which two prostitutes claim to be the mother of the same child. Solomon says that justice will be served only by cutting the child in half and dividing him among the two women. One woman cries out to stop him, and Solomon awards the child to her, reasoning that the true mother would have protested the murder of her child.

On the bus back to Michigan, Milkman ponders the names that "hid from view the real names of people, places, and things." The narrator says the Algonquin Indians originally called Michigan "Great Water." Milkman reconsiders the name of No Doctor Street. He thinks one's name will perish upon death unless it is written down. Also, Milkman realizes there never was any missing gold. He wonders if human relationships can be boiled down to two questions: "Would you save my life? Or would you take it?" He realizes that the only two people in his life who did not want him out of the way were his mother and Pilate.

Back in Michigan, Milkman goes to visit Pilate, who breaks a bottle over his head and knocks him out. When he awakes, he realizes that she hit him because of Hagar's death and his flight from Michigan. He now knows what his grandfather meant by saying, "You just can't fly on off and leave a body." Milkman tells Pilate that the ghost of Jake was calling for his wife, Sing. Milkman also deduces that Pilate's bag contains the bones of her father, not the bones of the old white man. Milkman tells Pilate they should bury the bones in Shalimar, on Solomon's Leap. Pilate agrees, saying she would also like to bury a box of Hagar's hair.

Meanwhile, Corinthians has moved into a house on the Southside with Porter. Macon listens closely to all of Milkman's stories, uninterested in the flying but intrigued by the fact that places were named for people. Macon and Pilate still have not reconciled, and neither have Macon and Ruth. Milkman assumes that the Seven Days will be looking for a new Sunday man now that Guitar has disappeared.

Milkman and Pilate drive down to Virginia to bury Jake's bones. Shalimar greets them, and Pilate blends into the town seamlessly. At twilight, they climb up to Solomon's Leap, and Milkman digs a small grave. Pilate yanks the brass box from her ear and uses it as a grave marker. Suddenly, a shot rings out, and Pilate falls to her knees. She asks Milkman to take care of Reba, and says she wishes she had known more people in her life, because she would have loved them all. With her dying breaths, Pilate asks Milkman to sing.

Milkman can think of nothing but Pilate's song. He sings, "Sugargirl don't leave me here / Cotton balls to choke me." As Pilate dies, Milkman sings louder. Two birds circle around them. Milkman realizes that he has always loved Pilate so much because "without ever leaving the ground, she could fly." As he kneels over her body, Milkman realizes that Guitar will shoot him as soon as he stands up. He stands and shouts and waves at Guitar. Guitar puts down his rifle.

Milkman yells, "You want my life? You need it? Here." He leaps from the cliff toward Guitar without a thought about whether he or Guitar will die. In the final sentence of the novel, Milkman reflects that he now knows what Shalimar knew: "If you surrendered to the air, you could *ride* it."

UNDERSTANDING AND INTERPRETING

Chapter 15

You Can't Just Fly Off: When Milkman returns home, he must do penance for Hagar's death before he can rejoice. After Pilate knocks him out with the bottle, he searches his soul and realizes that his abandonment of responsibilities has had grave consequences. He sees the connection between Solomon's flight from his twenty-one children and his own abandonment of Hagar and his family. He understands that Jake's ghost, who said "You can't just fly off and leave a body," was pleading with his father to stay. Jake's ghost was also stating the fact that flying away and attaining complete freedom is impossible. The people you leave behind will always weigh on you. The body Milkman left behind was Hagar's, and now he knows he must be punished for his flight.

Noted Down and Remembered: Throughout the novel, Morrison explores what names signify, and Milkman's epiphany on the bus adds another layer to this exploration. Milkman considers those original names lying under the surface of imposed names. The original names have meaning and history that new names gloss over. Milkman has come to realize what his father considered in the first chapter when he wondered if *his* father ever had a name that was "not a joke, nor a disguise, nor a brand name." Now Macon Dead's father, Milkman's grandfather, does have a real name: Jake. Jake is possibly a slave name, just as the name Solomon was a slave name, but at least it is not a meaningless mistake made by a drunken soldier. At least it has history. Milkman even sees No Doctor Street in a new light. He now understands that even if Dr. Foster as a man did not deserve to have a street named for him, the black achievement that he stood for did deserve its own street. Renaming the street gave the people of Southside a small way of reclaiming their identity. Milkman puts all these ideas together and comes to the conclusion that names should be "noted down and remembered" lest they get lost in the sweep of history. By burying Jake's bones together, Milkman and Pilate reclaim Jake's name. The only marker they need at the grave is Pilate's brass box, in which she has kept a written record of her own name.

> "In Milkman's leap there is the pure motion of flight, a dance to the heaves, witnessed by the rocks and hills near Solomon's Leap and Ryna's Gulch, where 'Life life life life' is the chorus that echoes to those of us in the community and beyond."
>
> KATHLEEN O'SHAUGHNESSY

The Keepers of History: When Pilate falls to the ground, Milkman realizes that she has always been his connection to the history of the Deads, to Jake and Sing and their past in Virginia. Like Pilate before him, Milkman went back to Virginia in search of a family legacy. At first he thought that it was the gold he was looking for, but his search became more personal and more rewarding than any material treasure could have been.

Pilate was always the member of the family who, through her songs and stories, flew back and forth from the Deads of Michigan to their past. It was she who kept the Deads alive. Pilate's final words show her need for human connection, knowledge, and love. Milkman knows that he must carry on the family legacy in her place.

> "It builds, out of history and language and myth, to music. It takes off. If Ralph Ellison's Invisible Man went underground, Toni Morrison's Milkman flies."
>
> JOHN LEONARD

Flying in Circles: The final scene connects us with the opening scene of the novel. Pilate sang before Robert Smith leaped to his death, and now Milkman sings while Pilate dies, symbolically taking over her role as storyteller and chronicler. Milkman plays not just the role of Pilate the singer, but, later, of Robert Smith the jumper. But whereas Robert Smith's flight was the act of a madman, Milkman's leap is one that reclaims his family legacy. He sheds his vanity and takes to the sky, in a triumphant and defiant test of his newfound power and self-identity. It is not a prideful display of power, nor is it an escape or an abandonment. It is a flight of commitment, of responsibility, and of action directed at his opponent, Guitar.

An Ambiguous Flight: We do not know whether Milkman's leap kills himself, Guitar, or neither. Morrison intentionally leaves the ending open to show us that Milkman finally thinks of others just as much as he thinks of himself. In amazing contrast to his old, self-involved ways, now Milkman can think of someone else, Guitar, even though it means risking his own life. He jumps not for fun, not for revenge, but to defend his family. His heroism, predestined by his birth on the day after Smith's leap, expresses itself not in the leap itself, but in his own willingness to sacrifice himself. In the final sentence, Milkman "surrenders" to the air without any concern for himself and opens himself to the new possibilities of a meaningful life.

Toni Morrison

Conclusions

Song of Solomon chronicles a black man's discovery of his cultural, racial, and family identity. The protagonist, Milkman Dead, grows up valuing only material things and simple pleasures, but he comes to realize that his life is meaningless. The "Song of Solomon," which Pilate and the children sing, is the means by which Milkman learns of his ancestry.

By the novel's end, Milkman comprehends the contradiction of flight, which is both escape and navigation. He learns that by flying away, one gains freedom by abandoning responsibility. Milkman also learns that family names deserve to be examined and cherished, because they link us to our ancestors. As Milkman ventures into his family's past, he learns to appreciate his family and his African roots.

V

BELOVED

Beloved

An Overview

Key Facts

Genre: historical slave novel; novel of memory

Date of Publication: 1987

Setting: 1853–1873, on the outskirts of Cincinnati, Ohio, and the Sweet Home Plantation in Kentucky

Narrator: omniscient (all-knowing) third-person

Plot Overview: An escaped slave is haunted by memories of her past and by the ghost of her own child.

Style, Technique, and Language

Style—Unraveling the Past: *Beloved* is divided into three parts, the first of which reveals, piece by piece, the horrible truth about Sethe's past. Part Two shows how powerfully the past can affect the future, as Beloved begins a reign of terror over Sethe and Denver. Part Three brings the novel's themes and action to a climax, when Beloved confronts the future.

The action of the novel takes place in the 1870s, with some flashbacks to the 1850s. The years of the Civil War (1861–1865) are hardly mentioned, perhaps because the gruesome, long-term effects of slavery on slaves far outweighed the bloody but shorter-lived war.

Technique—An Act of Memory: Toni Morrison's storytelling technique in *Beloved* is uniquely linked to the themes of the novel. By revealing small clues bit by bit, the narrative unfolds in a way that resembles the act of remembering. The novel works as memory does, by piecing together shards of recollections to create a story. The novel begins with scattered bits of information that only cohere in later chapters, when Morrison fleshes them out and characters fill in the narrative blanks.

Morrison's methodically fragmented approach shows the insufficiency of language as a means of conveying the horror of slavery. Throughout the novel, the reconstruction of memory is associated with reclaiming one's body, heritage, family history, and language.

Language—Imagery and Metaphors

Beloved: Beloved, resurrected from water and endowed with "race-memory" of the Middle Passage, symbolizes the terrors of the past. She stands for the legacies of slavery that linger in the present. Just as memories of slavery can overwhelm any meaningful way of living in the present, Beloved compels Sethe to relive her past instead of looking toward the future.

The Bit: The bit, a torturous harness Sethe's mother is forced to wear, represents the silencing of the characters. One of the many grotesque, dehumanizing torture devices used on slaves, the bit pressed down on the tongue and literally prevented speech.

Paul D's Tobacco Tin: Paul D keeps the memories of Sweet Home buried within him, as if locked inside a real tin box. When he sleeps with Beloved, the metaphorical tin splits open, and he is forced to confront his past.

Names: The characters' names, and the way they received those names, represent their identities. Baby Suggs claimed ownership of herself by refusing to go by the name "Jenny Whitlow," her slave name. Stamp Paid renamed himself after being forced to let his wife sleep with his master's son. Paul D and his two brothers, Paul A and Paul F, were named by Mr. Garner after their arrival at Sweet Home. As adults, Paul D and his brother lack identities, which is symbolized by their meaningless names.

Characters in *Beloved*

Beloved: The ghost who returns in human form. Beloved, about nineteen years old, is the incarnation of the baby Sethe murdered. Beloved obsessively craves Sethe's love.

Edward Bodwin and Sister Bodwin: White brother and sister abolitionists. The Bodwins originally rent a house to Baby Suggs after she gains her freedom. They provide food and supplies to help runaway slaves.

Brandywine: The slave trader who buys Paul D from schoolteacher. Paul D tries to kill Brandywine in Georgia, and is sentenced to work on a chain gang as a result.

Brother: Paul D's favorite tree at Sweet Home.

Buglar: Sethe's son. Buglar runs off with his brother, Howard, after the baby ghost scares him away.

Denver: Sethe's daughter. Denver, about eighteen years old, is lonely. She was named for Amy Denver, the woman who helped Sethe give birth. After her brothers Howard and Buglar leave, she becomes even lonelier until Beloved shows up in the flesh. Eventually, Denver takes responsibility by finding work and getting help from the community.

Amy Denver: A white indentured servant about eighteen years old. She helps Sethe give birth to Denver. Her dream is to get to Boston and buy velvet.

Ella: An Underground Railroad worker and the wife/companion of John. She is the first to help Sethe in Ohio. When the women of the community gather at the end of the novel, Ella lets out a primal shriek that spurs on the others.

Paul A Garner: Paul D's oldest half-brother. Paul A is lost after the escape attempt and never found. After Sethe escapes, she sees his decapitated torso hanging from a tree.

Paul D Garner: The "last of the Sweet Home men," a former slave, and the youngest of the three Paul Garners. He is about forty years old in 1873. After the failed escape attempt, he is sold and ends up working on a Georgia prison chain gang. Years later, he shows up at Sethe's door in Ohio.

Paul F Garner: Paul D's half brother. Paul F is sold by the Garners before the escape attempt.

Mr. Garner: The benevolent owner of Sweet Home. Mr. Garner treats his slaves like paid labor, teaching them to shoot and letting them talk freely to him. He rents out Halle on Sundays so that Halle can earn Baby Suggs's freedom. After Mr. Garner dies, his brother-in-law schoolteacher takes over Sweet Home and treats the slaves badly.

"Morrison is one of the great, serious writers we have. Who else tries to do what Dickens did: create wild, flamboyant, abstractly symbolic characters who are at the same time not grotesque but sweetly alive, full of deep feeling."

ANN SNITOW

Mrs. Lillian Garner: Mr. Garner's wife. She dies shortly after schoolteacher takes over Sweet Home. She gives Sethe a pair of crystal earrings as a wedding gift.

Hi Man: The leader of Paul D's Georgia chain gang. He got his nickname because he yells out "Hiiii!" when the gang moves.

Howard: Sethe's son. He runs off with his brother, Buglar.

John: Ella's husband and an Underground Railroad worker.

Lady Jones: Denver's teacher. Lady Jones is the first in the community to help Denver when she comes looking for food and work.

Nan: The one-armed woman who cares for Sethe after Sethe's mother is killed.

Nelson Lord: A schoolmate of Denver's who asks if Sethe was really put in jail for killing Beloved.

Mister: "King of the roosters" at Sweet Home.

Nephews: The depraved relatives of schoolteacher. The nephews make scientific diagrams of the slaves, listing their "animal and human characteristics" in two columns. They rape Sethe at schoolteacher's command.

Sawyer: The owner of the restaurant where Sethe works.

Schoolteacher: Mr. Garner's wicked brother-in-law. After Mr. Garner dies, schoolteacher takes over Sweet Home and treats the slaves cruelly. At his insistence, his two nephews rape Sethe and take her milk while she is pregnant with Denver. He writes down observations about the slaves' lives in his notebook.

Sethe: The mother of Beloved, Denver, Howard, and Buglar. Sethe is the former wife of Halle and the daughter-in-law of Baby Suggs. She runs away from Sweet Home and kills Beloved, then a baby, to prevent Beloved from being reclaimed by schoolteacher. She has whipping scars on her back in the shape of a tree.

Sethe's Mother: We know Sethe's mother only through Sethe's vague memories. For undetermined reasons, Sethe's mother was hanged, along with a group of other slaves. Of all of her children, she "kept" only Sethe, meaning she perhaps killed or abandoned her other babies.

Sheriff: One of the "four horsemen" who come to take Sethe and her children. The gentle sheriff turns his head away when Sethe has to nurse Denver.

Sixo: The "wild-eyed" slave at Sweet Home. He carries on a romance with the Thirty-Mile Woman, with whom he tries to run off. After schoolteacher's maltreatment, Sixo stops speaking English. When caught trying to escape, he burns himself to death while laughing.

Slave Catcher: One of the "four horsemen" who come to claim Sethe and her children in Ohio.

Stamp Paid: The Underground Railroad worker who helps Sethe get across the river after she escapes from Sweet Home. Stamp Paid is also a fisherman, boatman, tracker, "savior," "spy," and the most respected black man in town. He names himself "Stamp Paid" because he feels he paid his dues by letting his wife sleep with his master's son.

Baby Suggs: Halle's mother and Sethe's mother-in-law. Halle buys Baby Suggs's freedom from the Garners by working on Sundays for five years. Baby Suggs settles at 124 and often gathers together the black residents of the area for spiritual revivals. The Garners call her Jenny Whitlow, which was the slave name used by Baby's previous master.

Halle Suggs: Sethe's husband, the father of Sethe's children, and Baby Suggs's son. On the night of the escape attempt, Halle apparently witnesses Sethe's rape, and it drives him mad. Paul D last sees him next to the Sweet Home churn, screaming and covering himself with butter and clabber.

Thirty-Mile Woman: Sixo's girlfriend and fiancée. She gets her nickname because Sixo travels thirty miles to see her.

Vashti: Stamp Paid's wife. When Vashti and Stamp are slaves, their master's son takes Vashti as a mistress.

Janey Wagon: The Bodwins' servant.

Weaver Lady: The woman with whom Paul D lives in Wilmington, Delaware, after escaping from the chain gang.

Beloved

Reading *Beloved*

PART ONE

Chapter 1*

It is 1873. On the rural outskirts of Cincinnati, at 124 Bluestone Road (known as "124"), live a former slave, **Sethe**, and her teenage daughter, **Denver**. Sethe's two oldest children, **Howard** and **Buglar**, ran away from the house many years earlier, driven away by the ghost of Sethe's other daughter, who haunts 124.

When the boys ran off, **Baby Suggs**, Sethe's mother-in-law, was already confined to her sickbed. In her final years, Baby asked Sethe to bring her different shades of fabric. Baby died two months after the boys left, when Denver was ten. This left Sethe and Denver to fend for themselves against the baby ghost. Sethe and Denver try to call out the ghost, but it will not budge. Sethe says the ghost is no more powerful "than the way I loved her."

---

* N.B. Chapters are unnumbered in the novel, but for clarity of analysis, they will be discussed as if they are numbered.

INSPIRED BY MARGARET GARNER

Beloved is loosely based on the true story of escaped slave Margaret Garner. In January 1856, Garner escaped from plantation owner Archibald K. Gaines of Kentucky, taking her four children to Cincinnati. Gaines and a posse of other white men pursued her and surrounded the house to which she had fled. Margaret's husband, Robert, fired shots at them before being tackled. Margaret, seeing that their freedom would soon be lost, grabbed a butcher knife and cut the throat of her baby daughter. She tried to kill her other children and herself, but the men overpowered her. The story was reported in the Cincinnati newspapers, and later in the abolitionist paper *The Liberator*. John Joliffe, a famous anti-slavery lawyer of the era, defended Margaret Garner at her trial, describing her as an American hero on par with those who fought in the Revolutionary War. In the years that followed, abolitionists used the story of Margaret Garner as an enduring symbol of their cause. Into the twentieth century, activists held her up as an icon.

Sethe gave ten minutes of sexual favors to the gravestone engraver in exchange for seven letters on the gravestone of the dead baby: BELOVED. Sethe had wanted the gravestone to read "Dearly Beloved," words the preacher used at the baby's funeral, but she thought that the seven letters would be "enough to answer one more preacher, one more abolitionist, and a town full of disgust."

Sethe often wonders how a baby girl's soul could be filled with so much rage. She and Denver should have moved away from 124 long ago, she thinks, but Baby Suggs warned Sethe that every house in the county contained the sadness of a black ghost. Baby wonders if the ghosts of her own husband and children might come back to haunt her, too, although she barely remembers them.

Sethe tries to remember as little as she can about the family she lost. The memories of Howard and Buglar fade fast, although she thinks she could recognize Howard if she met him again, because he had an unusual-shaped head. Yet, she finds herself overwhelmed with memories. For example, she has sudden flashbacks to Sweet Home, the Kentucky plantation where she was a slave. She remembers both the beauty of the place with its sycamore trees, and the brutalities visited upon her there, the men nursing her, and the destroyed nerves of her back. The memories of beauty overwhelm the memories of horror, which makes her wonder "if hell was a pretty place too."

One day, outside the house, Sethe encounters **Paul D Garner**, the "last of the Sweet Home men," sitting on her front steps. They have not seen each other for eighteen years, and Paul jokes that he has been walking for most of them. Sethe asks if he has any news of **Halle Suggs** (her husband, and Baby's son). Paul has no news. An image of Halle and a butter churn flashes into his mind, but he says nothing. Sethe remembers that it was 1855 when she ran off from Sweet Home, pregnant with Denver. She thinks if it "hadn't been for that girl looking for velvet," she might never have gotten away.

Paul enters the house, and a pool of red, undulating light surrounds him. He asks what kind of evil exists in the house, and Sethe says the energy is sad, not evil. Paul D thinks back to the last time he saw Sethe. When she first arrived at Sweet Home, all the men eyed her with desire and raped cows in their sexual frustration. Sethe eventually chose Halle as a mate. She was pregnant every year after they married. When they escaped, Sethe sent off her first three children in a caravan that was crossing the river to Cincinnati from Kentucky.

There were six slaves at Sweet Home: Paul D, Sethe, Halle, **Sixo** "the wild man," **Paul F Garner**, and **Paul A Garner**. Sethe was the only woman, bought after Baby Suggs got her freedom. **Mr. Garner**, the owner of Sweet Home, allowed Halle to work for someone else every Sunday for five years. With the money he saved, Halle bought Baby's freedom. Mr. Garner always thought of his slaves as men, not boys.

Paul D settles into the house, and Denver unenthusiastically welcomes him. He is their first guest in twelve years. Guests of theirs used to appear repulsed by the house and its residents. Denver listens to Sethe and Paul D reminisce and feels excluded. She wishes the baby ghost would appear, despite its venom. Interrupting, Denver tells Paul about the ghost in the house. Suddenly, Denver begins sobbing and tells Sethe she cannot stand to live in the house anymore, because no one ever visits them or talks to her.

Paul D suggests they move, but Sethe says no. She refuses to run away again. Sethe mentions that she has a tree on her back. On the night she ran away from Sweet Home, she was pregnant with Denver and still lactating from nursing her last baby. Some boys held her down and took her milk. She told Mrs. Garner of the attack, and schoolteacher ordered Sethe whipped for telling. The scars from the whipping formed the image of a tree on Sethe's back.

Paul D opens the back of Sethe's dress and tremblingly looks at the scars. The house begins to shake violently. Paul D remembers that the last time his hands shook like this was in 1856, when he was chained down for eighty-three days. Paul D shouts to the ghost to leave or come out and fight. The quaking eventually slows, and silence falls. Apparently, the ghost has vanished.

Sethe and Paul D go upstairs. Denver sits alone in the kitchen, missing her brothers and Baby Suggs. Her mother is upstairs with the man who just shooed away the ghost, Denver's only company.

UNDERSTANDING AND INTERPRETING
Chapter 1

Scraps of Memories: From the very first page, *Beloved* zigzags through time, revealing bits and pieces of the past while narrating the present-day lives of the characters. We begin the novel in 1873, when only Sethe and Denver live in 124. Within a few sentences, we jump backward a number of years to the time when Denver was ten and Howard and Buglar ran off. By the end of the paragraph, we regress seventy more years, to the beginnings of Ohio's statehood. Morrison constructs her novel from a main narrative woven with memories and flashbacks. Her characters slowly begin to unearth long-repressed memories, pulling up scraps of recollection that initially seem confusing. We do not yet know the whole story, because the characters do not yet want to remember the whole story. Paul remembers a mysterious butter churn, and Sethe recalls a girl searching for velvet. Neither of these details makes sense yet, but both will appear in future chapters and begin to make sense as the stories are gradually fleshed out. As characters reconstruct the past, we also begin to understand the present-day state of affairs at 124. The slowly unfolding stories mirror the extensive, sometimes torturous, process of remembering the past.

Families, Destroyed and Remade: The opening paragraph of the novel reflects the disintegration of Sethe's family—one of the legacies of slavery. Slaves abducted from West Africa did not enjoy the basic right to know their family's whereabouts. Families were torn apart as husbands, wives, and children were sold off to different owners, and sometimes killed. According to Paul D, Sethe's husband Halle disappeared and was never heard from again. Baby Suggs has died. Now, in 1873, Sethe's family has disintegrated so thoroughly that she now has only Denver, when once children surrounded her. Paul D represents the possibility of a new family, a new unity, and a reconstruction. He arrives and disrupts the current state of affairs. When he holds Sethe and opens her shirt to look at her back, he starts the process of examining the past, in this case literally, and looking to the future. By exorcising the baby ghost and taking Sethe upstairs to bed, Paul D brings a new calm and life to the house.

Cincinnati, North and South: *Beloved* takes place in 1873, an appropriate year for a novel that explores memory, identity, and family. In 1873, Reconstruction was taking place in the South. Reconstruction marked a period of great change, rebuilding, and sometimes bitter violence. During these years, American society tried to stitch itself back together after its bloody, divisive Civil War. The novel's setting, Cincinnati, is an "in between" city. Like the characters in *Beloved*, who straddle memories of slavery and the difficult present of emancipation, Cincinnati straddles North and South. Officially, it belongs to the North, but Cincinnati sits in the southern portion of Ohio, on the border of Kentucky, and probably has more in common with the South than with the North. Just as the city sits between both worlds and belongs to neither, the former slaves of *Beloved* sit uneasily between the uncertain stability of their new freedom and the horror of their memories.

124: *Beloved* begins in a haunted house that no one visits on the outskirts of town. 124, as the house is called, is a lonely place, far from both Cincinnati and from other houses and people. The house itself is like a pariah, an outcast from the rest of the community. Even when people visited it in the past, they could hardly hide their revulsion. 124 is a place of secrets, memories, and the ghost of a child who infects the present with her bitterness. Significantly, the number "124" lacks the number 3 in its sequence, a sign that Sethe's third child is missing.

THE BLACK BOOK

One of Toni Morrison's triumphs as a book editor at Random House was the 1974 compilation of a work entitled *The Black Book*. The book, assembled in scrapbook form, is a "folk journey of Black America" that spans 300 years of African-American history, from slavery through Reconstruction and into the twentieth century. Among the items included in the text are old news clippings, photographs, letters, bills of sale for slaves, patterns from slave-made quilts, poetry, and other cultural works that document the shared experiences of African-Americans. Perhaps most striking are the stories of ordinary people who have been forgotten by history. It was while researching and editing this book that Morrison first came upon the newspaper story about Margaret Garner that served as the inspiration for *Beloved*.

With One Mind: The community shuns Sethe and Denver, angry about a crime committed long ago. It is because of this anger that 124 stands isolated. The neighbors avoid it, fearful of the ghost and repulsed by the evil history of the place. This community solidarity surfaces throughout the novel, sometimes to harm, sometimes to help. The way black Cincinnati treats Sethe and her family shows that often, communities act with a single mind.

Sethe's Tree: One of the novel's early symbols of memory is the scar on Sethe's back. She refers to her scar as if it is a real cherry tree, albeit one that has no scent of cherry gum. It is a "lifeless" tree, just like the lifeless nerves in the scarred tissue on her back. Sethe has willfully deadened the memory of how she got the scars. The assault at Sweet Home is a psychological scar from her past that she keeps hidden away, just as she hides her physical scars under her clothing.

Defiant but Silent, Angry but Repressed: Sethe is a study in contradictions. She is defiant, but she also suffers silently in the face of unspeakable horrors and pains. She is strong and angry, but she represses her rage. She struggles with her life at 124, pushing down the memories of her past, yet she refuses to leave or to run away from the ghost. Motherhood defines her. Sethe's love for and protectiveness of her children seems endless. Her memories of being assaulted at Sweet Home seem so disturbing partly because the boys took the milk she needed to get to Cincinnati to feed her baby. Sethe's powerful love for her dead baby girl almost matches the power of the ghost's anger. Sethe even sells herself to the gravestone engraver, accepting a proper marker at her baby's grave as payment. Even the marker is an act of defiance. Most observers condemn Sethe's killing of her child and would argue that to such a mother, a child is not beloved. However, Sethe truly loves her baby. The word "Beloved" on the gravestone is deeply meant.

The Unexpected Paul D: Paul D appears on the scene after wandering for eighteen years. His unexpected arrival at 124 disrupts the house and its inhabitants. He wants companionship, a soul mate, and a connection with someone from his past. While willing to examine the past, Paul D approaches it with apprehension. Like Sethe, he seems wary of unearthing painful memories. Despite this wariness, however, Paul D makes an effort to look at Sethe's back, which signifies a commitment to revisit the past. Paul D feels an immediate affection for Sethe and tries to be upbeat, perhaps because he is optimistic about putting down roots and starting a new life. When he feels the ghost of 124, it reminds him of his own painful past, a time when he was in chains and felt powerless. Despite the pain of these memories, however, Paul D confronts the ghost head on, trying to protect Sethe and Denver, as well as his dreams of a future in a new home.

Denver's Isolation: Denver has lived her whole life at 124, enduring eighteen years of loneliness, isolation, and exclusion. Denver's strongest relationship is not with her mother, but with the ghost, which, despite its "venom," is the ghost of her late sister. The angry, disembodied spirit is the closest thing Denver has to a companion and playmate. As soon as Paul D arrives, Denver feels further isolated. She senses that Paul D and her mother share history, which excludes Denver. She finds herself wishing the ghost would make an appearance. Worsening her detachment, Denver never knew her father, and the stories she hears about him have nothing to do with her. Baby Suggs claims Halle as a lost son, Sethe claims him as a lost husband, and now Paul D claims him as a lost friend and companion. Denver gets no piece of him. Sethe's protectiveness is like a jail, but Denver knows no other way to live. She depends fully on her mother, and craves her attention.

Baby Suggs's Disintegration: Like a memory, Baby Suggs seemed to disintegrate. She faded away late in life, and eventually she was confined to a bed, where she daydreamed about colors. Baby's own memories show that she practiced the same intentional forgetfulness that Sethe does. In order to minimize her pain, Sethe remembers only small details of her past, intentionally blocking out most memories of her children.

A Furious Ghost: True to the process of remembering, we learn about Sethe's dead baby through small clues. Howard and Buglar brought the infant across to Ohio before Sethe made the trip. The baby was murdered, slit across the throat. From this death comes the ghost's fury. The infant's ghost, a powerful, territorial presence that harbors a grudge, haunts 124 for eighteen years. The appearance of Paul D angers it, and it sends strong tremors in an attempt to frighten him.

PART ONE
Chapter 2

Sethe and Paul D lie in bed together upstairs after hurriedly making love. Each silently reminisces about Sweet Home. Paul D remembers that all the men desired Sethe except Sixo, who used to plot out trips to see a woman who lived thirty miles away, known as his **Thirty-Mile Woman**. He would walk seventeen hours in each direction just to spend one hour with her. Then he would return to Sweet Home, exhausted, and sleep next to a tree that was nicknamed **Brother**. Paul D admires Sixo's tenacity, thinking, "Now *there* was a man, and *that* was a tree." Now, after his lovemaking, Paul D lies next to Sethe's tree and feels disappointed. The actual act of sex with her did not live up to his twenty-five years of longing.

Sethe remembers that the men and women at Sweet Home "were moved around like checkers." Baby Suggs had eight children with six different fathers, and all of the fourteen fathers and sons ran off or were hanged, stolen, or seized. Halle was the only one Baby kept for any amount of time. Unusually, Sethe got to spend six years with Halle, who fathered all four of her children. She remembers that he first looked at her with an interest that "suggested a family relationship rather a man's laying claim." He was more like a brother than a husband. When he asked her to marry him, Sethe agreed but did not know what to do next.

Sethe approached Mrs. Garner and told her that she and Halle wanted to get married. The young fiancée wondered if they could have a wedding. Mrs. Garner quietly laughed at Sethe's naïveté and asked if she were already pregnant. There was a small celebration with Halle, Paul D, and the other slaves. They roasted corn over the fire. The corn opened up easily after one husk was pulled down, exposing the "shy rows" inside. Whenever Sethe heard husks ripping, she felt as if she were hurting something. But it was a simple joy once the corn was opened, and she noticed "how quick the jailed-up flavor ran free."

UNDERSTANDING AND INTERPRETING Chapter 2

Separate and Silent: In this chapter, Paul D and Sethe revisit memories of Sweet Home, but they do so silently and separately. The two lie next to each other in bed, but they do not think of themselves as a couple. Instead, they remember the idea of love and marriage as they knew it in the past. Paul D thinks of Sixo's passionate pursuit of the Thirty-Mile Woman, a desperate love that makes his current experience seem pale. Sethe thinks of her marriage to Halle, a good man.

Family Destruction: Sethe and Paul D must deal with the pain of their destroyed families. Slaves were moved around from slave owner to slave owner with no thought of family ties, and denied the right to nuclear families composed of husband, wife, and children. Paul D's memories of Sixo and his Thirty-Mile Woman shed light on the way one slave desperately tried to hold on to a version of family and love, bucking the efforts of his owners. Sethe felt that in marrying Halle, she gained a brother more than she gained a husband. A man who could instantly provoke a feeling of family ties was a desirable, safe man.

Be a Man: Throughout the novel, Paul struggles with his self-worth and his masculinity. Here, he compares himself to Sixo, "a real man" who proved that he could make a commitment to something. In order for Paul to feel truly manly, he seemingly needs to define himself as a husband, father, or brother. Both Baby Suggs and Sethe subscribe to the notion that "a man ain't nothing but a man." Although Paul has not heard these words, they seem to echo in his consciousness. He is a man, but he is not a son or a husband, as Halle was. Mr. Garner boasted about treating his slaves like men, but this meant that he controlled their manhood and they did not. Paul searches for his manhood as a source of identity.

Sweet Trees: In his story about Sixo, Paul remembers the beautiful tree, nicknamed "Brother," at Sweet Home. Trees appear throughout the novel as sources of comfort and solace. Like Sethe's dream of the beautiful sycamores, Paul's memory of beautiful Brother soothes the other, harsh memories of Sweet Home. In the first chapter, Sethe imagines the scar of slavery on her back as a beautiful cherry tree. She allows Paul to look at the scar as if it is a self-made decoration, not just an unwanted legacy of her time at Sweet Home.

Golden Corn: The "feast" of corn at Sethe and Halle's wedding reflects one of the few moments of freedom and love that the slaves felt at Sweet Home. In this chapter, the corn symbolizes the slaves. The corn makes a painful sound when ripped from its husk, but then it comes off freely. Similarly, the slaves will suffer during their desperate escape, which comes after years of pain and restraint. The pain of the journey, however, culminates in a mostly sweet freedom. In addition, the corn-husking is a metaphor for the painful process of remembering, of pulling away layers to find the golden truth.

PART ONE
Chapter 3

Denver thinks back to her childhood. She used to play in a thicket of boxwood trees, alone with her imagination. One night when she was young and in the boxwood, Denver thought of the story of her own birth.

Sethe was nine months pregnant with Denver when she wandered along the "bloody side" of the Ohio River, trying to get across to her other children, who had escaped earlier from Sweet Home. A young, poorly dressed white woman named **Amy Denver** found Sethe crouching in the grass. Sethe admitted that she was running away, and Amy said she was on her way to Boston to buy some velvet. Amy massaged Sethe's feet, which were bloody from hours of walking barefoot, and Sethe's eyes filled with tears of pain. Amy said, "Anything dead coming back to life hurts."

The narrative continues to relate Denver's past experience. After remembering the story, Denver walked back to the house. Through a window, she spied Sethe kneeling on the floor and praying, the form of a white dress kneeling beside her. Later, Denver asked Sethe what she was praying about. Sethe said she "talking about time." She talked of her "rememory"—suddenly remembering some forgotten thing. Places, Sethe said, are always there, even after their physical presence is gone. Sweet Home is always a real place for her because the image of it is still in her mind.

Denver asked to hear more about the story of her birth. Sethe told her about **schoolteacher**, Mr. Garner's brother-in-law. Schoolteacher took over the plantation after Mr. Garner died. He brought his two **nephews** with him and took a strange interest in the slaves, writing about them in a notebook. Telling this story, Sethe got lost in remembrance and fell silent. To break the silence, Denver told Sethe that she thought the baby ghost "had plans."

Now, when Paul D arrives at 124, Sethe wonders if she can make new plans of her own. The simple idea of having plans is something she has not contemplated for eighteen years. The last plan she made was to escape from Sweet Home, and its failure terrified her. Sethe notices how barren 124 looks. No wonder, she thinks, Baby Suggs was so "starved for color." The two orange squares on Baby's quilt are the only patches of color in the house. Sethe realizes that blood and gravestone are the last colors she remembers seeing. Paul D brings new life to the house, and suddenly Sethe notices appearances. "Drabness looked drab; heat was hot. Windows suddenly had a view." Paul fills the house with his singing, hard-edged prison hollers that clash with his little chores of mending a table leg or fixing the windows.

Paul D has never before been able to live with a woman for more than a few months. However, he feels that Sethe and 124 are not normal. He thinks back to his time on a chain gang in Georgia. He stopped thinking then, only meeting his basic human needs. He was still in this state of mind when he arrived at 124. Any more consciousness than that, he thinks, would have required him to remember his last vision of Halle and Sixo. The chain gang made him crazy enough to keep his mind off the past, but now he is beginning to remember again.

Paul D tells Sethe that he wants to stay at 124, although he is worried that Denver will not like it. Sethe tells Paul that years ago, schoolteacher tracked them down at 124, and she went to jail with Denver to avoid going back into slavery. If Denver could survive that, she thinks, she can survive anything. Soon enough, Sethe and Paul D seem like a couple.

UNDERSTANDING AND INTERPRETING

Chapter 3

Alone in the Boxwood: Denver, an isolated soul, pursues solitary pleasures. She plays alone in the boxwood—like most of the trees in the novel, a comforting place—and she remembers stories Sethe told her. Not surprisingly, Denver's favorite story is the one about her own birth. By fixating on this story, which involves her and Sethe, Denver lays claim to her mother, whose past at Sweet Home so preoccupies her.

"Rememory": Sethe uses the word "rememory" to explain what happens when you suddenly remember something that was buried, almost forgotten, in your mind. Rememory is a form of memory that can damage those who remember, inducing them to relive the terror they experienced. As Denver knows, Sethe can tell stories about the past only up to a point. When the terrifying parts creep up, the stories come to a halt. Paul D copes in his own way. He goes slightly mad on the Georgia chain gang, shutting his brain down in order to keep the past out of his mind. Now that he is at 124, however, his mind opens up to the past of which Sethe was a part, and he feels his forgotten memories coming back into his consciousness.

> "Morrison reveals herself, when she shucks the fuzziness born of flights of poetic imagery, as a writer of a considerable power and tenderness, someone who can cast back to the living, bleeding heart of childhood and capture it on paper."
>
> HASKEL FRANKEL

Shadowy Schoolteacher: Schoolteacher is described only in passing, but Sethe's sketch leaves the impression that there is more to his story. The man's mysterious notebook makes him sound like a scientist or scholar. All Sethe initially tells Denver is that schoolteacher made cold, rationalistic observations of the slaves, as if they were a living experiment. The brief description of schoolteacher is an ominous taste of what we will learn of him in future chapters.

Craving Colors: At the end of her life, Baby Suggs craves color, a simple pleasure, but one that speaks of a zest for living. Baby Suggs, like Sethe, lived a life of hardship and drabness, and the small indulgence of color makes her happy. Sethe, for years too unhappy to see color, begins to taste life again once Paul D arrives—a slow transformation symbolized by a new appreciation for color. Sethe realizes that since the time of the baby's death, she has been oblivious to the small pleasures in life. She now truly looks at and sees her house and the view from the windows.

Making Plans: The arrival of Paul D heralds a rebirth of 124. Sethe begins to imagine making plans. For years, she has been afraid to make plans, worried that if she did, she would jinx herself. Also, refusing to make plans means refusing to think about the future, or even to count on the existence of a future. Plans indicate renewal and the willingness to look forward. In the same way that Paul D opens the back of Sethe's dress, he now opens up possibilities for her. But making new designs means forgetting old ones. For the moment, Sethe forgets that the vision of the white dress might be, as Denver suggested, a sign that the baby ghost has plans of its own, plans for its own resurrection.

PART ONE
Chapter 4

As the days go by, Denver struggles against Sethe and Paul D. When Sethe passionately defends Denver, Paul D thinks to himself that you take a risk by loving someone as much as Sethe loves Denver. The best thing, he believes, is to love "just a little bit," so that if you lose something, you have a little love left over for what is next. Sethe says she would always choose Denver over Paul. Paul D says he wants to stay, but not to replace Denver.

A few days later, the three of them walk to a carnival in town. It is the first social outing in eighteen years for Sethe and Denver. Sethe notices that the shadows of their figures on the ground make it look like the three of them are holding hands. She thinks the shadows are a good sign, one that suggests they could make a life together. Denver is still sullen. At the carnival, Paul D hops gleefully from attraction to attraction with infectious enthusiasm. Denver begins warming to him. She notices people smiling at them. On the way home, she is positively delighted. The three shadows again appear to be holding hands.

UNDERSTANDING AND INTERPRETING

Chapter 4

Mother and Protector: When Paul D argues that Denver is old enough to care for herself, Sethe shows the powerful instinct for protection she feels toward her children. "I don't care what she is. Grown don't mean nothing to a mother," she says. Sethe clings to Denver because Denver is her only remaining child. Even when Denver treats Paul rudely, or acts immature, all of Sethe's complicated feelings for her children—her guilt, her love, her desperation, her anger—mean that Sethe automatically sides with Denver. She makes it clear to Paul D that her child will always come first.

The Promise of Shadows: The hand-holding shadows on the road make Sethe wonder if making plans is such a bad idea. Followed by the happy family picture painted in the shadows, Denver's defenses finally come down when the three of them visit the carnival. They naturally begin to form a family unit, and the people at the carnival see them as one. The promise of a new life seems at hand. It is a resurrection, a reconstruction of family.

On the Outside: Sethe and Denver have not been out for a social engagement in years. In fact, Denver has never in her life been outside the property. The land beyond 124 is almost foreign. Denver has a happy first experience, however. She is the first to notice that their new family unit receives smiles and friendly glances. A life outside 124 is a new life, without a baby ghost haunting their minds, and without the history of that baby's death held over their heads.

PART ONE

Chapter 5

The narrative goes back one day in time. The day before the carnival, a fully dressed woman walked out of a stream near 124. She rested on the streambed, struggling to breathe. The day after the carnival, the woman makes her way to a stump near the front porch of 124, her eyes barely open. Sethe and the others find her there when they return from the carnival. Sethe sees her, runs to the back of the house, and urinates profusely, almost involuntarily.

Inside the house, the woman drinks cup after cup of water. She is about nineteen or twenty and dressed in fancy clothing and shoes. Her skin is flawless except for three small scratches on her forehead. Denver notices that her eyes are expressionless. When Paul D asks her name, she moans, "Beloved." Paul thinks of asking who her family is and where she is from, but he stops when he remembers all of the people he saw during his eighteen years of wandering. All of them were running, "from dead crops, dead kin, life threats, and took-over land." The women and children usually stuck together, and the men were mostly solitary. No one ever asked about people's families or what brought them out on the road.

Beloved sleeps for four days, waking only for water. Denver tends to her "out of love and a breakneck possessiveness." Sethe watches the two of them together, noting that Beloved's neediness helps Denver's lonesomeness. Beloved seems to like only sweets. Paul D thinks there is something strange about her. She acts sick and frail, but he and Denver saw her pick up a rocking chair with one hand. When Paul asks Denver to confirm what they saw, she says she saw nothing.

UNDERSTANDING AND INTERPRETING
Chapter 5

A Baby Born Again: The text never says so explicitly, but we are meant to surmise that Beloved is a human reincarnation of Sethe's dead baby girl. The way Beloved appears, emerging from dark water and struggling for breath, replicates a birth. Sethe's first reaction upon seeing Beloved is to let loose a torrent of water, as if her water has broken. The name "Beloved," the same word that marks the baby's gravestone, is another clear sign of Beloved's identity. Sethe does not seem to notice the coincidence in names. She is happy to have a new guest in the house and content to let Beloved stay indefinitely, like family.

Budding Beloved: Although in body she is a young woman, in some ways Beloved takes on the appearance and characteristics of a newborn. She is frail, her skin is perfectly smooth, and her eyes have trouble taking in the light. At first, she seems like a harmless presence in the house, sleeping for days on end and needing constant attention from Denver. She is about nineteen years old—the age Sethe's baby would have been had she lived.

A Ghostly Sister: Denver, craving attention and missing the companionship of the baby ghost, feeds on Beloved's needs as a way to fill her own life with meaning. When confronted with the story of the rocking chair, she even lies and covers up for Beloved. She wants to protect this new guest in the house at all costs. Not only is Beloved a companion close to Denver's age, she is the sister Denver never had, even if Denver does not know it yet.

THE MIDDLE PASSAGE

The Middle Passage is defined as that portion of the Atlantic Ocean between West Africa and the Americas through which European ships transported Africans into slavery between the fifteenth and nineteenth centuries. The Middle Passage is also defined as the actual journey from Africa to the Americas, one leg of the infamous Triangular Trade that included Europe, Africa, and the Americas. Africans forced to travel on these ships encountered horrific brutality. The men and women were piled on top of one another. Food was scant, and sometimes withheld until the final days of the trip. Fresh water was rationed. Disease spread quickly and easily, and death rates averaged around twenty-five percent. Slaves were occasionally thrown overboard when food supplies ran low or disease became a risk for the entire ship. Women were periodically raped and impregnated by the ships' crews. Sethe's mother endured such a journey, and her hatred for her captors and rapists caused her to throw overboard those children conceived by rape.

A Past of Horror: Paul again thinks of his years of wandering—another indication that he has been searching for an identity. The men, women, and children he met on the road, all ravaged by slavery, do not explain where they are from or what brought them on the road, and they do not ask other people about their origins or stories. The past is a taboo subject, because it is full of horror.

PART ONE
Chapter 6

As the days go on, Beloved never takes her eyes from Sethe. She waits for Sethe to come home from her job in town. Each night, she goes farther down the road to greet Sethe. Sethe basks in the new attention, which she never received or wanted from Denver. One night, Beloved asks Sethe where her diamonds are, referring to a pair of earrings Sethe once owned. Sethe says she never had diamond earrings, just crystal ones that were a wedding gift from Mrs. Garner. Usually telling stories from her past hurts Sethe, but this time she tells Beloved the story of her wedding, saying, "They said it was all right for us to be husband and wife and that was it." She says the earrings are long gone.

At Beloved's urging, Sethe also reveals what little she remembers of her own mother. She rarely spoke to her mother and did not sleep in the same cabin with her at night. Her mother had a mark below her chest, like a brand, and she told Sethe that if ever something happened to her, Sethe could identify her by the mark. Later, Sethe's mother was hanged. Sethe never knew why.

After telling the story, Sethe jumps up from her chair and begins folding sheets. She remembers a long-forgotten memory. After her mother was killed, a one-armed woman named **Nan** took care of her. Like Sethe's mother, Nan spoke a different kind of language. She explained that Sethe's mother and grandmother were both "from the sea" (they came on a slave ship) and had been raped many times by the ship's crew. Sethe was the only child her mother had with a black father, and she was named after him. She "threw" all the other children to whom she gave birth, because their fathers were white. These memories make Sethe angry.

Denver is bored when her mother's stories do not involve her. She only likes to hear the story about Amy Denver. Beloved, however, hangs on every word and keeps asking questions. Denver wonders how Beloved could have known about Sethe's earrings.

UNDERSTANDING AND INTERPRETING

Chapter 6

Greedy Beloved: Beloved devours all the attention she gets from Sethe. Like an infant, she thinks of herself as a part of her mother, and she shapes her identity around Sethe's existence. When Beloved goes farther down the road to meet Sethe each day, it is as if she wants to *be* Sethe, or at least to remain attached to her, like a baby still in the womb. Her neediness is further expressed in the series of questions she asks about Sethe's past, as if Sethe's past were her own. Beloved's needs become more possessive as time goes on and she tries to claim ownership over Sethe as her mother.

Identifying the Body: The story of Sethe's mother continues the series of vague but chilling clues about Sethe's family history. Given the impossibility of Sethe and her mother spending much time together, they were not close, and Sethe's mother knew that her cattle brand was the only way Sethe could identify her. Now, Sethe wonders if she could identify her son, Howard, by recognizing the shape of his head. Sethe's knowledge of her family members is so thin that she must rely on distinctive markers to recognize them. Also, the mention of identifiers carries the sinister suggestion that Sethe might need to identify her family members after they have died. This is the case with Sethe's mother, who was hanged from a tree.

Losing Language: The way language is used, and who controls it, is central to the novel. Sethe does not learn the African language her mother speaks—a reminder that slaves' lives were controlled in every conceivable way. To rob someone of her native tongue is to rob her of her history and the ability to pass on that history to her children. When Sethe loses the language of her ancestors, she breaks her link to them and loses her cultural grounding.

Denver's Jealousy: While Beloved desperately tries to claim Sethe for herself, Denver becomes more and more isolated. She finds a new friend in Beloved, but she is hurt that Sethe opens up to Beloved, telling stories about her past that Denver has never heard. Beloved's eagerness to know all about Sethe's past shows an intimacy that Denver has never shared with her mother. Denver likes to hear only the story of her own birth, and now Beloved crowds her out, soliciting stories that remind Denver how rigorously she has been sheltered from the harsh realities of the outside world. Beloved's questions also make Denver suspicious, for Beloved seems to know more about Sethe than a stranger would.

PART ONE
Chapter 7

Paul D, wary of Beloved, peppers her with questions. Her answers never satisfy him. He secretly wishes she would leave or that Sethe would throw her out of the house. He wonders if Beloved has forgotten everything about her own past, like so many of the people he has met. She seems different from the others, however. Paul's vexation with Beloved leads to another argument with Sethe, who does not mind having Beloved around. Paul D wants Beloved sent away, but Sethe thinks Paul is acting like a typical male, wanting to harm women.

The two have a conversation about Halle. Sethe believes Halle abandoned her. He was supposed to run away from Sweet Home with her, but he did not show up. Paul now reveals that Halle witnessed schoolteacher's nephews raping Sethe, and it broke his will. The last time Paul saw him, Halle was sitting by the butter churn at Sweet Home, dousing himself in butter, out of his mind.

That night, Paul D was forced to wear "the bit"—a painful metal harness that schoolteacher forced the slaves to wear, keeping their tongues pressed down and their lips yanked back. While Paul was locked in the bit, he saw the Sweet Home roosters hopping around the yard. Schoolteacher's evil deeds changed Paul D that night. He was no longer a human being, but something less than a rooster. The king of the roosters, which Paul D calls **Mister**, looked especially noble compared to him.

Paul keeps the rest of his thoughts to himself, refusing to show Sethe what he has hidden in the "tobacco tin buried in his chest . . . its lid rusted shut." Sethe has done all she can to suppress the memory of the two boys sucking on her breasts while schoolteacher observed the scene and wrote in his notebook.

A TORTURE DEVICE

Toni Morrison first read about "the bit"—a metal device that locks around the head and pushes down the tongue—in the journals of a slave owner. She had to go to a museum in Brazil to find an actual example of the implement. Not quite like a horse's bit, "the bit" was a steel plate that forcibly opened the mouth of the slave who was harnessed in it. The bit, which could be tightened or loosened, left scars and welts on the lips and mouth, and prevented swallowing and proper breathing. It was ostensibly designed to prevent slaves from eating any of the crops that were being picked, but it also had the effect of maintaining silence and performing slow torture.

Now she adds Halle to the gruesome image, and she decides she cannot possibly add anything more to it. She concludes she would rather think about the future, even though her brain will not let her.

UNDERSTANDING AND INTERPRETING

Chapter 7

Less than a Rooster: Paul D questions his own manhood first during the argument with Sethe, when he protests that he is not the type of man who would harm women. He again wonders about his manhood when he recounts his story about the night of the escape from Sweet Home. Locked in the bit as he watched the roosters, Paul thought of himself as a lower form of life than even the roosters. That was the night that schoolteacher broke his spirit. Mr. Garner used to call him a "man," but schoolteacher permanently erased the idea of manhood from his mind.

Tobacco Tin of Secrets: Paul D treats his dangerously painful thoughts as though they were locked away in a tobacco tin inside him. Prior to his arrival at 124, he considered the tin rusted shut, but parts of his past have now slipped out. Paul does not want to open the tin any further and risk feeling more pain.

The Silencing Bit: One of the most powerful metaphors in the book, this device restrained, silenced, and humiliated. The bit not only makes the wearer feel like an animal, it also imposes silence and results in the absence of language. The bit, which physically silences Paul, metaphorically silences his ability to talk about his experiences. Instead of discussing his life as a slave, he seals up his memories, hiding them in the tobacco tin and remembering as little as possible. Paul's day-to-day survival, like Sethe's, relies on his ability to remain quiet, to forget, and to impose on himself the silence that the bit originally imposed.

PART ONE

Chapter 8

Denver and Beloved dance happily together. Denver now knows that Beloved is the reincarnation of the ghost that used to haunt 124. She asks Beloved what her old home was like. Beloved says it was dark and hot, with no room to move around. She was surrounded by people, some dead, but she did not know their names. Beloved came back to see Sethe, who left her alone. Denver begs Beloved not to leave or to tell Sethe her true identity. Angry, Beloved says Sethe is the one she needs, not Denver.

Beloved asks Denver to tell the story of her (Denver's) birth. As Denver tells the story, she sees it through Sethe's eyes. Denver explains that Sethe and Amy, a runaway servant, arrived at the Ohio River and found an old rowboat half-filled with water. As they got into the boat, Sethe's water broke, flooding the boat even further. Amy helped Sethe give birth as the boat moved across the water. Later, huddled by the shore, Amy tended to Sethe's wounded back. She told Sethe that the whipping scars looked like a "chokecherry" tree, and she traced her fingers around the many "branches" and "blossoms." At twilight, Amy Denver, Denver's namesake, continued on her journey to Boston.

UNDERSTANDING AND INTERPRETING
Chapter 8

Sisters and Rivals: For the first time, Beloved explains why she came back to world of the living: she wants to possess Sethe. Sethe's face haunts her, and she insists that Sethe belongs to her and her alone. When Denver tries to enter Beloved's fantasy, Beloved lashes out like selfish child who has a new toy that she refuses to share.

Chokecherry Tree: In this chapter, we learn that it was Amy Denver who initially thought that Sethe's scars resembled a tree. Amy Denver's kindness, and her willingness to see beauty in Sethe's scars, comforts Sethe. After giving birth to Denver—a hopeful, lucky experience—Sethe takes the positive image of the tree with her and tries to forget the source of the pattern on her back. The tree's branches give it the appearance of a family tree, perhaps a symbolic way Sethe can keep with her the family she has lost. Her new child, Denver, is represented by one of the blossoms on the tree.

Blessed Child: Throughout the novel, Denver is the one character who symbolizes the future. She is the first of Sethe's children born out of slavery and, as Sethe says, she seems impervious to danger. From the time of her birth, Denver flouted disaster. Her mother lay bleeding and exhausted on the wrong side of the river, but help came along in the form of Amy. Sethe, Amy, and the unborn Denver needed to cross the river, and they somehow stumbled upon a boat. Denver was then immediately baptized by the river water as Sethe gave birth to her, a sign of cleansing and regeneration.

TRAVELING ON THE UNDERGROUND RAILROAD

Beloved illustrates the secret efforts to bring thousands of fugitive slaves to freedom in the North. The network of people striving to help slaves escape was known as the Underground Railroad. The Railroad was an unorganized confederation of individuals, both black and white, who worked spontaneously in different parts of the country to shuttle escaped slaves to safety. There was a loose system of "stations" (hiding places), "passengers" (escapees), and "conductors" (organizers). **Harriet Tubman** (1820–1913) escaped via the Underground Railroad and went on to help free three hundred slaves via the Underground Railroad. Cincinnati and other parts of Ohio were active regions for the Railroad because of their proximity to Canada and to Kentucky, a "border" state still allowing slavery but allied with the Union North during the Civil War.

PART ONE
Chapter 9

When Baby Suggs was alive, before Sethe arrived from Sweet Home, 124 was the center of black life in the area. Strangers spent the night, and food was always on the stove. During the warm months, Baby Suggs held spiritual meetings in the Clearing, a wide-open space in the woods. There, she talked to the crowd from atop a rock. She urged her listeners to dance, cry, raise their hands in the air, and love their bodies. She told them the only grace they could have was the grace they could imagine.

Sethe decides to revisit the Clearing with Denver and Beloved. While they walk to the spot, Sethe remembers that after Amy Denver left, she waited by the river until a raft showed up. It was ferried by **Stamp Paid**, a river pilot and agent of the Underground Railroad, who took her across the river to an abandoned hut. Another Railroad worker, **Ella**, took her to Baby Suggs. When Sethe arrived at 124 with the newborn Denver, her other little girl was already crawling. (She came to be known as the "crawling-already? baby.") Soon afterward, 124 was silenced by what happened to Sethe and the "crawling-already? baby." Baby Suggs died believing there was no bad luck, just white people.

In the Clearing, Sethe stands on the rock and considers Paul D's return to her life. Before he arrived, she felt satisfied with the companionship of Denver and the baby ghost. Paul D brought with him "new pictures and old rememories that broke her heart," such as the image of Halle and the butter churn. Still, she can count on Paul, and she was lonely for male companionship.

Sethe imagines Baby Suggs caressing her neck, as she often did when she was alive. Suddenly, Sethe feels like she is being strangled. She tumbles forward and the ghostly grip on her neck loosens. Sethe thinks it might be the baby ghost. Beloved massages Sethe's neck, then kisses her passionately on the lips. Sethe pushes her away, noticing that Beloved's breath smells like new milk.

Later, back in the house, Sethe sees Paul D and smiles. She considers the idea of a new family comprised of him, Denver, and Beloved. As Sethe prepares a large meal, she remembers arriving at 124 full of hope. She now feels the same way, thinking of her own abundance and ability to provide for them. Upstairs, Denver accuses Beloved of choking Sethe, but Beloved denies it and dashes out of the house. Denver remembers being seven years old and attending grammar school classes taught by **Lady Jones**. She learned to read and, for the first time in her life, had peers. One day, one of her schoolmates, **Nelson Lord**, approached her and asked if her mother was jailed for murder, and if Denver went there with her. These questions, especially the second one, made Denver dread returning to school.

Denver was too frightened to ask her older brothers about Nelson's questions. As she grew older, she realized that her mother was a murderer. Denver began to have nightmares about Sethe decapitating her. One day, she finally worked up the nerve to ask Sethe and Baby Suggs if it was true that Sethe had killed the baby. Suddenly struck deaf, she could not hear their answer. For two years after that, Denver remained deaf. She regained her hearing the first time she heard the baby ghost crawling up the stairs of 124. After that day, the ghost began spitefully abusing everyone in the house.

> "*Beloved* is a calculated series of shocks."
>
> HAROLD BLOOM

When Beloved first appeared at the house after the carnival, Denver suspected she was the baby's ghost reincarnated in human form, come to belong to her. Now, when she sees Beloved using her powers to choke Sethe in the Clearing, she realizes she needs Beloved more than Sethe does.

UNDERSTANDING AND INTERPRETING Chapter 9

Baby Suggs's Revival: Baby's spiritual gatherings in the Clearing were aimed at getting the black community of Cincinnati to feel whole again, as a community and as individuals. Baby preached neither morals nor religious dogma, but how to love one's body. As slaves, the people to whom Baby preaches were owned by others, their bodies and their lives abused. In Ohio, they had freedom, but many of them could not embrace it. Like Paul D and Sethe, the former slaves kept their memories and emotions locked inside, questioning their own identity and right to exist and never convincing themselves that their flesh and blood belonged to them alone. Baby said, "Cry. For the living and dead. Just cry," ordering the people listening to her to feel and desire.

You Are Mine: Beloved becomes increasingly needy and, for the first time, shows her capacity for malevolence. When she chokes Sethe, she performs a malicious act of will aimed at preventing Sethe from soaking up the goodness and freedom of the Clearing. Beloved, a reincarnation of the baby that Sethe killed, is one of the memories Sethe would have been able to put aside if the Clearing had continued to do its restorative work. Beloved cannot let that happen, however. Her sole reason for returning is to make sure that Sethe never forgets the past. Beloved's kiss, typical of her greedy desire for her mother, ratchets up the tension. The kiss is passionate and incestuous, as if Beloved now wants to own Sethe sexually. Beloved's ownership is of a different kind than the one Baby Suggs advocated. Beloved seeks not ownership of herself, but full control and possession of Sethe.

"On one level *Beloved* might simply be read as a hair-raising parable of mothers and daughters everywhere; on another it could almost be a genuine folk tale of the period, discovered in some old trunk—the writing is timeless, and the characters epic; on any level at all it is also a unique piece of living social history."

WILFRED SHEED

Milk and Motherhood: Sethe warms to the idea of constructing a new family consisting of Paul D, Denver, and Beloved. While she cooks, she imagines that she can provide for them all. This generous impulse echoes Sethe's thoughts on the night schoolteacher and the nephews attacked her. As they raped her and took her milk, her only concern was how she was going to get breast milk to the baby who had gone on ahead of her. When Sethe finally made it to 124, she was ready to nurse that baby, Beloved, and her new one, Denver. Now, eighteen years later, she is ready to do the same.

Denver's Deafness: Again, we see how Denver has been sheltered from knowledge of Sethe's actions. Only when outside the house at Lady Jones's school does she learn of her mother's past and her own. Although Denver has an impulse to find out about the past and asks about what really happened, her fear makes her unable to hear the revelations. She actually goes deaf rather than hear that her mother killed Beloved. Only when the baby ghost begins to make noise does Denver's hearing return—perhaps a hint that the baby ghost may help everyone in Sethe's household face the past. Instead of avoiding the pain and horror through deafness or suppression of memories, Denver and her mother can confront what has happened by confronting Beloved. At this point in the novel, however, Denver is impaired in a new way, seduced by Beloved's companionship. Instead of helping Sethe when Beloved chokes her, Denver stands aside, silent, feeling that she needs Beloved's friendship more than she needs to help her mother or think about the past.

PART ONE
Chapter 10

Paul D thinks back to the time immediately after he left Sweet Home, brutalized and trembling uncontrollably. Eighteen days after the escape attempt, schoolteacher sold Paul D to **Brandywine**, whom Paul D tried to kill. For his murder attempt, Paul was put on a chain gang and forced to live in a thousand-foot-long ditch with bars. Twenty-four hours a day, Paul was chained to forty-five other men. Sometimes the guards abused the men sexually. At dawn, the lead man on the chain called out, "Hiiii!" (Paul called him the **Hi Man**), and the gang began work breaking rocks.

Once, it rained for nine straight days and the prison ditch filled with water. Wordlessly, a plan formed. The men tugged on the chain, alerting one another. Then they dove through the mud and under the bars, helping each other, since if one man died, all would die. The escape was successful. Still chained together, they made it to a camp of Cherokee Indians who freed them. Weeks later, Paul D was the only one still in the Cherokee camp. He finally got directions to follow the tree blossoms north. In Delaware, he met a **weaver lady** who took him in. Eighteen months later, he was back on the road.

UNDERSTANDING AND INTERPRETING
Chapter 10

Paul's Manhood and Identity: Paul D's treatment in Alfred, Georgia was so inhuman that he has not told anyone about it, including Sethe. The stories are so firmly lodged in his tobacco tin that "nothing in this world could pry them out." In Georgia, Paul D had traveled so far beyond humiliation that he felt nonexistent. After eighty-six days on the chain gang, he felt that "[l]ife was dead." Any memories of his allegedly respectful treatment at Sweet Home were crushed, and he became just another faceless man in a chain of forty-five. He bore no name, only a number. As Paul remembers the story, he repeats numbers: eighty-six days, forty-six men, one thousand feet of earth, five-by-five cells. The guards raped the prisoners, robbing them of their sexual rights and their manhood. Prison life destroyed Paul's ego, reducing him to a state of nothingness.

Chains of Community, Responsibility, and Solidarity: The chain gang was forced to work together to escape during the flood. Although the men's spirits had been broken, their survival instinct was intact. The chains, previously a symbol of oppression and incarceration, became during the escape a symbol of interconnectedness and solidarity. The chain gang showed a unity of purpose and spirit in the face of overwhelming odds.

PART ONE
Chapter 11

Beloved, using supernatural powers, urges Paul D to leave the house. Paul starts falling asleep in an armchair downstairs instead of sleeping with Sethe. Then, he begins staying in Baby Suggs's first-floor bedroom. Paul loves Sethe and cannot understand his strange behavior. Soon enough, he moves to the storeroom outside.

One night, Beloved visits him in the storeroom and tries to seduce him, saying "I want you to touch me on the inside part and call my name." Paul D tries to stop her, scolding her for being an ungrateful guest. He says Sethe loves her, but Beloved cries out that Sethe does not love her the same way she loves Sethe. Beloved finally succeeds in seducing Paul. He feels the lid fall off his tobacco tin. He calls out "Beloved," but when that does not satisfy her, he screams, "Red heart. Red heart. Red heart."

UNDERSTANDING AND INTERPRETING
Chapter 11

Beloved's Malevolence: Paul D stands in the way of Beloved's quest for Sethe's affections, so she tries to hustle him out of the house. She works her powers subtly, so Paul does not suspect what is happening. She makes Paul think that he is voluntarily staying away from Sethe. Beloved wants Sethe to love her and only her. She will never be satisfied with Sethe's affection until it equals the obsessive passion that Beloved heaps on Sethe. She unhappily tells Paul that Sethe "don't love me the way I love her. I don't love nobody but her." As long as Sethe loves Paul, Beloved cannot be happy.

Opening the Tin: Paul D's metaphorical tobacco tin splits open when Beloved seduces him. When he calls out "red heart," he could be referring to Beloved, the bloody baby and obsessive lover, or he could be referring to his own heart, finally laid bare after years hidden away in its tin.

PART ONE
Chapter 12

Denver, desperate to get Beloved's attention, fears that Beloved will leave her and that if she does, Denver will have "no self." Sethe has not yet realized that Beloved is her daughter reincarnated, so she still wonders about Beloved's past. Beloved says that all she remembers is one white man standing on a bridge. Sethe concludes that some white men kept Beloved locked up as a sex slave, which happened to Ella.

One afternoon, Denver and Beloved go out to the cold house, where ice is stored. Beloved goes in first, and when Denver enters, Beloved has disappeared. Denver, crushed, believes Beloved has left for good. Beloved reappears and asks Denver if she sees "her face" in the darkness in the corner. Denver sees nothing. Beloved, mysteriously, says, "Me. It's me," and smiles.

UNDERSTANDING AND INTERPRETING
Chapter 12

Sisters Intertwined: Denver cannot live without Beloved. When Beloved vanishes in the cold house, it is as if Beloved's very essence has disappeared. Denver, sheltered her whole life, has never had a chance to develop an identity outside the confines of 124, or to make a friend close to her age. Denver has had no one against whom to define herself but her mother and her ailing, depressed grandmother. Beloved's arrival comes as a relief to Denver. Suddenly, Denver has a sister and a friend. The thought of losing this new, comforting presence terrifies Denver.

PART ONE
Chapters 13–14

Paul D thinks of himself as the "last of the Sweet Home men." Mr. Garner allowed Paul D and the others—Sixo, Halle, and Paul A—to defy him. He let them determine the best way of doing things around the plantation. They learned how to shoot guns, and Garner offered to teach them to read. Yet Paul D asks himself, "Is that where the manhood lay? In the naming done by a white man who was supposed to know? Who gave them the privilege not of working but of deciding how to?" Schoolteacher's actions revealed the fraud behind Mr. Garner's respect. Schoolteacher took away their manhood and humiliated them, reminding them that they never had any power to begin with.

Paul D wonders if schoolteacher was right to say they were never men. This would explain why he had no power to stop Beloved. Paul D leaves work early one day to visit Sethe on her job at Sawyer's restaurant. He plans to tell her about Beloved and ask for her help. He finds he cannot tell her, however, and instead finds himself saying he wants to have a child with her.

Sethe laughs, but Paul D tells her to think about it. They have a happy walk home. It begins to snow. Later that night, Sethe saves Paul D by asking him to sleep upstairs with her. Denver and Beloved sit in the kitchen, where Beloved commands Denver to make Paul D leave for good. Denver says it might anger Sethe. Beloved reaches into her mouth and pulls out a tooth. She thinks her whole body might start falling apart. It takes great effort to keep herself together every day. She cries heavily, holding the tooth in her hand.

> "There's a lot more to Beloved than any one character can see, and she manages to be many things to several people. She is a catalyst for revelations as well as self-revelations; through her we come to know not only how, but why, the original child Beloved was killed. And through her also Sethe achieves, finally, her own form of self-exorcism, her own self-accepting peace."
>
> MARGARET ATWOOD

UNDERSTANDING AND INTERPRETING

Chapters 13–14

Being a Man: Paul D questions the meaning of the word "man" when he thinks back to the way Mr. Garner and schoolteacher granted and rescinded the slaves' manhood as if manhood was an object in their power to control. If the slaves were actually men, Paul reasons, schoolteacher could not have done what he did. Mr. Garner told them they were men, but this was not true, 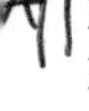 because Mr. Garner could have robbed them of their manhood at any time. Paul D concludes that Mr. Garner was a fraud, "a scarecrow in the rye." Paul D strikes at the heart of the question of identity by deciding that self-definition must come from an individual himself and cannot be bestowed upon that individual by someone like Mr. Garner. The slaves' names at Sweet Home, much

> "The growing of food and the growing of children are both vital to the family's survival."
>
> DEBBIE TAYLOR

less their manhood, were forced on them by some careless boss, some slave owner. When Paul D realizes that Garner robbed him of his ability to define himself, just as schoolteacher did, he wonders if his own manhood ever existed. He has never had a chance to call himself a man or to name himself.

Denver's Maturity: Denver shows her first sign of independence by not immediately agreeing with Beloved's command to force Paul D from the house. This small resistance marks the first time Denver does not unhesitatingly jump to make Beloved happy and convince her to stay. Denver is beginning to become a force for redemption, for looking past the present to a hopeful resolution of the haunting of 124 by Beloved.

PART ONE
Chapters 14–15

The narrative returns to 1855. Twenty days after Sethe's arrival at 124 with Denver, Baby Suggs cooks up a huge celebration feast. Ninety people attend the feast, secretly deciding that it is extravagant.

The partygoers hold Baby Suggs in quiet contempt, wondering if she ever suffered the slave's life they all lived. They resent her for living in a two-story house and enjoying freedom bought by her son. The day after the feast, Baby Suggs realizes she may have offended people. While hoeing in the yard, she smells resentment and has a sudden premonition of something terrible about to happen.

> "A feast is made for laughter, and wine maketh merry: but money answereth all things."
>
> ECCLESIASTES 10:19

Baby remembers arriving at Sweet Home from the Carolinas. The Garners seemed to run a "special kind of slavery, treating them like paid labor, listening to what they said, teaching what they wanted known." Before going to Sweet Home, she was forced to have sex with other slaves to "breed" another generation of slaves. Mrs. Garner called Baby "Jenny," because on her bill of sale she was called by her slave name, "Jenny Whitlow." When Mr. Garner asks why she calls herself Baby Suggs, Baby says, "Suggs is my name, sir."

After Halle bought her freedom, Mr. Garner drove Baby to Ohio. Baby looked down at her hands as if she was looking at them for the first time, realizing they were hers. She started feeling her heartbeat. Garner said she must feel grateful to Halle for buying her freedom, but Baby kept silent, thinking about Halle still trapped at Sweet Home.

Mr. Garner put Baby in touch with the **Bodwins**, a brother and sister who rented 124 Bluestone Road to Baby. The Bodwins' servant, **Janey**, asked her where the rest of her family was, and Baby thought about all of her children on the Whitlow plantation. She could not stand to hear herself say their names. Janey and the Bodwins tried to help her get in touch with them, but after leaving a few messages, they received sad news, and Baby gave up trying to find any more members of her family.

UNDERSTANDING AND INTERPRETING
Chapters 14–15

Owning Hands and Heart: When Baby Suggs obtained her freedom from Sweet Home, she felt human for the first time. She examined her hands and felt her heartbeat, realizing that for the first time that her body belonged to her. Never again would people who "owned" her treat her like a horse or a dog in heat, breeding her and forcing her to carry a new generation of slaves. The heart beating in her chest was a sign of a new life, a new freedom. Baby learned to love her own flesh and blood, and she would preach this at the Clearing. Baby's name also signifies her ownership of herself. From the time of her freedom, she would only be called Baby Suggs, never Jenny Whitlow. Suggs was the name of Baby's first husband, and she carried the name with her to her death. Her husband's name was all she had left of him, his only legacy to her, and she passed it to her son, Halle, even though Halle was the son of another husband.

A Fraud Unmasked: The fraud of the Garners' benevolence is revealed once again in Mr. Garner's assumption that Baby felt grateful to be free, as if freedom was something to which she was not truly entitled. For all of Garner's moral posturing, we never sense that he was a good man doing the best he could in a difficult time. Garner had other choices. He did not have to own slaves. At the very least, he could have joined with his friends, the Bodwins, in actively helping the slaves. It did not cross his mind to grant Halle's freedom, allowing him to join his mother, so Halle stayed at Sweet Home and Baby never saw him again.

The Crowd Resents: After Baby's lavish feast, the community turns on her for acting prideful. Overjoyed with her own freedom and happy to have a family with her again, Baby does not think carefully about how her happiness may affect those who have much less than she does. The townspeople resent her seemingly easy departure from slavery, they resent the fact that Baby's son was able to buy her freedom, and they resent her house. Morrison suggests that the townspeople's collective disapproval is what makes Baby's bad premonition come true.

PART ONE
Chapter 16

What Baby smelled that day was the "four horsemen" coming down the road: schoolteacher, his nephew, a **slave catcher**, and the local **sheriff**. They cornered Sethe in a shed behind the house. Inside, they found two infant boys bleeding in the sawdust on the floor. Sethe was holding one blood-soaked baby to her chest and trying to throw the other against the wall. Schoolteacher immediately realized that "there was nothing there to claim," and he stormed away.

The sheriff shooed off the nephew and the slave catcher. He saw that the two boys and the infant were still alive, while the older baby girl was dead. He took Sethe into custody and gently removed the living baby, Denver, from her arms. Sethe held tight onto the "crawling-already? baby," refusing to let go. She told the sheriff that she needed to nurse Denver, and the sheriff obligingly looked away out of respect for her privacy. As Denver nursed from Sethe's breast, the blood of the other baby mixed in with the milk. In front of the house, a throng of black people watched as the Sheriff led Sethe away with Denver in her arms. Everyone was silent.

FUGITIVE SLAVE LAWS
Sethe and her children were hunted down and captured, a legal action under the Fugitive Slave Laws, first passed by the United States federal government in 1793 and reconstituted as part of the Compromise of 1850. According to the Compromise, all citizens in southern and northern states were required to report any suspected escapees. Fugitives, if caught, did not have the right to a trial. The federal government nullified these laws in 1860, an act that led to the secession of South Carolina from the Union, hastening the Civil War. In 1864, Congress permanently repealed the laws.

UNDERSTANDING AND INTERPRETING Chapter 16

Forced Into Racism: For the first time in the novel, a third-person narrator relates events from the perspective of white people. As the four horsemen enter the realm of 124, foreign territory, we see through their eyes. Instead of seeing Baby Suggs, they see a "nigger with a flower in her hat"; instead of seeing Stamp Paid, they see a "crazy old nigger" in the woodpile. When they leave, they see a crowd of nameless black faces on the road watching them. As soon as these whites appear, blacks are reduced to namelessness and facelessness, as if they are slaves again, deprived of all humanity. By narrating the chapter from the whites' point of view, Morrison forces us to inhabit their racism.

> "*Beloved* proclaims that apocalypse and change are not necessarily at opposite poles: an apocalypse—the lifting of the veil on whatever lies beyond—can stimulate change. Its catharsis can be the beginning of transformation; apocalypse can thus become a bridge to the future, passage to freedom."
>
> SUSAN BOWERS

Sethe Sits in Judgement: The number of horsemen, four, refers to the Four Horsemen of the Apocalypse, as prophesied in the Book of Revelations in the New Testament. The Book of Revelations says that after the apocalypse, the end of the world, humanity will be judged, and the "worthy" will be let through the gates of heaven. If we interpret the horsemen's arrival as the apocalypse of *Beloved*, we can interpret Denver as the worthy one, the new baby born without sin. She survives, but the other children are struck down. The arrival of these four horsemen heralds the end of the new world of freedom for Sethe, and the end of Baby Suggs's faith.

Twenty-Eight Days: The four horsemen appear twenty-eight days after Sethe arrives, a gap in time suggestive of a lunar cycle and a menstrual cycle. This symbolism draws attention to Sethe's role as mother. It is as if her motherhood is tested during each cycle. A month before the horsemen come for Denver, Sethe goes through the test of escaping and giving birth to Denver. The menstrual cycle also symbolizes renewal, marked by blood and by the release of an unfertilized egg. The number twenty-eight foreshadows the bloody murder of the baby and the conclusion of an unrealized life.

THE FOUR HORSEMEN OF THE APOCALYPSE

Morrison's four horsemen directly allude to the Apocalypse, the stages of which are detailed at the end of the New Testament. In Revelations 6: 1–8, the seven seals on the scroll of God are broken, releasing four men on horses that represent the plagues of humankind: Famine, War, Pestilence, and Death. These horsemen bring the judgment of God, determining who will be saved and delivered into God's kingdom in heaven. The Four Horsemen are often represented in so-called endtime prophesies as the harbingers of doom for humankind. A famous Renaissance woodblock print by the German artist Albrecht Dürer (1471–1528) captures the biblical story. It depicts Death trampling a bishop, Famine swinging the scales of justice, War wielding a sword, and Pestilence drawing his bow to destroy the wicked.

PART ONE
Chapter 17

Back in the present, Stamp Paid shows Paul D an old news clipping about Sethe's arrest. Paul refuses to believe that it is Sethe depicted in the story. Stamp tells him about Baby Suggs's party, not mentioning that no one warned Baby or Sethe that the four horsemen were on their way to 124. He describes how Sethe grabbed her children and ran into the shed, where there was nothing but a saw and shovel. Paul D still refuses to believe Stamp's story.

UNDERSTANDING AND INTERPRETING
Chapter 17

Condemning its Own: Stamp makes the bitter revelation that the neighbors of 124 did nothing to warn Sethe or Baby about the arrival of the horsemen. The community, annoyed by Baby's pride, collectively failed. They allowed their anger and envy to overcome them, and decided, in effect, to turn over Sethe to the white men because of their irritation about Baby's party. They betrayed themselves by betraying Sethe, who as a slave had suffered exactly the same brutality that the townspeople suffered. Because the community falls apart, condemning its own rather than standing together, it shares in the blame for what happened to Sethe and the children.

> "When a village ceases to be a community, it becomes oppressive in its narrow conformity."
>
> PAUL GOODMAN

Stamp Paid: Just as Stamp pilots people back and forth across the river, here he shuttles between the community and Paul D, providing Paul with the news clipping. He is a respected member of the community, and a symbolic archivist of black Cincinnati, but he keeps to himself his opinions about the community's role in what happened that day. Perhaps he feels guilt or regret.

PART ONE
Chapter 18

Paul D confronts Sethe with the story from the newspaper clipping. At last, she comes clean, pacing around the room as she recounts the story. She explains that the baby was crawling already when they arrived at 124. She wondered if she was ready for solid food. Sethe says that in Kentucky, her children were not hers to love, but once she got to Ohio, she could love whom she pleased. Paul thinks back to the chain gang, where he protected himself and "loved small." A big love—a wife, a brother, a child—would "split you wide open." He understands what Sethe means, that true freedom is the freedom to love a big love.

Sethe says she collected the children she loved and put them in a safe place. Paul D tells Sethe, "Your love is too thick." She counters, "Love is or it ain't. Thin love ain't love at all." Paul says her love failed. The boys ran off, the baby girl died, and Denver hides in the yard. Sethe says she had to keep them from schoolteacher. Paul D says, "You got two feet, Sethe, not four." He turns and leaves without saying goodbye.

UNDERSTANDING AND INTERPRETING
Chapter 18

Thick Love: When Sethe escaped Sweet Home, she could finally and truly love her children. She no longer had to rein herself in or hold back her love because the children could be killed, sold, or lost at any time. Finally, her babies belonged to her, not schoolteacher. Paul D has never felt the kind of thick love that Sethe feels for her children. He has "loved small." As he said in Chapter 4, he thinks it is best to love everything just a small amount, so that if anything goes wrong, you have love left over. Paul also seems to recognize that Sethe's brand of love stifles children by pulling them in so close they become a part of their mother. Denver can hardly set foot outside the grounds of the house, and Beloved clings to Sethe with violent ferocity.

An Ambiguous Murder: Morrison does not suggest that by killing her baby Sethe made the right decision, nor does she suggest that Sethe made the wrong decision. By killing Beloved, Sethe gives herself and her other children their freedom. Freedom has cost them tremendously, however. Sethe's family has disintegrated, and the baby she killed has haunted her for eighteen years. The new family unit Sethe dreams of forming with Paul D, Beloved, and Denver is an illusion built on the repressed truths of the past—truths that Beloved will force Sethe to confront.

PART TWO
Chapter 19

It is the present, and 124 is noisy. Standing on the road, Stamp Paid can hear unintelligible voices inside the house. He has gone to check on Sethe five times, but each time he lacks the courage to knock. He wonders whether he did right in showing Paul D the news clipping. Stamp Paid has spent his life helping people in Cincinnati and on the Underground Railroad, but now he wonders if he is truly the "high-minded Soldier of Christ" he thought he was.

After Sethe killed the baby, a day he calls the "Misery," Stamp Paid went back to 124 only once, when Baby Suggs died. A memorial gathering for Baby took place in the yard, since no one dared enter the house. The neighbors hoped bad things would happen to Sethe. Baby Suggs "was buried amid a regular dance of pride, fear, condemnation and spite."

Stamp Paid walks up the steps to 124 in another attempt to talk to Sethe, and again he hears the chorus of voices inside. The only word he can make out is "mine." Most people in town know Stamp Paid and owe him their lives, so he drops in without knocking. However, he has the impulse to knock at the door of 124, which makes him realize that he does not know the inhabitants. He turns and leaves again.

Inside, Sethe recalls her twenty-eight days of freedom at 124, which were followed by eighteen years of solitude and disapproval. Beloved and Denver go ice skating. Later, they sit in front of the fire, and Sethe hears Beloved humming a song she made up years ago to sing to her children. Sethe seems to realize that Beloved is her daughter.

Stamp Paid goes to 124 a few days later. On the way there, he remembers that after the "Misery," Baby at last let the exhaustion of life get to her. Stamp remembers asking Baby why she had not come to the Clearing in weeks. Baby responded that she had nothing left to say to the people. Stamp was indignant then, but now he thinks he should not have taken such a high-and-mighty tone. Stamp is getting tired, too. White people still destroy black people any way they can: lynchings, school burnings, rapes, whippings.

Meanwhile, Sethe sees that she, Beloved, and Denver make up a new threesome that replaces the one she saw in the shadows on the day of the carnival. For the first time in eighteen years, Sethe feels as if she can live with her two daughters in the "timeless present," instead of worrying about the past. Stamp Paid knocks on the door at last. No one answers, so he walks over to the window, where he sees the backs of Denver and Beloved. He is puzzled by the identity of Beloved. After neither of them answers the door, he gives up trying to see Sethe again.

Later, Stamp visits Ella and John and asks if they know whether anyone is staying with Sethe and Denver. They do not know, although they suspect one may "see anything at all at 124." They tell him that Paul D is still in town, sleeping in the church basement. This upsets Stamp.

Sethe remembers how after Mr. Garner died, schoolteacher took over the plantation. Sixo stole a small pig (a "shoat") from the farm. Schoolteacher confronted him about it, and Sixo admitted to killing, butchering, and eating the pig. He insisted he had not stolen it, however, because he would be a better worker after a good meal. Although schoolteacher thought Sixo's answer was clever, he beat Sixo "to show him that definitions belonged to the definers—not the defined." One day, Sethe heard schoolteacher giving a lesson to his nephews. They were making scientific diagrams of the slaves' human and animal characteristics.

Stamp Paid believes that the noises clamoring around 124 were the "mumbling of the black and angry dead." Most black people he knew died after spending their whole lives trying to disprove the white perception that blacks had a "jungle" inside them. Yet the more they tried to persuade whites that they were gentle, clever, and loving, the more the jungle grew. This was a jungle planted by white people. It grew and spread, changing everyone, including whites, making them "bloody, silly, worse than even they wanted to be," scared of what they had made. At 124, you could hear the jungle's rumblings, mixed in with the secrets of the women inside.

UNDERSTANDING AND INTERPRETING Chapter 19

Voicing Rage: The voices Stamp Paid hears in 124 foreshadow the coming turmoil inside the house. They also show that Beloved embodies the bloody legacies of slavery. The voices emanating from the house are the "mumbling of the black and angry dead." They express the concentrated anger of the slaves who died before Beloved and those who died after. The rage planted in the slaves by whites is a legacy of silence, since the slaves can never express their rage. Thus, the language usually goes unspoken, and when Stamp Paid actually hears the noises coming from 124, he cannot decipher them. One of Beloved's many roles is to facilitate an examination of the past horrors of slavery, and to allow silenced, now dead black people to speak their thundering rage and sorrow.

Stamp's and Suggs's Solidarity: Both Stamp and Baby play elemental roles in the black community of Cincinnati. Both fought back the exhaustion brought on by the "struggle" (Stamp's with the Underground Railroad, Baby's with the Clearing), but Baby was finally defeated after the day of the Misery. Her refusal to go back to the Clearing was akin to silence, a self-imposed muzzling of the language she once used to enliven the spirits of those at her revivals. She told them to love their mouths, but then she closed her own mouth. Stamp now regrets his indignant attitude toward Baby, as he feels his own exhaustion coming on. When he finds himself about to knock at 124, he thinks of the great failures of his black community—its neglect and spite, which led to Sethe's murder of her daughter. Stamp thinks of Baby Suggs, remembering her exhaustion, which pained him, and of his need to continue doing his own work. When Stamp Paid visits John and Ella, he is still trying to mend fences, recharge the spirit of the community, and show sympathy for the outcasts at 124.

Who Owns Language?: The exchange between Sixo and schoolteacher gets to the heart of the way language was manipulated under slavery. Schoolteacher's premise, which says definitions belong to the definers, not to the defined, shows that even slaves' words were owned by the slave owners. In Chapter 2, Paul D told another story about Sixo at a time when Sixo had "stopped speaking English because there was no future in it." After schoolteacher beat Sixo, Sixo realized that the act of speaking—and, by extension, language itself—was futile. Schoolteacher was threatened by Sixo's smart use of language, and whipped him as a violent reminder of who owned the definitions. Meanwhile, Sethe made a similar discovery about the futility of language after encountering schoolteacher's lessons. She found herself dehumanized and defined as an animal. She did not entirely understand the language they used against her, but she knew that something evil was lurking in their words.

Creating the Jungle: Stamp's idea is that white people, by insisting that black people are animalistic, stupid, violent, and filled with a jungle, actually create that jungle in black people. Then, after creating a jungle where none existed before, whites are terrified. Whites make themselves violent, scaring themselves with their own creation. Stamp Paid's theory of the jungle marks the only mention in *Beloved* of how slavery affected whites. The passage reflects Morrison's view that slavery was an evil to all involved in it, both slave and master. The institution of slavery dehumanized the owners as much as it did the oppressed, since the owners lost their human compassion and became bloody animals. Everyone in the novel, black and white, must reckon with the past before they can hope to understand racial problems.

PART TWO
Chapter 20

The next four chapters are stream-of-consciousness narrations by Sethe, Denver, and Beloved, followed by a "conversation" among the three of them.

Sethe knows now that Beloved is her daughter. She celebrates Beloved's return, relieved that she does not have to explain anything to the girl. She wants to show the entire world to Beloved. Sethe remembers taking care of Mrs. Garner during her illness as if the woman was her own mother. After Sethe saw her mother hanged, she stayed as long as she could, looking for the brand mark that would confirm that the body was her mother's.

"At the heart of this astounding book, prose narrative dissolves into a hypnotic, poetic conversation among Sethe, Denver, and the otherworldly Beloved. Morrison casts a formidable spell."

WALTER CLEMONS

During Baby Suggs's final years, she could enjoy seeing colors for the first time. She started with blue, then moved on to yellow, then green. At the moment of her death, she had made her way to pink. She never wanted to get to red; Sethe and Beloved had provided enough red for one lifetime.

Sethe says that on the Misery, she planned to kill all of the children and herself, so that she could finally be reunited with her own mother in the afterlife. Her mother, she remembers, had been forced to wear the bit so many times that her face was disfigured into a permanent smile. She wonders why her mother was hanged, and thinks that it could not have been for running off, because a mother would never run off and leave a child.

After Sethe got out of jail, she considered suicide so she could join her dead baby girl. She thinks she could not live with her children. Now that Beloved has come back to her, Sethe thinks she can live in peace.

UNDERSTANDING AND INTERPRETING
Chapter 20

A Conscious Stream: Sethe's narration, like the narrations that follow this chapter, is a first-person stream-of-consciousness monologue. These are the voices that Stamp Paid heard when he approached 124—Sethe, Denver, and Beloved all talking at the same time, mixed in with "mumbling of the black and angry dead."

Mother and Daughter: Sethe is preoccupied with motherhood and, in particular, with her relationship with Beloved and the bond that she felt with her own mother. She clings to her lost daughter, happy to be reunited with her. It is as if this reunion has proved to Sethe that she was right to kill her baby. Sethe even remarks to herself, "My love was tough and she back now. I knew she would be." Now that Sethe has her daughters with her, she feels that she will never have to provide for anyone else but them. Sethe loved her mother and wanted to tend to her. Since she could not, she transferred her affection to Mrs. Garner. Now, Sethe wants to do everything she can for Beloved and give her the things that her own mother never could. Sethe's commitment to her children runs so deep that she would rather kill herself and all of them than be separated from them, or allow them to come to grief. She could not bear to let her own children suffer the same brutalities she suffered at Sweet Home.

Mine, Mine, Mine: The only word Stamp Paid heard from outside 124 was "mine." All of the women want to claim someone in the house: Sethe wants to claim Beloved and Denver; Beloved wants to claim Sethe; Denver wants to claim Beloved and Sethe. The idea of claiming her daughters recurs in Sethe's monologue and in the two that follow. She feels that her freedom from slavery now grants her the right to claim ownership of her children. This kind of possessiveness is a destructive form of love, now as much as it was when Sethe killed her baby. A person who tries to possess another depends on the love and emotions of the other in order to feel worthy. Sethe's worth is now based on the love given to her by her children. Beloved also wants to consume and possess Sethe. None of the women in the house have a true identity of their own. They depend on each other entirely.

PART TWO
Chapter 21

Denver begins her monologue by saying, "Beloved is my sister. I swallowed her blood right along with my mother's milk." Denver has always feared Sethe because she killed the baby girl. Denver's brothers, also frightened, were prepared to kill Sethe, if necessary. Now, Denver watches carefully, making sure Sethe never tries to kill Beloved again.

Denver thinks that Beloved came back from the afterlife for her alone. She dreams of being with Beloved and Halle, letting Sethe and Paul D go away and leave them alone. Denver believes that Halle would no longer want Sethe since she has slept with Paul D. Baby Suggs said that people look down on you for sleeping with more than one man. Slaves were not supposed to have pleasure, only to have as many children as possible.

Baby Suggs died thinking she had made a mistake. The white people came for Sethe despite Baby Suggs's grace and faith. Baby Suggs warned Denver that the ghost in 124 was after Sethe, not Denver. She had told her to watch out for the ghost, because it would be greedy. But Denver concludes, "She's mine, Beloved. She's mine."

UNDERSTANDING AND INTERPRETING Chapter 21

Unrealistic Dreams: Denver's life has been contained within the house and the yard. She has been at 124 her whole life, on guard against Sethe and scared that Sethe would kill her. Denver had only the baby ghost for company before, and now she has only Beloved, a more satisfying companion because she is flesh and blood. Denver's dreams, which emerge from her lonely reveries and her time alone in the boxwood, are unrealistic. She wishes Sethe and Paul D would go away, so that she, Beloved, and their lost father, Halle, could be together at last. Like a small child, Denver harbors unrealistic hopes that her father will magically return. She has not spent enough time in the world beyond the house to understand anything but the emotional territory of 124—a blank space, haunted for reasons that always puzzled her. Denver's identity is stunted. When Beloved arrives, Denver clings to her madly. Solitary and abnormal, Denver longs for someone to love and depend on her.

PART TWO
Chapter 22

Beloved's narration begins with the words, "I am Beloved and she is mine . . . I am not separate from her." She voices fragments from her unconscious, remembering a dark, cramped place, somewhat like a grave. Other people, alive and dead, are with her in this place. It is always the present. Beloved says, "All of it is now there will never be a time when I am not crouching." Beloved talks about being underwater and outside of water. In this place, she gets just a cup of water each day, so little that she cannot cry. Beloved remembers emerging from the water and seeing Sethe's face.

UNDERSTANDING AND INTERPRETING
Chapter 22

Face Value: Beloved still fixates on Sethe's face. She equates her existence with her mother's, saying, "I am not separate from her." Beloved refers to Sethe's face as if it stands for life itself, saying she once lost Sethe's face but has now regained it. Only when Sethe's smiling face appears does she feel she has been found and she and Sethe can come together. Beloved's resurrection from the afterlife depends solely on possessing Sethe. Beloved's possession knows no limits and will begin to resemble a type of consumption, as she is a disease devouring Sethe's entire being.

"*Beloved* is a reminder that the process of consciously remembering not only empowers us to tell the difficult stories that must be passed on, but it also empowers us to make meaning of our individual and collective lives as well."

MARILYN SANDERS MOBLEY

"Race-Memory": Beloved's descriptions of the cramped compartment in which others surrounded her, and men mistreated her, sound like descriptions of a journey from Africa on a slave ship. She describes surroundings of ocean and water, as if referring to an ocean voyage, and she says she only came back to life after emerging from the water. Beloved connects herself to her grandmother and great-grandmother, both of whom came through the Middle Passage. By her death and afterlife, Beloved gathers the strands of her family's experience, from the ships, to the land, to slavery, to Sethe's freedom, and to her own murder.

PART TWO
Chapter 23

The final chapter of this group of internal monologues takes the form of a conversation among the three women, although no one seems to be listening to anyone else. Sethe reassures Beloved that she is safe, that the "men without skin" are far away and will not come back, and that she will continue to be a good mother. Denver says she will take care of Beloved and she hopes Beloved will never leave them. She also warns Beloved that Sethe is dangerous. Beloved says she wants Sethe's face, but blames Sethe for hurting her. The conversation starts coherently, but disintegrates into single sentences and fragments. It becomes unclear who is saying what. The passage ends with the repeated phrase, "You are mine / You are mine / You are mine."

UNDERSTANDING AND INTERPRETING

Chapter 23

A Trinity: The structure of this chapter, in which the three women talk at once, shows the failure of communication and the disintegration of identity. It is this ominous, haunting chorus of unintelligible voices that Stamp Paid could hear from outside the house.

Owning the Others: Each woman claims ownership of the others, repeating the refrain, "You are mine." Just as it is impossible to discern who is saying what, it is futile for each of the women to claim an identity of her own, since each prefers to rely on the others for identity.

Assigning Blame: For the first time, Beloved casts blame on Sethe for hurting her and for leaving her when she was an infant. This foreshadows her revenge, in which she will try to consume Sethe's existence.

PART TWO

Chapter 24

Paul D has been sleeping the basement of the Holy Redeemer Church since he left Sethe. He now believes that he should have gone to the fire with Sixo. Paul D was the youngest of the three half-brothers, Paul A, Paul F, and himself, who worked for Mr. Garner at Sweet Home. Once, Paul D met a family of slaves who had stayed together for a hundred years. They were of all races—black, half white, part white, part Native American—but they could catalog their relationships with ease. He watched them enviously and asked each to explain his or her relationship to the others in the family.

At Sweet Home, none of the slaves expected Mr. Garner to die. Paul now thinks about Mr. Garner and the way he called them men, wondering, "Was he naming what he saw or creating what he did not?" Paul D wonders if he acted like a man on his own, or because Garner allowed it.

When Sixo proposed escaping to the North, they all pitched in to make the plan work. Problems arose, and nobody knows what happened in the end. The night of the escape, Paul D met the Thirty-Mile Woman in the woods, and they waited for Sixo and Paul A to show up. Only Sixo came. Suddenly, schoolteacher, his nephews, and four other white men were upon them. Paul D and Sixo were captured and tied up. Sixo grabbed the nearest rifle and began to sing. When the men tied Paul D to a tree, Sixo hit one of them with the gun. The other men knocked Sixo out cold. Schoolteacher decided that he was a lost cause, and they let him begin to burn in a hickory fire. Sixo laughed and yelled out, "Seven-O! Seven-O!" The men shot him in order to silence him.

> "I never thought I had the emotional resources to deal with slavery.... I thought I was writing a story about self-murder, the ways in which we can sabotage ourselves with the best of all possible intentions."
>
> TONI MORRISON

They took Paul D back to Sweet Home in chains. He overheard them discussing his worth, setting it at $900. They put a "three-spoke collar" on him to prevent him from lying down. He overheard that two of the others were dead, deducing that Paul A must be one of them. Sethe came to see Paul D in slave quarters, and he told her the news. Paul D now realizes that the nephews must have attacked her shortly after she left him. When he heard later that they had tracked Sethe to Cincinnati, he was not surprised, since "her price was greater than his; property that reproduced itself without cost."

UNDERSTANDING AND INTERPRETING Chapter 24

Masculine Identity: Paul D continues to struggle with his self-esteem. For the first time, we learn that the three Pauls of Sweet Home were brothers. By naming them all Paul, Mr. Garner treated them as if they were interchangeable. Every aspect of the slave men's identities, including Garner's unorthodox insistence on their manhood, was imposed on them by Garner. They did not have the privilege of making choices for themselves or defining their own identities. Garner did not beat them; he dominated them much more perniciously, by implying that their manhood was a generous gift from him. Even now, Garner's legacy of total control poisons Paul D's mind. Paul believes it possible that Garner truly did grant him the gift of manhood. He wonders if manliness would have sprung up from naturally. When Paul D heard the monetary figure that labeled his worth, he understood it as another way his self-worth had been defined by someone else. Accustomed to other people defining him, Paul D now struggles to define himself. He wanders because he wants to find a home and an identity.

Sixo's Name: As Sixo dies in the fire, he screams out "Seven-O!" The numbers perhaps refer to the escape attempts (white men 7, black man 0) or perhaps indicate the number of generations in his family that perished under slavery. Sixo gave up on language and died not speaking but laughing. Numbers, not letters, made up his own name, numbers that signified nothing but death and defeat at the hands of white men.

PART TWO
Chapter 25

Stamp Paid apologizes to Paul D and invites him to stay at another house in town. He tells Paul D that when he was a slave, his wife, Vashti, was taken away from him and forced to sleep with his owner's son. When she came back, Stamp Paid, then called Joshua, almost broke her neck out of rage at the owner. Instead, he decided he had paid a debt to his master, changed his name to "Stamp Paid," and dedicated his life to helping slaves escape.

Stamp tells Paul D that he was in the yard at 124 the day of the Misery. He says Sethe loved the children and was only trying to "outhunt the hunter." Paul D says he fears Sethe, but the new girl in 124 scares him the most. Stamp is curious about the identity of this girl, but Paul D cannot explain it. Stamp asks if he ran off because of Beloved. Paul D thinks back to all the horrors in his life—the bit, Sixo laughing in the fire, Halle in the butter, Sethe's scar—and asks Stamp, "How much is a nigger supposed to take? Tell me. How much?" Stamp replies, "All he can. All he can."

UNDERSTANDING AND INTERPRETING
Chapter 25

Debt Paid: By naming himself, Stamp claimed ownership of his life, something Paul D has struggled to do. After suffering the horror of having his wife forced to become another man's sex slave, Stamp Paid's anger caused him to seize control of himself. His insistence on naming himself recalls Baby Suggs's insistence on keeping her own name instead of using the Garners' name for her. Stamp's work on the Underground Railroad also relates to his name. When he takes people across the river on his raft, he charges no money and considers their journey paid in full because of their suffering under slavery. Like Sixo, Stamp wears his name as a badge. He continues to serve his community, as if by his actions, he helps cancel the white man's outstanding debt to the ex-slaves.

Community Solidarity: By rescuing Paul D from his life in the basement of the church, Stamp forces a new life on Paul D. Paul D's emotions, once locked in his tobacco tin, come flooding out at the end of the chapter. He breaks down under the weight and strain of his memories. Stamp Paid wants to prevent Paul D from becoming another defeated person like Baby Suggs.

PART THREE
Chapter 26

A month after Paul D left 124, the house becomes quiet. Sethe starts going to work later and later each morning until she is fired. Instead of looking for another job, she stays at home doting on Beloved, who always wants lullabies, games, and stories about the past. She begins wearing Sethe's clothes and imitating her every movement.

At first, Denver is allowed to join in the games with Sethe and Beloved, but as time passes, and Sethe spends their life savings on fabric and ribbons for Beloved, Denver drifts away and watches them from a distance. Arguments begin breaking out. Beloved complains, and Sethe apologizes, but Beloved is never satisfied. Beloved tells Sethe that the afterlife was horrible and that Sethe never loved her. Sethe's excuses do not interest Beloved. She slams things on the table and breaks windows. Food begins to run low, and Sethe eats less so that Beloved can eat more. Sethe becomes weaker and weaker.

> "Toni Morrison may well be the most formally sophisticated novelist in the history of African-American literature. Indeed, her signal accomplishment as a writer is that she has managed, uncannily, to invent her own mode of literary representation."
>
> **HENRY LOUIS GATES, JR.**

Denver realizes that "if Sethe [doesn't] wake up one morning and pick up a knife, Beloved might." Sethe's health fails rapidly. By April, Denver goes out into the world to get a job and food. She goes to her old teacher, Lady Jones, and tells her that she needs a job. She explains that Sethe is ill and they need food. Two days later, food starts showing up at 124, left by women in Lady Jones's church group, all of whom knew Baby Suggs and used to dance at the Clearing.

By June, Denver has learned to read with the help of Lady Jones. While her life in town improves, the situation at 124 grows worse. Beloved sometimes claws at her own throat until blood appears, making Sethe rush to her. Denver cooks, washes, and cleans the house. Sethe's greatest fear is that Beloved will leave before Sethe can teach her the important truth of life: white people can "dirty you so bad you forgot who you were and couldn't think it up."

Finally, Denver goes to the Bodwins to ask for help. She tells the Bodwins' servant, **Janey,** about what is happening at 124, identifying Beloved as a cousin. Janey hires Denver to work for the Bodwins as a night maid, concluding that Sethe's pride drove her to madness. Denver cringes at this criticism. Janey asks if Beloved has any lines on her hands. When Denver says no, Janey understands the truth. When Denver leaves the house, she notices a ceramic figure of a black boy. His pedestal says, "At Yo Service."

Janey tells the community about Sethe and Beloved. People wonder how they should feel about it. Ella previously considered Sethe prideful and misdirected, and since the day of the Misery, she has left Sethe alone. With the news of the ghost, however, Ella reconsiders. On the hot, humid night that Denver is to work at the Bodwins for the first time, the heaviness of the devil hangs over the land.

OHIO AND THE CIVIL WAR

The state of Ohio was part of the Union during the Civil War, though it saw little action within its borders. Parts of Ohio were involved in what was known as Morgan's Raid, in which a Confederate force of 2,500 soldiers led by General John Hunt Morgan created havoc by raiding and burning train depots and boats for three weeks throughout Ohio, Kentucky, and Indiana. It was the farthest north a Confederate army penetrated into Union territory during the War. Morgan and his men were defeated at the Battle of Buffington Island, on the Kentucky border—the only Civil War battle to take place on Ohio soil.

Mr. Bodwin is scheduled to fetch Denver at 124 with his carriage. As Denver sits on the porch waiting for him to arrive, a group of thirty women gradually assembles in front of the house. Some have brought crucifixes or bibles to help expel Beloved from the house. Denver waves and wonders what is going on. Some of the women drop to their knees and begin praying. Ella arrives and starts to holler at the house, and soon the others join in with a primitive noise. The narrator says, "They stopped praying and took a step back to the beginning. In the beginning there were no words."

Inside the house, Sethe continues to serve Beloved, who is in bed with a fever. Both women hear the hollering of the women outside. Sethe opens the door, holding hands with Beloved. It is as if the Clearing had come to her: "It broke over Sethe and she trembled like the baptized in the wash." Beloved has now taken the shape of a beautiful pregnant woman, towering over the malnourished Sethe. Sethe sees a man with a black hat approaching the house on horseback. Sethe is gripped by a terror that the man has come for Beloved, "her best thing." Sethe races off the porch toward the man, pulling the ice pick out of her apron pocket. Denver runs after her.

Beloved watches as Sethe dashes toward the man. She thinks she is being left alone again—that Sethe is joining the women and leaving her behind. She sees the man on horseback, whip in his hand. It is the "man with no skin," and he is looking at her.

UNDERSTANDING AND INTERPRETING Chapter 26

Denver Redeemed: Denver's loyalty finally switches away from Beloved, her companion and sister, and back toward her mother. It is Denver's own motherly, protective instincts that make her realize that she and Sethe are in danger. Beloved's whims and increasingly aggressive behavior could lead to Sethe's murder. Denver has listened to all of Sethe's explanations and has finally come to grips with the family's dark past. After years of staying inside the house, she ventures outside of the sheltered world Sethe created for her and finds the community she desperately needs. Denver's step is a brave one. She has had virtually no contact with anyone besides her mother and Beloved, so social interactions of any kind present a challenge. Still, in her bid to help her mother, Denver finds the strength to march up to near-strangers, explain her plight, and ask for employment.

Greedy Woman: Beloved's greed and neediness begin to spiral out of control. Her behavior turns aggressive, and her plate-rattling and window-breaking resemble the vengeful behavior she exhibited when still in the form of an unseen ghost. She has returned for revenge. Her all-consuming rage is not hers alone; it stands for the eternal legacy of slavery. She represents the haunting of the past, which bars the possibility of looking to the future. Sethe's guilt and desperate need to tend to the past, represented by Beloved, prevent her from living her life. The frantic attention she provides has exhausted her physically, just as her memories of the murder of the baby have exhausted her emotionally for eighteen years. Beloved's ongoing presence in Sethe's life, if unchecked, would have killed Sethe by depriving her of the chance to set aside the legacies of slavery. Beloved forces Sethe to relive the past and repeat the same stories over and over,

> "I never liked books about slavery.... They were always so big and so flat and you could never get close to them. So I thought if I did something narrow and deep, it would be successful."
>
> TONI MORRISON

which makes Sethe constantly remember the pain of her enslaved past. Beloved literally sucks the life from Sethe, wearing her clothes, depriving her of food, and swelling in size.

Community Solidarity: The women of Cincinnati now make up for their past wrongs. They failed to act eighteen years earlier when the four horsemen arrived, but now they gang up on Beloved as a force for good, trying to exorcise the demon in their midst. The women represent the community's desire to rise up and contend with Beloved, to confront the specter of slavery. Even those women who have considered Sethe prideful and self-righteous do not expect her to contend with the ghost single-handedly. When Sethe sees them outside, she thinks of the Clearing, the place where Baby Suggs preached enjoyment of life. When confronted with the love of her community, Sethe is "baptized."

Primal Scream: Ella begins the holler that summons Beloved from the house. It is a primal call that does not involve words. Beloved represents the legacies of slavery, including the legacy of a language defined by the slave owners, so the women stand back from the language of their repressors and use a primitive sound "from the beginning." The sound echoes the yelling at the Clearing, voiced at the urging of Baby Suggs, who told people to love their mouths. Clever words could not beat schoolteacher, but this holler defeats his legacy.

Mr. Bodwin as Horseman: The man on horseback is Mr. Bodwin, who has come to take Denver to work. But the image of Bodwin as a potentially malevolent force shows that even he, an abolitionist, is not blameless. The ceramic figurine at the Bodwins' house is a racist caricature, which shows that even good white people can harbor racist ideas.

Beloved's Pregnancy: Beloved's pregnancy has several possible meanings. Some critics argue that Beloved has consumed Sethe's identity and that she has become Sethe in a pregnant state. According to this theory, Beloved has become the Sethe who gave birth to Beloved. Beloved is due to give birth to the baby (Sethe) that she will murder, just as she is currently killing Sethe by sucking away her energy.

Another possible interpretation is that Beloved is pregnant with a future that will be born if she is allowed to kill Sethe. This future would allow Beloved to carry out her aim of constantly and harmfully reminding people of slavery's horrors. A third, literal interpretation is that Paul D has impregnated Beloved.

PART THREE
Chapter 27

The next day, 124 is quiet again. Paul D comes back to the house after learning from Stamp Paid what had happened. Sethe tried to stab Mr. Bodwin with the ice pick, but Denver and the women wrestled her to the ground before she could attack him. They looked back at the house, and saw that Beloved was gone. A little boy who had been in the woods behind the house said he saw a naked woman "with fish for hair" run through the woods to the stream.

Paul D decides that he does not care what happened; he cares only about why he left the house in the first place. Running away has filled his life. He escaped from slavery five times, but was always caught. After leaving Sweet Home, he went to Brandywine, then to the chain gang in Georgia, then to the weaver in Wilmington, then to ownership by the Northpoint Bank and Railway, and then to the armies of both sides of the Civil War. After a few months on the battlefields of Alabama, picking up dead Confederate soldiers, he was finally sent to a foundry in Selma. After the War, he left Selma and started walking. He saw dead black bodies everywhere, including those of women and children. Finally, he arrived in New Jersey, where the living outweighed the dead. There, he started a life as a free man, wandering for seven years until he reached Ohio.

Paul D goes to 124. He sees remnants of Beloved's presence: ice skates, ribbons, the dress she wore the first day she arrived. He finds Sethe lying in Baby Suggs' bed, humming to herself. She is very ill. Paul D thinks she wants to follow Baby Suggs' way out, giving up and dying in bed with nothing but colors to ponder. Sethe says out loud that Beloved left her, and she lost her "best thing." Paul D, contemplating his feelings for Sethe, sits down and examines Baby Suggs's multicolored quilt. Suddenly he remembers what Sixo said about his Thirty-Mile Woman: "She gather me, man. The pieces I am, she gather them and give them back to me in all the right order."

Paul D says to Sethe, "Me and you, we got more yesterday than anybody. We need some kind of tomorrow." He leans over and holds her hand, then says, "You your best thing, Sethe. You are." Paul touches her face with his other hand, as Sethe asks, "Me? Me?"

THE COLORED REGIMENTS OF THE CIVIL WAR

Great numbers of black soldiers fought valiantly in Civil War combat on both sides. At the start of the war, President Lincoln feared that recruiting black troops into the Union army would cause the border states to secede. But by 1862, the numbers of white volunteers had dwindled and the numbers of free blacks and escaped slaves willing to fight had increased, so Lincoln instituted the United States Colored Troops. More than 200,000 black soldiers eventually served in sixteen regiments. The most famous battle involving the Colored Regiments was fought at Fort Wagner, South Carolina, where the 54th Regiment of Massachusetts lost half of its troops. The battle was later dramatized in the 1987 film *Glory*. By war's end, sixteen black soldiers had received the Congressional Medal of Honor. Yet, discrimination continued even in the military, where black troops received less pay and fewer rations than their white counterparts. After the war, the Colored Regiments were excluded from the two-day victory parade in Washington, D.C.

UNDERSTANDING AND INTERPRETING
Chapter 27

Wandering After the War: In this chapter, Paul D provides the last parts of his life story, all of which involve wandering from place to place. Paul saw horror at Sweet Home before the war, and piles of dead black bodies on the roadsides after it, but when he tried to serve, he never saw combat. His experiences, which bracket the war, highlight the absence of the actual Civil War in the novel. *Beloved* identifies the brutalities of slavery and Reconstruction as a legacy equally or even more horrible than the grisliest war in American history. The "Sixty Million and More" of Morrison's dedication reminds us that slavery claimed the lives of countless millions, a far greater number of people than were killed during the Civil War.

Sethe in the Balance: At the end of the novel, Sethe lies defeated, just as Baby Suggs had before her. She feels that her "best thing" has been taken away from her again, and she has no desire to work or to live. She is still lost in her belief that Beloved gave her an identity. But Paul D's presence, his assurance that she is her own "best thing," and his gentle touch hint that Sethe will eventually find her own identity, discover her own face, and face the future. Her final word shows that she may be able to claim her own self ("Me?"). Paul D has come to grips with his past and is ready to return to 124 and live with Sethe and Denver as a family again.

Rebuilding Memory: Sixo's words about the Thirty-Mile Woman provide a vivid expression of the theme of reconstruction. Sethe and Paul D have assembled the pieces of their memories and now may rely on each other to gather the fractured pieces of their lives. The phrase "right order" suggest that Sethe and Paul will succeed if they find a way to remember the past without allowing the memories to continue a life of their own.

Gone for Good?: *Beloved* is, among other things, a ghost story. In the tradition of ghost stories, we are left wondering if Beloved truly has departed forever. Although she seems to have vanished, reminders of her existence linger in the house, and we have only the word of a small boy to suggest that she has banished herself to the water. Still, her spirit and her human incarnation seem to have vanished.

PART THREE
Chapter 28

In the final chapter, the narrator explains that the community forgot Beloved over time. People forgot her name and "[d]isremembered" her. The people who actually saw Beloved made up tales about her. Soon, though, they determined to forget her. People who knew Beloved, such as Sethe, Paul D, and Denver, remembered her for quite a while; in the end, however, they decided that "remembering seemed unwise."

UNDERSTANDING AND INTERPRETING

Chapter 28

A Storytelling Paradox: The end of the novel presents a paradox. The story of Beloved is not one to pass on, the narrator says, yet the novel passes it on to the readers. Perhaps readers can hear of Beloved because they exist at a safe distance from her. It is those people close to Beloved, and to what she represents, who should not pass on her story. Beloved's story is one of "rememory," of the ways in which damaging memories can continue to do damage in the present if they are dwelt upon. People need to forget Beloved because they need to manage the past. Yet, at the same time, we must hear the story in order to learn about the dangers of memory. In some ways, *Beloved* is not a story at all, but a warning.

Dearly Beloved: Beloved becomes, as she was before, a person with no name, another unidentified victim of slavery. When she vanishes, she returns us to the dedication of the novel, "Sixty Million and More," which pays homage to the nameless, unnumbered victims of the Middle Passage. With her death, the name "Beloved" returns to its origins, which are the phrase "Dearly Beloved," addressed to the mourners at a funeral. Now that Beloved is truly dead, her community could again be addressed as Dearly Beloved.

Conclusions

Beloved explores memory and the ways people remember and forget the past in order to move into the future. The novel, written in a fragmented style, evokes the intricate processes of memory and the struggle to find a language with which to express the dark truths of American history. The fragmented narrative represents the inadequacy of language to articulate the experience of American slavery. Sethe and Sixo learn that the very meaning of words can be controlled by those in power.

For the former slaves in the novel, one of the most difficult problems is how to remember the past in a way that does not prohibit a peaceful life in the present. The character of Beloved represents the devastation that occurs when former slaves like Sethe must surrender their hopes for the future by endlessly reliving the atrocities and humiliations of the past.

SUGGESTIONS FOR FURTHER READING

Benson, Alan, producer and director. *Profile of a Writer: Toni Morrison* (videotape recording). Edited and presented by Melvyn Bragg. Chicago: Home Vision, 1987.

Bjork, Patrick Bryce. *The Novels of Toni Morrison: The Search for Self and Place Within Community*. New York: Peter Lang, 1992.

Bloom, Harold, editor. *Modern Critical Interpretations: Toni Morrison's* Beloved. Philadelphia: Chelsea House, 1999.

Gates, Henry Louis, Jr. and K.A. Appiah, editors. *Toni Morrison: Critical Perspectives Past and Present*. New York: Amistad, 1993.

Holloway, Karla F.C. and Stephanie A. Demetrakopoulos. *New Dimensions in Spirituality: A Biracial and Bicultural Reading of the Novels of Toni Morrison*. Westport, Conn.: Greenwood Press, 1989.

McKay, Nellie Y. *Critical Essays on Toni Morrison*. Boston: G.K. Hall U& Co., 1988.

Mobley, Marilyn Sanders. *Modern Critical Views: Toni Morrison*. New York: 1988.

Morrison, Toni. *Beloved*. New York: Alfred A. Knopf, 1987.

______. *The Bluest Eye*. With a new Afterword by the author. New York: Plume, 1994.

______. *Song of Solomon*. New York: Alfred A. Knopf, 1977.

______. *Sula*. New York: Alfred A. Knopf, 1973.

Otten, Tracy. *The Crime of Innocence in the Fiction of Toni Morrison*. Columbia, Mo.: Univ. of Missouri Press, 1989.

Samuels, Wilfred D. and Clenora Hudson-Weems. *Toni Morrison*. Boston: Twayne Publishers, 1990.

Smith, Valerie, editor. *New Essays on* Song of Solomon. New York: Cambridge Univ. Press, 1995.

INDEX

A

Ali, Muhammad 5
Allen, Samuel 90
Atwood, Margaret 179
Austen, Jane 11

B

Baldwin, James 3
Bambara, Toni Cade 5
Breedlove, Pauline 15
Bell, Roseann P. 76
Beloved 6, 143–205
biblical references 66, 113, 128, 138, 183, 184
bit, the 146, 169, 170, 190, 196
The Black Book 5, 156
Black Power 4, 9, 27, 28
Blackburn, Sara 54
Bloom, Harold 168
The Bluest Eye 4, 7, 13–50
  beauty in 17, 22, 23, 26, 27, 30, 31, 32, 33, 36, 41, 43–44, 50
  language in 17–18, 22, 23, 35, 50
"Bojangles" 16, 24, 25
Bontemps, Arna 65
Bottom, the 53, 54, 55, 56, 58, 59–61, 67, 70, 75, 78, 81
Bowers, Susan 183
Brooke, Rupert 106
Bryant, Jerry H. 83
Byerman, Keith E. 32

C

Carmichael, Stokely 4, 9, 28
Cather, Willa 11
Christian, Barbara 16, 36
Cincinnati, Ohio 145, 151, 152, 153, 155, 157, 172, 174, 185, 187, 188, 195, 200
civil rights 4, 9, 28, 108
Civil War, the 8, 104, 145, 155, 172, 182, 198, 201, 202, 203
Clemons, Walter 190
Cullen, Countee 65

D

Davis, Angela 5
Dee, Ruby 41
Dick and Jane 15, 17, 18, 22, 23, 29, 32, 36, 48, 50
Dixon, Melvin 98, 99
Dostoyevsky, Fyodor 11
dreams 70, 80, 81
Du Bois, W.E.B. 65
Dumas, Henry 5

E

Ellington, Duke 65
Ellison, Ralph 3
Emmett Dreaming 108

F

Faulkner, William 4, 10, 11
Flaubert, Gustave 11
Four Little Girls 120
Frankel, Haskel 17, 162
Freedmen's Bureau, the 8, 104
Fugitive Slave laws 182

G

Garner, Margaret 8, 152, 156
Gates, Henry Louis, Jr. 196

Grant, Robert 85
Great Depression, the 3
Great Migration, the 8, 38, 98

H

Harlow, Jean 16, 41, 43, 44
Hemingway, Ernest 11
Hill, Anita 6
Howard University 3, 4, 5, 104
Hughes, Langston 65
Hurston, Zora Neale 3, 6, 11, 74

I

identity 5, 16, 26, 27, 31, 40, 43, 47, 50, 53, 61, 69, 75, 80, 84, 85, 89, 90, 100, 109, 113, 114, 121, 127, 132, 140, 141, 142, 155, 160, 165, 167, 168, 175, 176, 178, 179, 191, 192, 194, 196, 201, 203
Invisible Man 31

J

Jazz 6, 65
jazz 65
Jim Crow laws 4, 8
Jones, Gayl 5

K

Kentucky 3, 8, 15, 38, 41, 145, 152, 153, 172, 186, 198
King Solomon's Mines 127
King, Martin Luther, Jr. 9, 28

L

Lee, Spike 120
Leonard, John 22, 141
The Liberator 152
Lorain, Ohio 3, 15, 42

M

MacTeer, Claudia 15
Maginot Line 34, 35, 39
Malcolm X 9, 116
Medallion, Ohio 53, 58, 61, 62, 64, 78, 84
Middle Passage, the 7, 146, 166, 193, 204
Middleton, Joyce Irene 91
Mobley, Marilyn Sanders 193
Morrison, Harold 4
Morton, Jelly Roll 65
Mules and Men 74
music. See songs

N

National Suicide Day 56, 59, 61, 65, 81, 83
Native Son 6
New Orleans 55, 56, 62, 64
Nobel Prize 6, 11

O

O'Connor, Flannery 68
O'Shaughnessy, Kathleen 140
Ohio 8, 23, 36, 38, 41, 43, 147, 154, 186, 198
  see also the Bottom, Cincinnati, Lorain, Medallion, Shalimar
oral tradition 3, 17, 22, 43, 89, 91, 99, 112

P

Paradise 7
Parks, Rosa 4
Playing in the Dark: Whiteness in the Literary Imagination 6

pregnancy 17, 19, 21, 22, 39, 41, 44, 45, 48–49, 95, 112, 149, 153, 154, 159, 160, 199, 201
Priestley, J. B. 48
Princeton University 6

R

Rancler, Alan 5
Random House 5
Reconstruction 8, 104, 155, 156, 203
"rememory" 161, 162, 204
Robinson, Bill. See "Bojangles"
Rogers, Ginger 16
Rubenstein, Roberta 26

S

Shakespeare, William 63
Shalimar 129, 136
Sissman, L. E. 5
slavery 7, 8, 10, 44, 94, 100, 102, 103, 115, 117, 126, 145, 146, 153, 155, 160, 162, 167, 172, 173, 180, 182, 188, 189, 200, 203
Snitow, Ann 148
Song of Solomon 6, 7, 87–142
songs 3, 10, 89, 90, 91, 99, 124, 135, 141
storytelling 17, 43, 89, 91, 99, 146, 204
Sula 5, 51–86

T

Tar Baby 6
Taylor, Debbie 180
Temple, Shirley 16, 24, 25, 26, 27, 40
Their Eyes Were Watching God 74
Thomas, Clarence 6
Tolstoy, Leo 11
Toomer, Jean 65
Tubman, Harriet 172
Tyler, Anne 110

U

Underground Railroad 8, 42, 147, 149, 172, 187

W

Walker, Alice 74
Willis, Solomon 3
Winfrey, Oprah 7
wings 95, 122
Wofford, Chloe Anthony 3, 4
Wofford, George 3
Wofford, Rahmah Willis 3
Woolf, Virginia 4, 11
World War I 34, 56, 58, 59, 60, 65, 93
World War II 9, 16, 23, 33, 34, 38, 49, 105
Wright, Richard 3, 6

SparkNotes Literature Guides

1984
A Passage to India
The Adventures of Huckleberry Finn
The Aeneid
All Quiet on the Western Front
And Then There Were None
Angela's Ashes
Animal Farm
Anna Karenina
Anne of Green Gables
Anthem
Antony and Cleopatra
As I Lay Dying
As You Like It
Atlas Shrugged
The Autobiography of Malcolm X
The Awakening
The Bean Trees
The Bell Jar
Beloved
Beowulf
Billy Budd
Black Boy
Bless Me, Ultima
The Bluest Eye
Brave New World
The Brothers Karamazov
The Call of the Wild
Candide
The Canterbury Tales
Catch-22
The Catcher in the Rye
The Chocolate War
The Chosen
Cold Mountain
Cold Sassy Tree
The Color Purple
The Count of Monte Cristo
Crime and Punishment
The Crucible
Cry, the Beloved Country
Cyrano de Bergerac
David Copperfield
Death of a Salesman
The Death of Socrates
The Diary of a Young Girl
A Doll's House
Don Quixote
Dr. Faustus
Dr. Jekyll and Mr. Hyde
Dracula
Dune
Edith Hamilton's Mythology
Emma
Ethan Frome
Fahrenheit 451
Fallen Angels
A Farewell to Arms
Farewell to Manzanar
Flowers for Algernon
For Whom the Bell Tolls
The Fountainhead
Frankenstein
The Giver
The Glass Menagerie
Gone With the Wind
The Good Earth
The Grapes of Wrath
Great Expectations
The Great Gatsby
Grendel
Gulliver's Travels
Hamlet
The Handmaid's Tale
Hard Times
Harry Potter and the Sorcerer's Stone
Heart of Darkness
Henry IV, Part I
Henry V
Hiroshima
The Hobbit
The House of Seven Gables
I Know Why the Caged Bird Sings
The Iliad
Inferno
Inherit the Wind
Invisible Man
Jane Eyre
Johnny Tremain
The Joy Luck Club
Julius Caesar
The Jungle
The Killer Angels
King Lear
The Last of the Mohicans
Les Miserables
A Lesson Before Dying
The Little Prince
Little Women
Lord of the Flies
The Lord of the Rings
Macbeth
Madame Bovary
A Man for All Seasons
The Mayor of Casterbridge
The Merchant of Venice
A Midsummer Night's Dream
Moby Dick
Much Ado About Nothing
My Antonia
Narrative of the Life of Frederick Douglass
Native Son
The New Testament
Nicomachean Ethics
Night
Notes from Underground
The Odyssey
Oedipus Trilogy
Of Mice and Men
The Old Man and the Sea
The Old Testament
Oliver Twist
The Once and Future King
One Day in the Life of Ivan Denisovich
One Flew Over the Cuckoo's Nest
One Hundred Years of Solitude
Othello
Our Town
The Outsiders
Paradise Lost
The Pearl
The Picture of Dorian Gray
Poe's Short Stories
A Portrait of the Artist as a Young Man
Pride and Prejudice
The Prince
A Raisin in the Sun
The Red Badge of Courage
The Republic
Richard III
Robinson Crusoe
Romeo and Juliet
Scarlet Letter
A Separate Peace
Silas Marner
Sir Gawain
Slaughterhouse-Five
Snow Falling on Cedars
Song of Solomon
The Sound and the Fury
Steppenwolf
The Stranger
Streetcar Named Desire
The Sun Also Rises
A Tale of Two Cities
The Taming of the Shrew
The Tempest
Tess of the d'Ubervilles
The Things They Carried
Their Eyes Were Watching God
Things Fall Apart
To Kill a Mockingbird
To the Lighthouse
Tom Sawyer
Treasure Island
Twelfth Night
Ulysses
Uncle Tom's Cabin
Walden
War and Peace
Wuthering Heights
A Yellow Raft in Blue Water